014569199 Liverpool Univ

KU-205-908

Understanding Modern Sociology

Understanding Modern Sociology

Wes W. Sharrock,
John A. Hughes
and Peter J. Martin

SAGE Publications
London • Thousand Oaks • New Delhi

First published 2003

SAGE Publications Ltd
6 Bonhill Street
London EC2A 4PU

SAGE Publications Inc
2455 Teller Road
Thousand Oaks, California 91320

SAGE Publications India Pvt Ltd
B-42, Panchsheel Enclave
Post Box 4109
New Delhi – 100 017

British Library Cataloguing in Publication data

A catalogue record for this book is available from the British Library

ISBN 0 7619 5706 5
ISBN 0 7619 5707 3 (pbk)

Library of Congress Control Number: 2002111619

Typeset by Mayhew Typesetting, Rhayader, Powys
Printed and bound in Great Britain by Athenaeum Press, Gateshead

Contents

The Background to Modern Sociology 1

BEGINNING CHAPTER ONE

In this chapter we will discuss some of the major social changes which had a bearing on the nature of sociology from the classical period to about the 1960s. These include:

- the rise of sociological schools
- the repoliticisation of sociology
- the rediscovery of European social thought

This volume continues the story of sociological theory begun in *Understanding Classical Theory: Marx, Weber and Durkheim* (Hughes et al., 1995). Roughly, it deals with the 'middle period' of sociology that can, again roughly, be dated from the 1920s to the late 1960s. This is not to say, as we shall see, that the work of the classic theorists was neglected or that the ideas that they put forward became moribund. Indeed, and as we pointed out in the previous volume, that Marx, Weber and Durkheim are classics is a result of the extent to which their ideas, through this later period, have been extensively adapted in the work of, or served as critical foils for, these subsequent theorists. Thus, their presence within the growing discipline of sociology became even more prominent. Of course, much happened in sociology since these classic theorists wrote, not least because much also happened in society itself.

Although industrialism had acted as the major stimulus to the rise of sociology, the industrial order was, as the classical theorists had seen, a dynamic one, with the power to extend its reach across the globe and to further transform its own nature. The nineteenth century saw the increasing penetration of industrialism to all walks of life in most European societies and in North America. The late nineteenth century also saw the spread of European influence throughout

Africa and Asia as a product of the competition between the 'Great Powers' of Britain, France and Germany.

These changes were marked by cataclysmic events whose legacies are still felt today. In the early twentieth century these were the First World War and its aftermath, namely, in 1917, the Russian Revolution and the creation of the Soviet Union, soon followed by the rise of Fascism and Nazism leading, in 1939, to the Second World War. The military conflicts bracketed the Great Depression of the 1920s and 1930s which raised the possibility that Marx's predictions about the demise of capitalism were about to be fulfilled, and attracted many intellectuals and social theorists to communism. Though the above events may have seemed to presage the final crisis of capitalism, the capitalist system was to prove more resilient than its critics expected.

For sociology, the aftermath of the First World War had significant consequences. The Soviet Union – a state avowedly Marxist in its revolutionary inspiration and ideology if not entirely in conformity with Marx's own hopes for the emancipation of the proletariat – became during this period a more or less permanent element in key aspects of sociological thought, particularly Marxist social thought. The Bolshevik Party seized power in Russia without any prior bourgeois revolution of the kind that Marx himself had claimed was a precondition for a socialist revolution. For many writers, political activists and scholars from a number of disciplines, the Soviet Union was a bastion against the rising forces of Fascism and Nazism. European political life became polarised between socialism, as represented by the communists, and Fascism as represented by Hitler's Nazis in 1930s Germany.

The First World War shattered German intellectual life, a situation made worse, in the 1930s, by the rise of Nazism, which not only stifled the freedom of intellectual expression but also forced Jews, for long one of the strongest mainstays of European intelligentsia, to flee, mostly to the USA. This exodus was to have a profound and long term effect on sociology. It enabled members of the Institut für Sozialforschung (Institute for Social Research) from Frankfurt, to survive. Max Horkheimer, Erich Fromm, T.W. Adorno and others left Germany, recreating the Institute at New York's Columbia University (returning to Germany only in 1949). They were the nucleus of 'the Frankfurt School', a major source of neo- or post-Marxist fusion of theory and political criticism which they termed Critical Theory.

The Cold War confrontation between the capitalist West and the communist Soviet Union also meant that it was difficult to keep politics out of sociology, not that many sociologists necessarily felt this to be a bad thing. It was a confrontation that shaped many of the then current concerns of sociology: for example, the conditions supporting democratic societies, the consequences of economic affluence, the Third World and its development, the nature of the state and its relation to the economy, and more. It is not that there was consensus on these questions: they were tackled by various approaches including Marxism, functionalism and, to an extent, structuralism.

The schooling of sociology

The classical period of sociology was dominated by individual thinkers, among whom Marx, Weber and Durkheim have proved the most durable, but the thinkers we will discuss here are included in 'schools', partly because of the large numbers of people involved, and partly as a consequence of sociology becoming established in universities. Of course, both Weber and Durkheim were university professors, but they were pioneering practitioners who did much to establish sociology as a discipline fit for higher education. Universities were now housing concentrations of scholars, so that, for example, the University of Chicago became the base for symbolic interactionists, while the luminaries of the American functionalist theory were associated with Harvard and Columbia, and Critical Theory initially with Frankfurt.

Sociology was becoming a discipline acquired through study and training with universities the main vehicle. In the USA in the 1920s there were moves to make sociology a profession as well as an academic subject. Durkheim, throughout his academic life, had stressed the importance of establishing scientific sociology and applying it to the successful management of complex industrial societies. Quite independently in the United States – and with perhaps more success than Durkheim's own efforts – the stimulus of movements for social reform facilitated attempts to bring sociological knowledge and research to bear upon social problems, and was an early influence on symbolic interactionism.

This period saw the rise of a distinctive American sociology rivalling European social thought, less philosophical in tone, more empirical, and to a significant degree developing independently. Simmel (1858–1918) was known and influential in America from the beginning of the twentieth century but it was not until the latter half of the 1930s that Durkheim and Weber, largely through the work of Talcott Parsons, became centres of attention. However, the distinctiveness of American sociology was the consideration it gave, beginning in the 1930s, to professionalising empirical research in sociology and to the curriculum of sociological training. Following the models of psychology and economics, efforts were made to develop methods of empirical research. Paul Lazarsfeld (1901–76), another exiled European, bringing ideas developed in Germany to the USA, together with colleagues at New York's Columbia University set out a research methods framework, building on earlier techniques used and developed at Chicago, that became known as 'variable analysis' and was the first basis for modern quantitative sociology and survey research.

The aim of variable analysis was to create a strategy for quantitative empirical research that would result in sociology ranking alongside the well-developed human sciences of psychology and economics. By the 1940s and 1950s, 'variable analysis' was established as an essential part of sociological training. Parsons (starting in the 1920s) sought to build a bridge between classic European social theory and American sociology by fusing some masterworks of European social thought into a single general sociological theory – his structural-functionalism –

that would be the organising theoretical framework for empirical research, bringing it closer to a bona fide scientific status.

There was always opposition to these developments, but for a time during the 1950s and 1960s sociological functionalism under the guidance of Parsons and Merton, along with 'variable analysis', could congratulate itself on making the breakthrough into a properly scientific sociology, becoming an accepted and respected profession.

The repoliticisation of sociology

Functionalism's predominance was, however, never an entirely comfortable one, and there were always critics (of its verbosity, if nothing else, but also of its unnecessarily abstract character, its 'conservative' inclinations and more) but it did seem to be taking over professional sociology as the most prominent theoretical framework. American sociology was, at that time, deemed to be sociology *tout court*, and it was in its further development that the future of the subject seemed to lie. Interactionism was a vigorous, dissenting, but very much a minority position, and the leaders of the Frankfurt School had – with the exception of Marcuse – returned home, but had done so in a defeatist and pessimistic mood, their intellectual careers effectively over. European social thought was considered of little interest and no relevance to the new developments, and it would have seemed unlikely, had people been aware of it, that Lévi-Strauss' linguistic-anthropological analytics would ever have any bearing on what sociology might be.

However, as mentioned earlier, the actual course of sociology was driven by socio-political developments even more than by the inner logic of its intellectual development. The institutional prosperity of sociology owed much to the 'long' economic boom originating in post-war reconstruction, and the expansion in higher education that this brought about following the 'baby boom' after the Second World War.

Both these developments – themselves complex social processes – were deemed to have major political consequences for at least the developed societies of the post-war world. In short, modern society had moved beyond capitalism though what this successor society was to be was a matter of some debate. An extreme version of the argument, developed in the 1930s and 1940s, was that there had been a managerial revolution (Burnham, 1945). The industrial corporation was no longer owned by an individual capitalist, but had become the possession of a large number of stockholders. Ownership and control had been separated. Those who owned shares in a company were not in control – at least, and for sure, they were not in *day to day* control of it. That task had fallen into the hands of professional managers whose interests, even though they did not own the company, would be protected and served by the well-being of the organisation itself and not by the systematic exploitation of the kind that the profit-taker of Marxist demonology might engage in. Others saw emerging a society which consisted of a partnership between capital and the pluralist state in which the worst excesses of capitalism would be ameliorated by welfare legislation, democratic institutions and economic growth – changes which marked the 'end of ideology'.

The Second World War had been a major confrontation with, and major defeat for, ideology. In this context, 'ideology' means fierce and extreme political beliefs of the sort that communists and Fascists espoused, and which saw political and social life as a struggle, a struggle with much of the character of a confrontation between 'good' and 'evil'. Conflict was seen as the main vehicle of politics and as the method of creating the will and the means of forcing through the necessary, and violent, changes to realise the believer's vision of the future. By the end of the war, it was argued, the fervour had gone out of politics in the West. The era of the 'end of ideology' was upon us, ushering in the development of a much more 'civil' politics in which there was a fundamental agreement on goals, in particular the endless improvement in the economic prosperity of the nation state and a continuous rising standard of living (Bell, 1960). Politics was moving toward a more 'technocratic' mode in which the big decisions were about the means to achieve ends, the best ways to manage the economy and social structure to sustain and accelerate economic growth, rather than the revolutionary transformation of political and social life.

The amelioration of social conflict was seen to follow from the increasing prosperity of the working classes as well as from the rapid and massive expansion of the middle classes through the provision of 'white collar' jobs in the increasingly prominent areas of administrative and service work. The new prosperity perhaps prefigured a changing relationship between home and work, signifying that the individual's life would become increasingly 'privatised'. That is, with greater leisure time and more personal wealth, the individual could make the home a much more congenial place, concentrating interest on personal and family life and withdrawing from what is nowadays called the 'public sphere' or, in more vernacular terms, taking less interest in public affairs. Whether this was a good sign was debated. Perhaps the 'apathy' that was spreading – as indicated by relatively low voter turnouts in the elections – was a good thing. People were contented and occupied, and bereft of the resentment and animosity that would drive them into political conflict. On the other hand, it might be that this showed a weakening of the ties between the individual and the society, involving not just voter apathy, but an alienated indifference to politics. If the latter, then this perhaps exposed democratic polities to the risk that unrepresentative minorities or technocratic state managers would gain control of society and could, in the worst case, lead toward totalitarianism.

American business corporations were often taken as a barometer of the wider culture, of society becoming increasingly composed of isolated individuals inculcated with a spirit of passive conformity. W. H. Whyte's *The Organization Man* (1957) was one popular sociology bestseller arguing that the modern corporation demanded dependence and conformity from its employees. The argument paralleled that of another popular book, David Reisman's *The Lonely Crowd* (1950). Reisman and his colleagues sought to identify a major change in the American character: the kind of rugged individual independence – the 'inner directed' character (that had been created by America's legacy from the Protestant religions) was giving way to the 'other directed' character, one driven by the need to conform and go along with the others.

Clearly, the above summary does not exhaust the diversity of analyses of post-war economies and societies – which were in any case predominantly about the United States – but it does highlight what is perhaps their dominant theme: class conflict was over. Or, to put it in terms of sociological thought: Marx had been made irrelevant by history itself. If there was ever anything to Marx's theory, then it had been superseded by events. It might have been true of the nineteenth century when, indeed, the business unit was owned and controlled by the individual capitalist who focused upon exploiting the workforce and maximising personal profit. However, the claim of the 'managerial revolution' was that the exploitative element had been removed from the employment relationship. Further, Marx had been analytically mistaken: he had confused 'power' in general with 'economic power', perhaps encouraged in his misjudgement by the conditions of his own time when the newly eminent force of business capitalism had been rampant, and when those with the economic power had also been able to dominate society. But now the distinctness of the two was apparent, and those with economic power were no longer able to influence political power as decisively as before (Dahrendorf, 1959). As for Marx's prognostications about revolution in Western societies, about the intensification of struggle between the workers and their capitalist exploiters, about the increasing 'proletarianisation' of its masses in the manual workforce, about the growing ranks of the unemployed, all of these had been refuted by the facts. The working class had not become increasingly impoverished. Anything but. It was increasingly prosperous. Far from becoming an ever more important political force, it was of diminishing significance. If anything, the working class was beginning to decline in at least relative importance when compared with the 'new middle classes' that were growing so rapidly and filling up the suburbs. Perhaps the final irrelevance of Marx's thought could be marked by the abandonment of the expression 'capitalist society' and its replacement by that of 'industrial society'.

However, even at the time – through the 1950s and into the 1960s – there were doubts about this diagnosis of the future of Western societies. Questions were raised as to whether economic prosperity was being bought at the cost of political disempowerment or cultural impoverishment. One of the most notable dissenters was C. Wright Mills, who called for a reuniting, through sociology, of 'private troubles' with 'public issues'. Many of his works developed a critique of the new complex of power in the United States – in a phrase first used by President Eisenhower, hardly a radical politician, 'the military-industrial complex' – which he felt was becoming increasingly concentrated in the hands of industrialists, the military and the managers of the state. However, Mills' critique largely fell on deaf ears and it was other political developments that were to transform the situation.

In the United States, the rising post-war prosperity brought into more prominent focus the position of the Blacks who still suffered major social, political and economic inequalities. In the 1950s and early 1960s Black Activist movements, some espousing revolutionary solutions, began to eschew traditional politics in favour of direct action against the socio-political arrangements of American society, especially in the Southern States. But it was the Vietnam War which became a focus not merely for opposition to war, especially on the university campuses, but also for much of the discontent about the supposedly benign nature of United States society. If the then influential sociologist, Seymour Martin Lipset, had pronounced America 'the good society', this quickly gave way to a fashion for spelling the nation's name with a K – Amerika – drawing not only on the image of the swastika, the emblem of the Nazi Party, but also on America's home grown racist movement, the Ku Klux Klan.

However, the groups who exhibited most discontent were not so much those who received the least from enhanced prosperity but those who stood to benefit most. The Black movements tended to be led by educated middle-class blacks, as were the student movements. On the whole, these were people who would normally be regarded as the beneficiaries of post-war changes and yet they were dissatisfied, often to the extent of engaging in direct action, including massive demonstrations and riot. How could it be that those who stood to benefit most exhibited the greatest dissatisfaction? The fact that they were threatened with conscription for the increasingly unpopular US involvement in war in Vietnam was a powerful spur to convert discontent into resistance.

The public life of American society might have seemed more prosperous, comfortably suburban and politically tranquil, but did this complacent picture represent how things really were? Might it be that the full reality of American society was less content and benign: what about the scale of racial oppression, to take one example? Even the positive features of American society could be a new form of oppression in which the mass of individuals were manipulated into quiet subordination, made into seemingly willing partners in their own suppression. Such a climate would, indeed, welcome the diagnosis of American culture as involving 'repressive tolerance' that was set out in Herbert Marcuse's *One Dimensional Man* (1991; first published in 1964).

The tremendous social turbulence in America and elsewhere – especially in Paris where the student disturbances of May 1968 were pivotal – led to a massive reaction in the academy. Sociology was seen as conformist and technocratic in spirit, willing to collaborate with the managers of the state and of business corporations in developing supposedly scientific methods for controlling and manipulating individuals. And, in some cases, willing to collaborate with the military. The prestige of science and scholarship, not merely of sociology, was massively dented by these developments, and, of course, the designation 'capitalist society' was rapidly reinstated, and the relevance of Marx instantly reasserted. The rediscovery of Marx was, from the point of view of Anglo-American sociology, in large part an affair of discovery, of becoming aware of the extensive European activity involved in remaking Marx for the twentieth century, something that was made even more potent by the events of May '68. The criticism of the dominant orthodoxy of United States sociology became a major pursuit and, accordingly, there was a tendency to draw upon the more subterranean traditions of American sociology, such as symbolic interactionism, as well as upon the Marxist and other traditions in European social thought. Resources were already available in the form of, *inter alia*, the Frankfurt School (and other strands of European Marxism), symbolic interactionism (also ethnomethodology) and in structuralism (especially its Marxist variants) for the formulation of alternatives to the orthodoxy.

During the 1950s, political objections to the dominance of structural-functionalism in sociology began, often made in the name of conflict theory, a general name for the views of an assortment of sociologists who were not necessarily connected with one another but were united in their opposition to functionalism, and broadly in accord with a line laid down by C. Wright Mills (1956). Mills, as we previously mentioned, launched a major attack on the military-industrial complex for its undemocratic dominance and ushered in a renewed interest in the study of elites and inequalities. Conflict theory complained that functionalism gave too little recognition to inequalities of wealth and power as sources of social conflict and, if anything, obfuscated the very existence of class rather than combating its injustices. The classic theorists were turned to again, with Marx and Weber seen as pioneering the ideas of conflict theory, giving the struggles over power and wealth a central place. Durkheim was condemned for his functionalist inclinations .

Herbert Marcuse, a long-standing member of the Frankfurt School, who had remained in American universities when many of his colleagues had returned home to Germany, came to prominence during the 1960s amongst student activists. The Frankfurt School – whose doctrines Marcuse had been updating in order to analyse the prosperous post-war Western societies – offered just the kind of sceptical, critical perspective on the role of knowledge that many had been looking for. The critical attitude of the Frankfurt School followed from Marx's ideas and, ultimately, through Marx, from G. W. F. Hegel. Marx had been removed from the agenda of mainstream social science, allegedly rendered irrelevant by the failure of any genuinely proletarian revolution to materialise, but suddenly he was back and in a central position.

Marx's notion of ideology provided a main stimulus for the renewed attack on capitalist society. But this attack was no longer on the exploitative economic arrangements of capitalism but on the forms of knowledge it had spawned. Acquiring knowledge was to be seen as an essentially *partisan* phenomenon, and the social sciences as being *politically* motivated, although this had been in a covert way and subject to a conservative agenda. The demand that social theories should have a critical, politicised cast has persisted, and the dominant ethos of Western sociology now takes an 'emancipatory' orientation as a *sine qua non*. Reactions against the social science establishment occurred in European societies as well as the United States, and did much, first, to initiate the breakdown of the sharp and strong boundaries that had kept European social theorists – other than Marx, Weber and Durkheim – apart from Anglo-American ones, and, secondly, to completely reverse the balance of prestige between Anglo-American and 'continental' theorising.

The rediscovery of European social thought

It would be quite wrong to see the reactions against the sociological orthodoxies of structural-functionalism and positivistic 'variable analysis' as giving the quietus to that mode of sociological thinking. Indeed, it is alive and well, especially in the United States. However, as far as sociological theory was concerned, in and after the turbulence of the 1960s the impetus passed to European or continental social theory, either of the German variety through the rediscovery of the Frankfurt School, or of the French kind in the newly burgeoning structuralism.

While this was, in one way, a major shift of orientation for sociology, both these directions can also be seen as ways of refurbishing the creaking doctrines of Marx. Marx had, as mentioned, been dismissed as irrelevant, his dire predictions about the fate of capitalist society disproved by history. As we have already said, the very term 'capitalism' had been one that many sociologists sought, in the 1950s and 1960s, to purge from the sociological vocabulary to be replaced by the more anodyne 'industrial society' in recognition of, they claimed, the fact that class conflict had abated, if it was not actually over. This, together with the claim that the so-called communist societies were hardly socialist paradises and fared badly in contrast with the affluence of Western 'industrial' societies, was seen to demonstrate that Marx was, at best, out of date. This dismissal of Marx was entirely reversed in the initial reaction against what was increasingly referred to as 'positivism'.

The revitalisation of Marx was not based on a defence of his specific analyses of capitalist societies. Instead, it was focused around the claim that his work represented a level and type of theorising which was much more sophisticated than that being offered in Anglo-American sociology of the time. More advanced theorising had been going on, relatively unnoticed or, if noticed, despised by Anglo-American sociology of this middle period, and much of this had been Marx inspired. It was theorising which took for granted the idea that the development of theory was politically motivated, with an emancipatory purpose. The British periodical, the *New Left Review*, played a major part by translating, publishing and commenting upon a range of European theorists – many of them neo-Marxist in orientation – then little known in Anglo-American social thought.

Anglo-American sociology was faulted by both the Frankfurt School and by structuralists – though in different terms – for its misconception of the nature and role of theory. Anglo-American sociology had been opened to this kind of attack through its own internal developments, developments that had engendered a sense of crisis. The symbolic interactionists and, later, the ethnomethodologists, were both crucially contributory to a rising tide of opposition to what became dismissively known as positivism. Whether this category was always justly applied is a genuine issue but not one there is space to consider here. Most simply, positivism can be understood as the idea of a basic unity of science, meaning that the social sciences should emulate the methods of the natural sciences. This view had long been contested but had tended to become the default supposition by the 1950s. There was, however, a powerful resurgence of the argument that the methods of the natural sciences, if replicated in social inquiries, would miss the essential nature of social phenomena. The appeal of the European theorists was that they could offer a critique of positivism or, as it was often known to them, 'empiricism', but with the additional element that symbolic interactionism and ethnomethodology lacked, namely, a political direction.

The European critique was that positivism confused the 'empirical' with the 'real'. Its idea of knowledge was too narrowly focused upon the immediate facts and its attempt to understand the nature of knowledge too preoccupied with methods for collecting facts. Reality is not just an assemblage of discrete facts, for facts get their character through being part of *some system*. As Marx had supposedly shown, the true nature of the facts could not be properly understood unless they were placed within an encompassing, and therefore deeper, picture. The Frankfurt School, for example, not only argued that the social sciences should be dissociated from the natural ones but were also critical of the natural sciences. If we do not merely occupy ourselves with figuring out how to collect facts about natural phenomena or human life but ask ourselves what our knowledge is being used for, then we will find, they claimed, that under capitalism knowledge of both natural and social phenomena is sought for and shaped by the need to dominate and control. Such knowledge obscures the potential for displacing capitalist oppression and exploitation and expanding human freedom. Both physics and the study of industrial relations may give us correct findings about how things are in the physical world or the industrial plant, but they simultaneously conceal from us the real, destructive and spontaneity-denying nature of capitalism. What is needed is an alternative approach, one that takes as its objective the exposure of the real nature of capitalism and, accordingly, brings out the limited and concealing role of what passes for empirical knowledge.

The suppositions of structuralism also made a distinction between the 'empirical' and the 'real'. The observable empirical facts should not, as the positivists imagined, be identified with the 'real'. The former may be determined by observation, but the 'real' is the domain of phenomena that underlie and give rise to the observable facts. The 'real', the underlying structure, can only be known through a theory, a scheme of thought that will abstract the essential constituents that make empirically observable things what they are. This was the basic idea of structuralism's founding figure, Claude Lévi-Strauss (b.1908), but his eventual influence was less immediately and potently influential upon Anglo-American sociology than that of Louis Althusser (1918–80) who trafficked in a radically reconstructed Marxism that, as 'structural Marxism', seemed to be part of a wider 'structuralist movement'. Althusser, too, insisted that grasping the 'real' was not a matter of accumulating facts but of developing the right theory, insisting that this had already been done. Marx had seen that capitalism was the social reality of the modern world, and had given powerful pointers to the true nature of capitalism. However, Althusser continued, what Marx's grasp of the 'real' consisted of was not immediately manifest in his enormous, wide-ranging, changing and ill-assorted writings. The truly scientific wheat needed to be separated from the ideological and pre-scientific chaff. This, too, was a theoretical task and could only begin once a theory of knowledge, especially scientific knowledge, was in hand.

Thus, both the Frankfurt School and the structuralists directed sociological argument to the level of theory, and much closer to philosophical debate, and away from the issue of methods of social research or whether the right emphasis was on conflict or consensus.

Some consequences

One of the main consequences of the demise of functionalism was the languishing of American social thought. American culture was never one to encourage abstract social and philosophical thought, therefore Parsons' use of European thinkers for abstruse theorising had provided a fertile ground for what was to prove but an interlude. The legacy of Parsons for sociology was the rejection of his ideas and dispute over the various critiques to which this gave rise. American empirical social research would remain as energetic as ever, but the theoretical initiative passed to European social thought .

The restoration of the necessary sophistication and critical edge involved a re-invocation of more classical theorists, especially, in the 1960s and 1970s, of Marx. The rehabilitation of Marx involved many competing re-readings of his work and very different interpretations of what it could mean to those that had been offered by sympathisers of autocratic communist regimes. The Frankfurt School held that capitalism had changed fundamentally by the 1930s, and, accordingly, critique had to move beyond Marx's initial framework which was essentially of the nineteenth century. To this end they had dissociated from Marx's 'economism' the idea that all social, political and cultural activities are to be explained in terms of the economic base. Indeed, the group emphasised cultural domination rather than economics and also incorporated Freudian psychoanalysis into its Marxism.

The centre of the other main movement, structuralism, was Paris and its intellectual life. Its roots, originating around the time of the First World War, were in the work of the structural linguist, Ferdinand de Saussure (1857–1913). However, it was readings of Marx and Freud which proved the most influential. Structuralism seemed to promise the fulfilment of the dream of a scientific human science by being able to eliminate the subject and substituting instead an analysis of the forces which determined human behaviour but of which human beings were unaware. At least for a while, structuralism appeared to offer the prospect of a rigorous science without positivism's ambition to quantify. The achievement of Marx and Freud, though in different ways, was the identification of the unconscious causal forces which shaped human behaviour.

The above account probably overemphasises the continuity of the arguments by making it seem that sociology was argumentatively relatively homogeneous. Of course, this is not the case. The picture we have painted, so to speak, is one which attempts to provide a *post hoc* coherence to a situation where there was a great deal of leapfrogging going on, drawing upon influences which had developed independently of each other, but were brought into the fray somewhat later, as in the case of French structuralism being brought into Anglo-American sociology some time after its mature but independent development. Nor is it the case that as one school emerged the others disappeared. Functionalism is certainly less prominent than it was – at least in sociology – though the methods of social research which were a parallel development are still very much alive and kicking. Symbolic interactionism is also alive though perhaps less vigorous than in its heyday.

The above points need to be borne in mind in what follows. For reasons of exposition we will discuss each of these schools of thought as a relatively self-contained development. We begin with functionalism – though historically any of the other schools could have served as a beginning – because it was mainly the reaction against functionalism which gave the other schools the prominence that they came to have even though their origins were earlier. As with the previous volume, *Understanding Classical Theory*, we will endeavour to give a full account of each school in its own terms rather than through the lenses of its critics. We will, of course, discuss some of the criticisms but the aim is to give each school its 'best shot' since, too often, the picture students get of an approach is that painted by its critics.

CHAPTER ONE SUMMARY

- The classic period of sociology starts to wane with the First World War and its aftermath: the Russian Revolution and the rise of the Soviet Union, the growth of Nazism and Fascism in Europe leading to the Second World War. Between the two conflicts was the Great Depression. Intellectual life became polarised between socialism and fascism.

- American sociology began to develop and rival European social thought. An important part of this process was the attempt to professionalise sociology including the creation of a strategy for the development of theory and methods.
- The post-Second World War prosperity raised issues about the nature of capitalism and whether it had been transformed into a new economic and political order representing a partnership between the capital and the pluralist state. Class conflict was over and ideology a thing of the past.
- By the 1960s Black Activist movements, and protests against the war in Vietnam, challenged the benign picture of modern society and the emergence of conflict theory opposed what was wrongly seen as the necessary conservatism of structural-functionalism. Sociology was repoliticised.
- The 1960s and 1970s saw a rediscovery of European social thought in the Frankfurt School structuralism – as a reaction against the positivism of the then sociological orthodoxy of functionalism and variable analysis. In the United States symbolic interactionism and ethnomethodology had a brief resurgence.

Select bibliography and further reading

In this selection we will ignore the more specific readings relevant to each school and refer to these after the appropriate chapters. It would be helpful to have read *Understanding Classical Social Theory*.

An interesting source on the developments in American sociology during this period is S.P. Turner and J.H. Turner, *The Impossible Science: An Institutional Analysis of American Sociology* (Sage, 1990). See also H.E. Barnes and H. Becker, *Social Thought from Lore to Science* (D.C. Heath, 1938) for an optimistic view of the development of sociology as a science, and L.L. Bernard and J. Bernard, *Origins of American Sociology: The Social Science Movement in the United States* (Russell and Russell, 1965). More of an historical curio these days but, again, a publication symptomatic of the optimism of positivist sociology, especially in the United States, is B. Berelson and G.A. Steiner, *Human Behavior: An Inventory of Scientific Findings* (Harcourt, Brace and World, 1964).

On conflict sociology see R. Collins, *Conflict Sociology* (Academic Press, 1975), R. Dahrendorf, 'Out of Utopia: Toward a Reorientation of Sociological Analysis' (*American Journal of Sociology*, 74, 1958) and I. Horowitz, *The Rise and Fall of Project Camelot: Studies in the Relationship between Social Science and Practical Politics* (Cambridge University Press, 1974), a major critique of the ideology underlying American positivistic social science. C.W. Mills' critique of the military-industrial complex was put forward in a number of his books, including *The Power Elite* (Oxford University Press, 1956), *The Causes of World War Three* (Simon and Schuster, 1958), *The Sociological Imagination* (Oxford University Press, 1959) and *Listen, Yankee: The Revolution in Cuba* (McGraw-Hill, 1960).

Relevant to the 'end of ideology' thesis are D. Bell, *The End of Ideology: On the Exhaustion of Political Ideas in the Fifties* (The Free Press, 1960); and Seymour Martin Lipset's, *The First New Nation* (Heinemann, 1964). C. Waxman's edited collection *The End of Ideology Debate* (Funk and Wagnalls, 1968) is also a useful source of material. The economist J.K. Galbraith explored some of the consequences of the growing affluence in the West in *The Affluent Society* (Riverside Press, 1960).

Functionalism 2

BEGINNING CHAPTER TWO

In this chapter we will present an account of functionalism, a sociological approach which was prominent in the United States particularly through the work of Talcott Parsons and Robert Merton. The chapter includes discussions of:

- early functionalist thought in British anthropology;
- Parsons' functionalism from: *The Structure of Social Action* to *The Social System*;
- some applications of the framework: professional roles and McCarthyism;
- Merton's adaptations of the framework;
- the fate of functionalism.

As we said at the conclusion of the previous chapter, we begin with functionalism mainly because it was the reactions to it which gave much of modern sociology its intellectual shape even though these reactions had their roots much earlier than functionalism's own rise to prominence in American sociology.

These days 'functionalism' is a dirty word in the social sciences, though it ill deserves this bad reputation when placed alongside other offerings in sociology, including more recent ones, and judged in its own terms. Whatever the true merits of the functionalist sociology pre-eminent in American sociology from the mid-1940s through to the early 1960s, the explosively critical reaction against it played a fateful role in the further development of contemporary social thought. The form of functionalism at the heart of the story was mainly contrived by, to use his own words, 'the incurable theorist', Talcott Parsons (1902–79). However, the idea of 'functionalist' analysis in social science certainly did not originate with Parsons. Elements of it can be found in the work of Durkheim, who himself was influential on two major figures in the British social anthropology tradition – A. R. Radcliffe-Brown (1881–1955) and the expatriate Polish scholar, Bronislaw Malinowski (1884–1942), each of whom developed a version of functionalism, as we shall see below.

However, the functionalism which came to dominate American sociology in the 1940s and 1950s was seen as a development of what American social theory had always been about. Early American sociology was much influenced by Herbert Spencer's (1820–1903) 'organicism' and evolutionary theory. Spencer's conception of the nature of scientific knowledge was that all the sciences rested on a common philosophical foundation and that the laws which governed the natural world also governed the social. For him the concept of 'evolution' was the unifying principle for the sciences, including sociology. Society should be studied as a systemic whole by analysing its component parts, the interrelationships between them and the functions that they fulfil for the total society.

So, functionalist ideas were already entrenched in American sociology prior to its emergence as the central perspective in the late 1940s and 1950s. Parsons dominates its more recent story because, in his attempt to resolve some of the basic problems in social thought, he created the most ambitious, sustained and systematic version of functionalism. Parsons meant his theories to be exceptionally far reaching, providing a general framework that would unify a large tract of the social and human sciences, integrating sociology with many other disciplines termed by Parsons 'the sciences of action' and including psychology, economics, political science and anthropology. At the time Parsons' work and that of his notable students, such as Kingsley Davis, Wilbert E. Moore and Robin Williams, were not seen as radical departures but as a reworking of familiar theoretical problems that had been the concern of American sociology since the late nineteenth century. However, functionalist thinking had wider antecedents than the United States, with sources in Durkheim's thought which had been developed prominently in British social anthropology in the period following the First World War.

Early functionalist thought in British anthropology

Functionalism is a very general idea that can be implemented in different ways. The essence of functional analysis is that of the part–whole relationship, with the nature of the part being understood in terms of its contribution to the whole. Thus, in anatomy, one understands the nature of lungs, heart, intestine and other organs in terms of their respective contributions – through processing and distributing the nutrients that other organs need, for example – to the well-being of the whole body. In other words, understanding what these parts are requires us to understand their place and their role within a larger entity. Accordingly, given the idea of society as some entity over and above individuals, as Durkheim argued for example, then it is not difficult to see a possible analogy here with the whole society and its constituent parts – the latter being understood in terms of the consequences of their existence and operation for the wider society. The analogy is that of society as an organism.

Functionalism's role in British social anthropology was meant to be revolutionary, making the discipline more scientific and properly empirical by rejecting its traditional way of explaining aspects of social life in terms of their history. The major complaint against such historical explanations, popular in anthropology during the nineteenth and early twentieth centuries, was that they were not proper historical explanations. Given that the majority of societies studied by anthropologists did not have writing, suitable historical evidence, such as documents and records, was absent as, on the whole, was archaeological evidence. Therefore, as functionalist critics complained, explanations that appealed to history could only be speculation, wholly imaginative and empirically baseless reconstructions of a supposed historical development. A properly scientific approach must be based on evidence, and the only evidence available to the anthropologist was that of observed contemporary practice.

A mode of explanation popular in late nineteenth-century anthropology was to explain present practices and institutions as survivals of earlier but discontinued ways. Thus, a puzzling, even apparently pointless practice is explained as having originally had some real use, but the practice had outlived the circumstances in which it had that use. For example, the handshake is explained as a survival of the period when males normally carried weapons and shaking hands was a means of showing that no weapon was concealed. This practice has 'survived' but the purpose it once had has been lost. But, for the functionalists, even if a 'survival' account were true, it would not be *explanatory* of contemporary practice. That people took up a practice because it was useful hardly explains why they keep it up today when it is no longer useful or even seems to make no sense. Instead, the functionalist recommendation was: Give up speculating about what point a practice might once have had in favour of asking, what keeps this seemingly pointless practice alive? What leads people to keep on engaging in it? This is a question that might be answered on the basis of the anthropologist's own observations. If a practice makes no real contribution to their lives, or only a negative one, then we would expect people to abandon it. So the sheer persistence of a practice is *prima facie* evidence that people must get something out of doing it, even if the 'benefits' are not necessarily immediately obvious.

Functionalism was initially designed to refocus the problems of social anthropology away from questions about the unrecorded, and therefore unknown, origins of tribal practices and toward questions asking about the contemporary conditions maintaining any given practice. Even though this idea could be dogmatically overstated, as in Malinowski's (1921: 214) assertion 'that every item of culture, every custom and belief, represents a value, fulfils a social function', it did not follow that functionalism need necessarily be wedded to such an exaggerated and self-discrediting doctrine. Malinowski himself, in a less assertive mood, would elsewhere insist that the notion of 'function' was only an exploratory one and, as we shall see later, Robert Merton (b. 1910), a contemporary and colleague of Parsons, was later to provide a cautious and discriminating statement of functionalism to dissociate it from such overstatement.

Radcliffe-Brown's version of functionalism consisted in establishing the necessary conditions for the existence of a society, or some one of its constituent parts. It was assumed, though the analogy was to be treated cautiously, that societies, like organisms, must satisfy such conditions for their continued existence. Radcliffe-Brown, unlike Malinowski, attempted to derive the needs of society from more basic biological needs, but focused upon the level of society's organisation, emphasising that society was a 'social system'. It was the need to generate and preserve the integration of the system that was the key analytical consideration. Very much in Durkheim's fashion, he explained how rituals serve to draw individuals together, creating or reinforcing feelings of solidarity, and viewed descent relations among kin in terms of the need of the society to define the rights that individuals had over one another in a relatively clear way that would inhibit conflict.

Radcliffe-Brown did not work out his functionalism in the more general and elaborate way that Malinowski did. The latter saw culture as developing in response to basic biological needs, but then giving rise to new patterns of social organisation and culture, producing fresh, or derived, needs. These patterns of social organisation assumed the form of 'institutions': an organised pattern of activities, carried out by associated personnel, directed toward some purpose, governed by rules, and involving material resources, such as tools or plant, and that serves some function. Institutions may serve the needs of human or cultural survival, but they too have requisites for their own persistence. The institution must:

- produce and reproduce its material requirements, that is, fulfil an economic function;
- specify and regulate appropriate human behaviour for the conduct of its affairs, a requirement of social control;
- shape its members to behave according to its specifications, an educational requirement;
- develop an authority structure to organise the institution, so meeting a political need.

Malinowski's identification of these functional preconditions was influential upon Parsons' later formulation of the 'functional prerequisites' of social systems.

Parsons' functionalism

The notion of part–whole relations, which we have said is an identifying characteristic of functionalism, implies a systematic rather than a chance relationship between the whole and its parts. For Parsons this relationship was to be thoroughly understood through the notion of a system, a conception which operated at the level both of theory construction and of sociological analysis. In Parsons' mouth, talk of 'systematic theory' would be a pleonasm. The very idea of a theory is of a body of ideas that is thoroughly systematic in a logical sense. For Parsons, a successful theory consists of a complex of general propositions that are logically interconnected through and through. Whatever the achievements of Parsons' great predecessors in social thought – he was influenced by anthropology, economics and political theory, as well as by the sociological greats – they had not produced any general, systematic, empirically well-founded theory comparable to the kind admired in the more advanced of the natural sciences, such as physics. Parsons aimed to work more assiduously toward such a theory than Marx, Weber and Durkheim and others had, though he would take much of the content of his theory from these great precursors, especially Durkheim and Weber.

The Structure of Social Action: *the interpretation of classical theory*

Parsons did not set out as a functionalist. His first main project was an interpretation of classical theory which appeared as *The Structure of Social Action* (Parsons, 1968; first published in 1937). In this work Parsons not only took a distinctive view of classical European social theory, but also provided a first introduction to it for many Anglo-American sociologists.

Parsons saw a decisive change in social thought occurring around the turn of the twentieth century. Four major thinkers were breaking out from the basic utilitarian framework within which social thought had been trapped for three centuries or more. Two of the four were the now familiar Durkheim and Weber. The other two remain less well known to us today: the Italian economist-sociologist, Vilfredo Pareto (1848–1923), and the British economist, Alfred Marshall (1842–1924). All four, Parsons claimed, had independently advanced toward a radically new approach to the study of social life. *The Structure of Social Action* would spell out and round out this outline in what Parsons dubbed as the 'voluntaristic approach to social action'. In the book Parsons gave a very sympathetic and approving rendition of Marx's portrayal of the exploitation of the worker under capitalism (ibid.: 119) but, nonetheless, excluded Marx from his theoretical synthesis as, in Parsons' view, Marx had not made the break with that outmoded way of thought – utilitarianism – as Durkheim and Weber had managed to do.

An individual performing an action in its most basic and irreducibly essential terms, Parsons claimed, has four elements. These are:

- an actor to perform the act;
- a situation, a set of given circumstances under which the act will be performed;

- an end or result that the action is directed towards bringing about, such as getting safely from this side of the road to the other;
- rules or standards which govern the selection of means to ends.

From the point of view of the person who will act to achieve the end, the 'situation' consists of two elements:

- features of the situation which are, from the actor's point of view, unalterable – call these conditions – which the actor will have to take into account if the action is to be performed;
- features of the situation which are within the actor's power to change: these can be manipulated to bring about a desired end and, accordingly, can serve as means.

Action is, therefore, the process of selecting means to alter situations – made up of conditions and means – to yield desired ends according to some standard of selection. Such standards involve choosing means not only on the grounds of practical efficacy but also on the grounds of whether they are 'right', 'proper' or 'appropriate'. In a word, a 'normative' element is built into social action.

This may now seem simple and obvious enough, but Parsons maintained that prior to the twentieth century social thought had failed to give a suitably rounded picture of the basic phenomenon of social life, namely, individual action. The main trends in social thought up until then had perhaps collectively recognised all of these irreducible elements but any given strand of thought had shown only a partial grasp of them, tending to give greatest (sometimes even exclusive) emphasis to only one of these equally necessary elements. In consequence, these trends provided an impoverished basis for understanding social organisation.

There were three main trends of earlier thought that interested Parsons. The first was utilitarianism which, for him, was the most important and influential theory. It rightly recognised that human action was a matter of choosing between possible means in order to achieve some end. However, it assumed that choosing means to some end was entirely a matter of *calculating* their practical effectiveness, and so excluded the fact of normative regulation. The second trend, positivism (though not the variant of positivism typically associated with variable analytic research methods) made too much of the undeniable fact that humans are biological beings among other animals, so giving excessive importance to our biological nature and treating heredity and the environment as the only determinants of conduct; that is, treating people as essentially driven by their biological constitution. The voluntaristic, or choice-making, nature of action as well as the 'ideal' component of normative regulation were both excluded. The third trend, idealism, was a corrective to positivism, but it placed too much weight on the 'ideal' side of human existence; that is, on the role of ideas, rules, standards and norms. Everything became a product of 'thought' or the 'mind' at the expense of the material side of our existence. Each of these approaches was on the side of right, but only partially so. A properly comprehensive conception was needed, and the makings of it were to be found in the achievements of the four theorists already mentioned.

The partiality of utilitarianism The deficiencies of the utilitarian tradition posed what was, for Parsons as it was for Durkheim, the key problem for sociology, namely, the problem of social order. Thomas Hobbes' (1588–1679) *Leviathan* had followed utilitarian assumptions to their logical conclusion and, in doing so, exposed their fundamental flaw. If one did not fudge Hobbes' argument – as he himself did – human society as we know it could not exist. There would be only what he called 'a state of war of all against all', each individual pitched in life or death struggle against every other individual.

If we assume, as Hobbes did, that people are strictly self-interested in that they will choose the most effective practical means to fulfil their ends, then other people are relevant only as possibly useful means – or hindrances – to the fulfilment of these ends. This leaves just two ways to relate to others – force or fraud (Hobbes, 1991; first published 1651). If others can be deceived into thinking that they are serving their own interests when they are really serving those of others, or can be coerced into doing what others want, then they are useful; otherwise they are just rivals in the competition for the naturally scarce resources available to satisfy human interests. Rationality, on Hobbes' conception, demands that others be eliminated when they are of no further use to us. Following out the theory, relations between individuals can aim only at deceit, enslavement or destruction. The world we live in may contain deceit and destruction but of course it is nothing like a 'war of all against all', as Hobbes himself was perfectly well aware. And so, at the very least, his pure assumptions have to be modified, allowing individuals to take the value of co-operation as a means of self-protection into account and to sign up to a 'social contract' that limits competition well short of the perpetual life-and-death confrontation of a 'war of all against all'. Strict 'utilitarian' assumptions are therefore incompatible with 'social order' as we know it, that is, the manifest solidarity of many person-to-person relations, which are not formed out of force and fraud.

Marx had stuck to the same broadly utilitarian assumptions as Hobbes in seeing individuals as motivated by their interests. His thought also had positivistic aspects to it in insisting upon the overriding importance of the material, animal being in human life, so underplaying the importance of 'ideal' elements in guiding action. Durkheim and Weber were, for Parsons, the two sociologists who made the crucial moves against Hobbesian utilitarianism.

In short, although Weber originated in the 'idealistic' tradition, he tried to secure a balance between 'idealistic' elements (by recognising the voluntaristic, choice-making nature of action) and the constraints arising from the material conditions of life. Durkheim moved from an original positivism (with its emphasis on the determining role of the environment in the form of the famous 'external' and 'constraining' nature of social facts) to accommodate a recognition of the importance of the normative, ideal, elements in social life. In the end, Durkheim may even have overcompensated, tending, especially in his late work on religion, to lapse into idealism.

The central point of the alleged theoretical convergence of these innovators was the rejection of the assumption, integral to Hobbes' scheme, that the ends of action are randomly distributed. Utilitarianism's theoretical problem was to understand how people select the best means to an end but there was no need for the theorist to ask how they came by the ends those means pursue: it is enough that they have ends. What these ends are, or how they are acquired, is irrelevant to the theorist's interests. The ends are, then, for utilitarianism, merely extra-theoretical givens, and therefore may as well be considered to be randomly distributed since their particular identity and distribution is irrelevant to the theoretical problem: *given* an end, *how* are the most effective means selected?

According to Parsons, Durkheim, Pareto, Marshall and Weber had all seen that ends are not randomly distributed, and that their distribution is theoretically vital, not irrelevant, to the solution of the 'problem of social order'. Indeed, it is the fact that the same ends are shared by many individuals that matters from the point of understanding social order. Further, the utilitarians' own theoretical problem had been exposed as too narrowly formulated, for the choice of means is not a purely practical calculation but is itself governed by 'ideal' considerations, especially moral rules. Thus, there are many perfectly practical and highly effective ways of doing things that we, most of us, just 'rule out'. These could certainly get us what we want, but their use would be repugnant. Force and fraud are surely ways of making use of other people, but they are not ones most of us could bring ourselves to consider, let alone use. The rules that regulate a choice of means are – like ends – socially distributed and widely shared.

The problem of social solidarity The 'convergence' Parsons sees among these theorists is, in its simplest terms, based on the idea that there is *agreement* on both ends and on the regulation of the choice of means among the members of society: agreement, in Parsons' terminology, on 'values' and 'norms', an agreement which is an essential ingredient of society, and the very basis of social solidarity. To show how society is organised so as not to collapse into a 'war of all against all', there must be an account of the ways in which values and norms are built into, and articulate with, social organisation to provide some *minimal* level of solidarity and integration among individuals; that is, there must be compatibility between the constituent parts of a society.

The 'war of all against all' was, for Parsons, a theoretical limiting case, an extreme condition that could not be expected to obtain in reality. It was one of two extreme conditions, at opposite – and equally unreal – ends of the continuum of theoretically conceivable societies. At the other extreme to the 'war of all against all' is the perfectly integrated society, in which there is no conflict whatsoever, but that, too, is impossible because of, at the very least, the sheer randomness of nature: there are irreducibly disintegrative tendencies at work in *all* natural phenomena, including social life.

As is plain to all of us, including Parsons, actual societies fall somewhere between these extreme limits, varying in the extent to which they exhibit internal disorder and conflict. Some societies show comparatively high levels of disorder and conflict, such as those divided by civil war. There is a limit even to this however, for beyond a certain point, civil war ceases to be war *within* a society since, if it persists, it is likely to lead to the falling apart of the society, as happened in the 1990s to the former Yugoslavia. At the other empirical limit are societies like those of Western Europe and the USA, where there is social conflict and internal disorder but at a very low level compared to Yugoslavia or Rwanda. There is a great deal of unity and coherence within such societies, and social and public relations are conducted in a prevailingly civil manner. The extent to which Parsons holds that actual societies are unified is often unfairly exaggerated by his critics.

Parsons follows Durkheim in making the conditions of social solidarity a main issue for sociological theory. We have, however, so far been talking about his views as they might mainly be extrapolated from his first major work, *The Structure of Social Action*, prior to his adoption of functional analysis. Parsons' 'structural functionalism' was for him a second best, a step back from his first ambition which was to build up a sociological theory that would treat social organisation as a composite of 'unit acts', the starting point of *The Structure of Social Action*. His ultimate aspiration was toward a mathematically formulated scheme, a system of equations like those making up the theory of classical mechanics in physics. This turned out to be much more difficult than Parsons first imagined and, realising that for the foreseeable future it was a totally impractical endeavour, he adopted a functional analysis as more manageable. Social life was to be considered from the 'top down', as it were, from the point of view of society-as-a-whole, rather than trying to work 'bottom up' from individual unit acts to the level of complex social organisation and of the whole society. Though this change took place in the 1940s, it was the early 1950s before the main statements of the new position began to appear.

The social system

Parsons' basic philosophical conception, that of 'analytic realism', of the relationship between scientific theories and the realities they portrayed remained constant in the transition from *The Structure of Social Action* to his later work. This doctrine held that the true – scientifically known – nature of reality is not immediately and empirically given. The phenomena that we see are, from a scientific point of view, composites of many different elements. An analogy here might be with the way in which chemistry works. The things we see around us are composed of chemicals, but we cannot identify these constituents until we decompose and isolate the things to determine what chemicals constitute them. The chemical constituents are real, but only knowable by breaking down empirically encountered phenomena. The same applies to social reality. As they are given to our everyday perception, social situations are composites of elements that are not immediately revealed in the empirical situation but which, nonetheless, are real.

From the point of view of Parsons' 'analytical realism' any empirical instance of activity was composed of different elements that needed to be isolated by scientific inquiry. These elements included what were the materials for many different disciplines, each with its own specialist focus upon a distinguishable aspect of the phenomenon. However, in the natural sciences although there may be a number of different disciplines – chemistry, biology, physics, astronomy, geology, etc. – there is a serious sense in which they are compatible with one another even if for many practical reasons they can be, and are, institutionally distinguished. Natural phenomena obey the same laws of nature, for example, and in many cases the most challenging research areas are those where disciplines overlap, requiring reintegration into an overall compatibility. The different social and cultural sciences could not, at least not for a long time, achieve the level of compatibility characteristic of the natural sciences, but since they deal with the same phenomena it is an ideal to which they should subscribe. Their different frameworks ought to be compatible and their findings complementary. The phenomena studied by sociologists were the same concrete empirical phenomena as those studied by the other social sciences from their own particular perspectives.

Take a meeting. Sociology's interest would be in the interrelationship of the members of the meeting. A person's conduct in a meeting, say, could be considered from the point of view of its relationship to the behaviour of others, and to the organisation of the meeting as a social occasion. The same behaviour could also be considered from psychology's point of view, as evidence of the individual's personality system.

Thus, sociology is only one of the social and cultural sciences. Though these sciences respectively concentrate on distinctive systems of organisation – social system, personality system, economic system, political system, and cultural system – those systems must interact with one another in the concrete empirical case. For example, someone's personality has effects on the social organisation of a meeting, and vice versa. Accordingly, these sciences ought to have interconnections. But if any serious integration of these sciences is to be achieved, what is required is a shared frame of reference for, to use Parsons' term for them, the 'sciences of action'. Sociology focuses upon a specific aspect of social phenomena, namely their organisation into a social system, the topic developed in *The Social System* (Parsons, 1952). Moreover, the title of a companion volume reflected the extent to which Parsons' aspiration was not just to a *sociological* theory, but reached *Toward a General Theory of Action* (1951). This collection co-edited with Edward Shils (1910–95) consisted of contributions from colleagues in disciplines such as anthropology and psychology whose work would also fall within the scope of Parsons' developing general theory.

Applying analytical realism, then, any concrete social situation is made up of four kinds of analytically distinguishable elements. A social encounter has:

1 A biological dimension; it is a relationship between human organisms.
2 These organisms have a complex psychological make-up in that they have personalities or, more technically, personality systems.
3 Since the situation involves them addressing their actions to each other, they are in a social relationship.
4 To no small extent the medium of that social relationship is their culture, for these transactions are typically conducted in a language the parties share, and in accord with the conventions of their culture.

Thus, a concrete interaction situation is (at least) a composite of biological, psychological, social and cultural elements. It is the product of the intersection of systems. However, although our biological make-up is indispensable to our conduct, and the arrangements of our social and cultural affairs compatible with this, biology is a natural science, not one of the 'sciences of action' and, accordingly, it must be mainly taken for granted.

We have mentioned how important the notion of 'system' was for Parsons, and how the idea of a theoretical system guided his plans. The notion of 'system' was also to be a key notion *within* his theoretical system. For Parsons, sociological thought sought to understand how social phenomena are organised into systems, into integrally interconnected arrangements. This is, of course, what the functionalist approach, generally at least, tacitly supposes. If the parts of a society are to be understood in terms of their effects upon other parts of the society and, ultimately, in terms of their impact upon the well-being of the whole, then this implies that all the parts of the society are mutually affecting, that they possess the properties of a system. For Parsons, a system is anything which is capable of persistence as an identifiable unit distinct from its environment, and whose unity consists in the integration of its internal parts. However, the business of the 'sciences of action' is to analyse the organisation of and interrelationships between different – social, psychological, cultural, etc. – systems.

The notion of system is meant to draw out the degree to which there is coherence in patterns of activity. At the level of individual psychology, for example, without coherence an individual's behaviour would be unpredictable from moment to moment. However, people exhibit much, if not complete, consistency in their behaviour. They may have a specific 'sense of humour', say, and will consistently find certain kinds of things funny. There are also consistencies between different dimensions of an individual's behaviour. A particular 'sense of humour' will fit with other tendencies such that someone with a strong sense of propriety will not find vulgar jokes funny. The notion of 'personality system' postulates an integrated structure of individual psychology, and the discipline of psychology seeks to understand the origins, nature and dynamics of such systems. The same point can be made about the notions of 'social system' and 'cultural system'. These, too, have to have internal order and a measure of coherent interconnection. We do not live in a social world in which we have to approach every social situation as a completely new one, having to work out in fine detail how we are going to behave. We, rather, can enter most social situations and carry on relationships without having to figure out from scratch how to behave. We expect a good deal of similarity in the ways people act across situations.

There are, of course, different bases for, and limits, to the extent of variation. The way in which people behave in church, for example, is different from the way in which they behave in the workplace, though not entirely so. The church can be thought of as a social system as can the workplace, for each has its own pattern of activity and its own distinctive requirements. We expect, however, that there is some consistency between both systems. The way in which people are required to behave at work cannot be massively at odds with the way their religious convictions call upon them to live without producing strain in the system.

In Parsons' usage, 'system' is a relative, not an absolute, term. Whether something is a social system or only part of another system (that is, a sub-system) depends upon the sociologist's point of reference. Any kind of unit showing organised persistence in, and differentiated from, its environment is a system. The 'systems' that figure in Parsons' scheme are 'open systems', ones which possess a distinct identity but are in transaction with – open to – their environment in the same way that living organisms ingest air and food from, and discharge waste into, the world around them. A system has relative closure, and can be identified as an autonomous unit at a given level of comparison. Thus, we could see a business organisation as a system, for a business is a unit separable from other businesses that, in a market economy, are part of its environment. But, if we were studying that business we might want to consider the different identifiable departments within the organisation – accounting, stock control, production, etc. – as systems themselves (or as sub-systems of the business). If we are studying 'small groups' we might take friendship cliques or working teams within a department as the systems (or as sub-systems of the organisational division in which they were found). The businesses, in their turn, are viewable as sub-systems of 'the economy' which, in its turn, might be viewed as a sub-system of 'the society', which itself is part of an 'international' or globalised system of relationships. Which we take as system, and which as sub-system, depends on our sociological purposes.

It is important to note here, though this warning is often ignored, that 'social system' in Parsons' terms does not mean the same as 'society', though the society in the form of the nation state is often treated as the point of reference, and thus as a system rather than a sub-system. Parsons himself, in the later part of his career, noted that the development of an 'international system' meant that the nation state would count as a sub-system relative to that, an observation that has an even greater cogency in a period of globalisation.

Parsons' idea, then, is of levels of social organisation standing in 'nested' relationships: a given system contains sub-systems which themselves contain sub-systems which themselves contain sub-systems, and so on down to the very small scale of a two-person relationship as the smallest scale of *social* system. The society-as-a-whole is, on this conception, a hierarchical structure of nested sub-systems.

Much of the consistency of different sub-systems derives from the common culture. Again, it is only to be expected that there will be consistency in the different ideas and beliefs that people have, the different rules that they respect and abide by. In short, their cultural commitments will also make up (more or less) a system. Weber's studies of the economic ethics of the world religions yielded good examples of such consistency by highlighting the extent to which there was often a continuity between religious ideas and economic activity. After all, religions give general instructions on how people should live and act and, therefore, must have a strong influence on the ethic that governs economic activity. Accordingly, not only will there be consistency *within* each of the personality, cultural and social systems, but, since they combine to make up elements of any concrete social situation, there must also be consistency *between* them; that is, to continue with the example, not only in the religious convictions people have, but also between their religious convictions and their views about other matters, such as how do business ethically.

It is important to reiterate that Parsons did not want to exaggerate the extent of consistency in any of the systems – personality, social or cultural – or between them. From a theoretical point of view, such consistency is not to be treated as guaranteed in advance, its production and maintenance rather being problematic and often only rather tenuously attained and a major problem for investigation in Parsons' approach. Nonetheless, in any 'ongoing' social system there *must* be a minimum degree of integration within the system's parts, with the culture, and with individuals' personalities, otherwise it could not be sustaining itself as a distinguishable unit. It would either be breaking up or dying out. Beyond that minimal level, the extent to which there is internal integration of a specific system, and the extent to which there is smooth articulation between it and the other systems it relates to, has to be determined empirically. Some systems will exhibit more integration than others, some parts of a system will be more integrated than other parts of it. For example, people have different personalities, and some will find a given pattern of social activity more satisfying than others. It may be that some will find a pattern of social activity so dissatisfying that they are reluctant – even flatly unwilling – to participate in it. Maybe they are so alienated that they will attempt to disrupt, even overthrow, the system. Similarly, a set of cultural ideals may well vary in the extent to which actual patterns of conduct fall in line with them. It is only to be expected that the needs of personalities and the demands of social systems can get out of line with each other, just as it is to be expected that the requirements of abstract cultural principles and of practical conduct will be in tension with each other. However, it cannot be the case that these misalignments are ubiquitous, and that people will not be able to fulfil any of the routines of social systems, or that the cultural ideals have no bearing at all on practical life, for this would deprive us of the very phenomena that so patently exist.

So, from the theorist's point of view, this minimal level of integration is not to be taken for granted, as automatically and magically provided. The theorist's job is to analyse the conditions under which, and the 'mechanisms' whereby, this minimal (and any greater) level of integration is generated, and it is with this that Parsons' work in *Toward a General Theory of Action* and *The Social System* was engaged.

Parsons is sometimes charged with idealism in giving excessive emphasis to 'ideal', or cultural, elements in his analysis. If this charge were true, then Parsons would have broken with his own fundamental strictures on the theorists who preceded him, namely, Durkheim, Weber, Pareto and Marshall, for their failure to keep in mind all four elements of the unit act. The criticism results from a reading into Parsons of conceptions, typically derived from Marx, of society as divided between a cultural 'superstructure' and a material 'base'. In such a theoretical context, it makes sense to ask whether one of these – the base or the superstructure – should be prioritised over the other; whether the superstructure could be the primary determinant of the base, or whether it should be the other way around. In Parsons' terms, however, this question makes absolutely no sense since the social system and the cultural system are not distinct entities to begin with. For Parsons' 'analytic realism' a real-world situation is composed of the different elements bound together. Cultural, personality and social systems are jointly constitutive of the empirical society: any social situation is then made up of social, psychological and cultural elements. These elements are, so to speak, *fused* with each other in the concrete case. The key relationship, in Parsons, between culture, personality and social system is therefore one of *interpenetration* rather than the causation of one by the other. Thus, the social system is made up of both personalities and cultural elements just as the interactions between persons are interactions between personalities subject to culturally prescribed procedures. Personalities are shaped by social relationships and therefore because they are socialised into the culture the personality is made up in important part of cultural elements. Cultures develop in and are perpetuated in social systems. However, among the various systems it is the social system which occupies a central position. This partly reflects Parsons' central interest in the sociological point of view, but also it is through the social system that the three systems are articulated with each other. Two basic mechanisms are involved here: institutionalisation and internalisation. It is culture which provides the terms in which social relationships are predominantly transacted; that is, the socially shared terms which specify how people should act toward each other.

Institutionalisation and internalisation

We have already discussed how Parsons' work grew out of the previous ideas of Durkheim and Weber, the functionalism of social anthropology and, as we shall see in a moment, a functionalist scheme from a colleague, Robert F. Bales, working in the field of small group behaviour. The same is true of another idea crucial in Parsons' scheme, that of 'social role', developed by, among others, Ralph Linton (1893–1953).

A 'role', or, strictly, in Parsons' terms, a 'status-role' is a key structural element in the social system but, in important respects, it is a cultural item. A social system is a network of status-roles (the idea of 'role' originally taken from the theatre), that is, of social positions – statuses – such as 'doctor', 'teacher', 'goalkeeper', 'wife', 'barman', 'father', 'teenager', etc. and the behaviour associated with and expected of those who occupy the role. The behaviour comprising a role is not, in the first instance, the actual behaviour of the individuals occupying the status, but is a set of prescriptions for appropriate behaviour that apply to whichever individuals might occupy the position. The prescriptions identify required conduct by expressing the expectations which are generally held by members of a social system about how the occupant of a given status should behave. A role is the set of expectations for behaviour standardly associated with a status, and expectations are, of course, people's beliefs about what behaviour is right and proper to the occupant of a given status. It is these normative beliefs which constitute a status-role as a cultural as well as a social system element. Status-roles are institutionalised in a social system; that is, built into, and shared throughout, the social system, and it is this which makes the expectations generalised or shared ones. Thus, a social system, as an arrangement of status-roles is, in important part, a matter of institutionalised cultural elements.

The notion of 'role' as comprised of shared expectations provides an important part of the solution to the problem of social order for Parsons. Social activities run smoothly because people do not have to work out their relationships with each other from scratch on every occasion. They can enter a great many situations with expectations as to what to do, expectations that will typically be fulfilled. Shared expectations have 'double contingency'. How a person acts depends upon how others react, and so, of course, each party has expectations not only about how he or she should behave, but about how the other will be expecting them to behave, as will the other also have conceptions of what the first will be expecting. If the expectations of both parties match then interaction can run smoothly and effectively.

Imagine getting into a cab and saying: 'Chorltonville, please'. In calling it 'a cab' we have already invoked expectations: that the parties to the transaction are 'cab driver' and 'passenger', that the driver will understand these words as an instruction to take the passenger to the named place. The passenger will expect, at the destination, to pay a fare, and so on. It is the capacity of the parties to rely on these shared expectations that enables 'taking a cab' to work as it does. The point can be generalised: the carrying out of most social transactions is extensively unproblematic, and there are unaccountably many situations where the parties can unreflectively interrelate on the basis of expectations about each other, each acting as the other expects them to.

The point about 'shared expectations' is that they are not merely cognitive, but moral. They are not empirical predictions about how the other will behave, but requirements as to how the other *should* behave. If, in a role-defined transaction, the other person does not behave as we 'expect' them to, that is, does not behave in what we regard as the 'right' or 'proper' way, then we do not merely react as if we have made a factual mistake, but in a personal way, with anger, resentment and so on. We are personally affronted by the fact they have not acted toward us in the way we are entitled to have them act. Or, if we behave inappropriately, then we experience embarrassment, shame, contrition, etc. These shared expectations have become part of our own personality. Parsons thought it one of Durkheim's main insights to have realised that social requirements do not constrain us just from the outside, but from 'within', that is, through their transformation from what others think is right and expect us to do into what we ourselves think is right. The 'external' standards of society are made 'internal' to the individual's own psychology; they are, in a word, 'internalised'. However, if Durkheim had seen the importance of internalisation (as it was later to be called), he had not provided an account of the psychological mechanisms that could produce this. It is Parsons' assumption that humans are 'sensitive' to each other, that they are responsive to the reactions of others for their own sake, that they are affected – rewarded or punished – by the approval or disapproval of others. It is on the basis of this that shared expectations are built up from the very beginning of our lives. It is the approving and disapproving reactions of others which are the foundation of internalisation.

Many years after *The Structure of Social Action* Parsons came to feel that the book could have been made more effective by the inclusion of another turn-of-the-century innovator, Sigmund Freud (1856–1939) who provided the account of the psychological dynamics of internalisation that Parsons felt was needed to fill out his general theory of action. Although these days Freud is perhaps regarded as somewhat less of an intellectual colossus, until recently it would have been difficult to overestimate the influence of his ideas on social thought. As we shall see in Chapter 3, in connection with Critical Theory and the Frankfurt School, as well as in connection with structuralism in Chapter 4, Freud was widely regarded as a pivotal figure who laid the basis for building the link between the psychological and the social although, it has to be said, this was often predicated on very different interpretations of his thought. For Parsons, the most important of Freud's ideas was that the basic personality is formed in the early childhood years through the nuclear family. Relations, rich in sexual undertones, between mother, father and child decisively shape the child's eventual mature personality. The development of the child's personality involves, in important respects, the child psychologically ingesting an image of its parents, especially the father, as the exemplar of proper behaviour and thus as a model for future conduct. This provides the core of the adult conscience.

However, Freud needed some reinterpretation for Parsons' purposes. Freud assumed that it was the image of the father as such that was 'internalised' by the child, providing the 'voice of conscience'. It is not, however, the father as the particular individual who is internalised, but rather, argues Parsons, the father as a symbolic representative of the wider society and its culture, and thus of the standards of that wider culture that he embodies. The child's personality is, accordingly, prominently constituted by cultural elements. A personality system is shaped within a social system and comprised of cultural elements which, in their turn, develop the attraction and attachment which the child can feel toward the social positions and responsibilities that will subsequently be imposed upon it. No more than one can treat social system and cultural system as entirely separate elements can one treat personality and cultural system as separate, for they too interpenetrate. As pointed out earlier, a social system is something which, in its concrete aspect, is carried out by individuals-with-personalities. For example, people in groups get along, or fail to do so, depending, in part, on the compatibility of their individual personalities.

Neither Parsons, nor Freud before him, sought to portray individuals as driven by forces of which they were unconscious and over which they had no control, be it role requirements imposed upon them by society, or psychologically unconscious forces. Freud's clinical work often involved clients who were subject to various kinds of compulsions that they were unable to control, such as perpetually washing their hands. Freud held that these individuals were driven by unconscious forces involving unresolved conflicts between, for example, what their unconscious really wanted them to do and what they could allow themselves to do: conflicts often expressed through their compulsions. Freud's therapy was meant to enable people so afflicted to gain control over their own behaviour by making them conscious of the underlying tensions causing their illness. If this was successful such persons could enjoy the same capacity for choice as other normal adults. However, Freud's general account of personality formation tells of the growth of autonomy from the unconscious by the mature, healthy personality. It is an account of the child developing away from being controlled by both its unconscious impulses and by its dependence upon adults. This is far from suggesting that individuals are mere puppets of their upbringing and social training. Parsons certainly understood Freud as providing an account of how the individual personality matured into that of the autonomous adult capable of making choices and decisions for themselves, and broadly motivated to conform to the normative standards institutionalised in the culture that they had internalised.

A picture of society

The picture of society developed to this point is of society as a network of status-roles which are combined to make up different social systems. Status-roles differ specifically in terms of the activities which the social system is engaged in, providing shared expectations of how parties to the system's affairs ought individually to behave. The shared expectations provide a basis for the orderly conduct of practical affairs. A complex society consists in a whole range of differentiated social sub-systems which are specialised in terms of the affairs they organise – educational, religious, political, and so on. The role expectations in each social system will be specific to the role that the system has in the larger system. The role expectations within each sub-system will also need to be compatible with role expectations in other sub-systems, otherwise social and psychological conflict will result. This compatibility is ensured by the shared ends, or values, to which *The Structure of Social Action* had given such prominence. These ends, or values, are institutionalised in the social system, and internalised in personalities. They are very general ends rather than specific practical ones, specifying the kind of 'good life' that an individual should seek, for example, or the kind of world that they would want to bring about. Below, in connection with Merton, we will mention the value Americans place on individual economic achievement, on seeking success through one's own effort. A value like that of material success is very general, and if widely shared among people, will induce compatibility between the role expectations constituent of all the different sub-systems. Individual achievement will be prized and encouraged in the family, in school, even in play, as well as in work. Though the role expectations in school will be shaped by the needs of educational instruction, the satisfaction of such instructional requirements will be organised in ways that accentuate competitiveness between pupils, emphasising the extent to which their educational attainments must be a product of their distinctive individual effort.

The society as a whole is centrally structured around a main set of shared values that possess the 'sacredness' that Durkheim had thought we attribute to the society itself. The society will be structured hierarchically: not merely as a set of inclusively nested sub-systems, but also in terms of stratification. Some parts of the society – and the individuals occupying statuses within them – will be regarded as superior to others, to the extent that they are recognised as being closer to, and more exemplary of, the main values of the society. Consider how prestigiously business is regarded in America, and the much more ambivalent view taken in the UK, and connect this to the strength of the American emphasis upon achievement and practicality: what Parsons dubbed 'instrumental activism'. The society will have to be organised in ways that both sustain and disseminate its main values throughout the sub-systems, so ensuring broad compatibility between them, and in ways that articulate them with the practical requirements of the various sub-systems themselves. This will ensure that newcomers are socialised into those values and expectations, and motivated to pursue and fulfil them. Of course, since a modern society is a very complex, highly differentiated structure there will be variations in the degree to which the values are thoroughly disseminated, the extent to which role expectations are coherent *within* a sub-system and mutually compatible *across* sub-systems, just as there will be variations in the extent to which individuals are 'successfully' socialised and motivated.

Parsons' schema does not claim that the social system is always integrated and that there is no conflict or strain. What he is attempting to do is present a tightly specified theoretical picture of the minimal conditions for an integrated social system. As such his schema is a theoretically limited case: one end of a dimension of integrated social systems. In Parsons' hands, trying to specify the conditions of social system integration also identifies the potential points at which system discontinuities – in Parsons' term, 'strains' – can arise. As we shall see more fully when discussing Merton's functionalist analysis of deviance, the pursuit of the value of success may well, especially for people disadvantageously placed to secure the means of success, lead to the use of illegitimate means for securing the value. This would set in motion machineries of 'social control' in an effort to 'correct' the insufficiently integrated elements of the system and try to motivate the deviant individuals to comply with role expectations or, more severely, contain or suppress them to limit their impact on the more inclusive system.

Parsons' framework is a 'top down' one beginning with the conditions necessary to secure the integrity of the social system as a distinguishable unit for analysis. Moreover, the framework was not only intended to encompass the other human sciences in addition to sociology, but also, in order to achieve this, was meant to be applicable at different levels of social organisation. To this end Parsons developed the pattern variable schema.

The pattern variables

Parsons' schema was intended as a general one encompassing all of the human sciences, and in order to make comparisons at all levels of social organisation, he introduced a scheme of dichotomies called 'the pattern variables'. These dichotomies were again largely derivative, mainly providing a condensation of the contrast made by numerous sociologists, such as Durkheim and Tönnies (1855–1936), for example, between 'traditional' and 'modern societies', reflecting, basically, the difference between the direct, individual-to-individual nature of relations in traditional society and the much more 'impersonal' character of transactions in modern society. The pattern variables are as follows:

Diffuseness–specificity

This pair refers to whether one is interested in another person in respect of all that might apply to them or only a specific aspect of them. With a close friend, for example, one might be interested in lots of things about them – what they did on their holidays, what kind of food they like, which book they are reading, how their parents are, and so on – whereas with a shop assistant, a bus driver or a doctor one is only interested in how well they do their specific job.

Particularism–universalism

This dimension refers to the kind of connection or relationship people might have between them. A kinship connection, for example, is a particular kind of relationship whereas being connected to someone on the basis of having passed a specific examination is to be connected on the basis of some general standard which goes beyond the particular person.

Affectivity–affective neutrality

This dimension refers to the issue of whether a person relates to another with feeling or neutrally. An example would be the way in which parents are expected to relate emotionally to their children in contrast with the dispassionate professionalism in which a doctor is supposed to relate to patients.

Quality–performance

This contrast is intended to capture relating to someone in terms of something that they are – a woman, a child, a member of an ethnic group, a relative, etc. – and relating to someone in terms of what they do or how they perform, such as whether they are successful in business, or in sport, or in education, for example.

Self–collectivity

This pair was a late addition to the set of pattern variables and denotes the difference between placing the individual first compared with putting the interests of the public or the collectivity first. An example is when professionals put their obligations to their professional group and, therefore, the public, before the interests of their individual client.

These contrasts provide an elaboration of the rather traditional sociological contrast between the 'traditional' and 'modern' society. In the former people relate to each other on the basis of kinship, know each other as individuals, give preference to each other because of their personal relationships and because of the feelings of solidarity, mutual liking (or disliking) that develop in such societies. The opposite extreme – the professional–client relationship, which is not found in 'traditional' society – exemplifies the nature of social relationships in 'modern' society. The professional should take on the client, regardless of the client's personal characteristics, should not have any interest in the client other than the specific problem which is the basis for the client's need of professional help, should not treat the client's case on any basis other than its technical merits and without regard for whether the professional likes or despises the client, and should handle the client's case in the way that any case should be handled, that is, according to the general standards of the profession not the idiosyncratic characteristics of the client.

The emphasis on 'the professional complex' also shows how far Parsons was from many of his critics, especially those inspired by Marxist social theory. They took it for granted that it was the business ethos which was dominant in 'capitalist' society. Parsons dissented from the view that it was the self-interested entrepreneur that was the epitome of modern society. He was impressed by the relentless growth of professional occupations that do not prioritise self-interest as business does but are oriented more to the 'collectivity' end of the self vs. collectivity pattern variable. It is the 'professional ethic', he argued, rather than the business one which is increasingly characteristic of modern industrial societies. Of course, whether or not Parsons was correct in his diagnosis of industrial society is arguable.

The four-phase model

After developing the above picture of society Parsons took its further analysis in a different direction by adopting the notion of 'functional prerequisites', a set of minimal conditions that must be satisfied if any system is to persist. The basic scheme of functional prerequisites was not initially developed from an analysis of society as a whole, but extracted from experimental studies of small groups by his colleague, Robert Bales.

Bales' scheme is simplicity itself, providing twelve categories for the direct observation of interaction amongst group members. Along with the kind of actions they refer to, the categories are as follows:

1. *Shows solidarity,* raises others' status, gives help, reward.
2. *Shows tension release,* jokes, laughs, shows satisfaction.
3. *Agrees,* shows passive acceptance, understands, concurs, complies.
4. *Gives suggestion,* gives direction, implying autonomy for other.
5. *Gives opinion,* evaluation, analysis, expresses feeling, wish.
6. *Gives orientation,* informs, repeats, clarifies, confirms.
7. *Asks for orientation,* information, repetition, confirmation.
8. *Asks for opinion,* evaluation, analysis, expression of feeling.
9. *Asks for suggestion,* gives direction, possible ways of action.
10. *Disagrees,* shows passive rejection, formality, withholds help.

11 *Shows tension*, asks for help, withdraws out of field.
12 *Shows antagonism*, deflates others' status, defends or asserts self.

These different observable activities could be examined in relation to their part in organising the group's activity. For one example, Bales divided the twelve categories into two more basic types, one related to the 'social-emotional' problem area which managed the 'integration' of the members into the group, the other with the 'instrumental' problem area, namely getting the group task done. Bales allocated items 1–3 and 10–12 to the first type, and 4–9 to the other.

The fact that Parsons should seek to formulate his comprehensive scheme for the analysis of the structure of whole societies, and of all societies, on the basis of small laboratory groups made up of a few individuals ought not to be surprising. For Parsons, there must be properties which social systems possess by virtue of their being systems, regardless of the scale or the nature of their activity. A laboratory group of six or seven is a social system, just as much as the whole of American or Chinese society. Admittedly, the experimental laboratory group is a small sub-system of a much larger system, but if it persists as a system then it must have met the same basic requisites for any other larger or more inclusive system.

Bales modelled the dynamics of small task-oriented groups as a cycle. Being task-oriented these groups would end a cycle of action when they attained their goal. But attaining the goal is not guaranteed. The group needs to organise itself in such a way that it can attain the tasks set for it. Moreover, attaining some of its goals is necessary if the group is to survive. Persistent failure would erode the group's entire rationale and motivation. Directly working toward its goal is only one phase in the overall activity cycle of any task-oriented group. When the goal has been achieved a group will not always immediately launch itself into another task. It may break up, its members temporarily going their separate ways, reassembling later for another round of goal-directed activity. The group continues to exist throughout its dispersal, for people remain members of the group even though they are not currently acting in their capacity as members of it. The group is then in a latent (or virtual) state. It is necessary if the group is to reassemble and effectively go about pursuing its goals again, that the group-required capacities of its members not deteriorate during latency. They must not lose their commitment to the group, nor exhaust the energies needed for the group's work. When the group reassembles to pursue further tasks, it must organise itself so that it can practically pursue those tasks and have to hand the resources necessary to accomplish the tasks. The pursuit of the goal is the main business of the group, but such a pursuit must be concerned with the 'technical' dimension of its activities. If a goal is to be attained then, virtually by definition, the way in which a group goes about getting to this must involve the use of practically adequate means. The business of seeking practical goals, however, has interpersonal consequences. Getting the group organised to meet the practical necessities of the task can give rise to enmity, dissent and disruption. Thus, it must be that there are periods in the task cycle of a group when attention will shift from getting on with the task itself to dealing with relationships internal to the group, trying to get people to co-operate in the practical procedures, stopping them from quarrelling with each other, calming heated feelings and so forth.

The group's operations can correspondingly be categorised in four basic phases: adaptation [A] goal attainment [G], integration [I] and latency [L]. Latency is also, more lengthily, called 'pattern maintenance and tension management' to differentiate two aspects: the first, maintaining value commitments necessary to the group's functioning and, second, managing the frustrations and disappointments which individuals are likely to experience in any group. The organisation of any functioning group must be a compromise between the individual members who make it up, a matter of give and take, and there may be a greater price for some participants than others. This is a fact that somehow the system must deal with.

This AGIL model, as it is commonly referred to, analyses the way the internal structure of social systems is organised to meet the 'functional prerequisites', bearing in mind that this may be instantiated at the level of the allocation of roles in small groups or in terms of the interrelationship of institutions of the whole society, or at any level in between or even beyond, including internationally. Parsons used the temporal sequence of the AGIL cycle from adaptation to latency as a scheme of structural differentiation too. That is, over a cycle of a system's activity these phases will be gone through, but within any system there will also be a tendency for units (individuals or sub-systems) to be *relatively* 'specialised' in one or other of these functions. In a small group, for example, those who are most active in leading the group toward its goals are likely to be less active than others in managing the problems of bruised sensitivities.

Another fundamental constraint on a system must be the interrelating of the four phases themselves. These too have a 'functional' aspect. For example, unless that part of the system specialising in 'adaptation' can provide sufficient resources for attaining goals, then the system will fail to achieve its ends. Those who create the resources the system needs will have to hand them over to those using them to reach the goals. But why should those putting effort into creating resources hand them over? They must receive some return for the output they sacrifice and others must input into their adaptive activities. If any sub-system only outputs, with no reciprocating input, then eventually it will run out of its own resources. Therefore, among the four phases, there must be exchanges and these must tend to balance or move toward equilibrium. After all, if in a process of inputting and outputting there is not sufficient equivalence to keep all parties motivated to play their part in the arrangement, then it will break down. There must, then, *in any ongoing system*, be relatively balanced exchanges among the four phases.

Two more ideas are needed to round out our account of the AGIL conception, namely, 'generalised media' and the 'cybernetic hierarchy'.

Generalised media

This notion relates to the four-phase model conceived as exchange, and inspired by an economic analogy between barter and money economies. Barter is restrictive, requiring the precise matching of the requirements of the exchanging partners. If A wants something that B has, but B does not want anything that A has, then they cannot exchange. A money exchange system is much more flexible. The point about money is that it has generalised properties. It will be accepted by anyone, and in exchange for almost anything. Parsons reasons that just as it is unimaginable that a complex economy could operate on the basis of barter, so it is inconceivable that any social system above the most minimal level of complexity cannot operate its four phases of exchange on a 'barter' basis. It must possess something that works in the same way as money, what he calls the 'functional equivalents' of money. These are the 'generalised media' of exchange. Clearly, 'money' is the generalised medium of exchange in economic transactions, which are the paradigm case of 'adaptive' functions, but there must be others corresponding to the different functions: to money, add power, influence and commitments.

These other media are, of course, very different from money; they do not have the specifically quantitative character that money has, which makes the judgement of equivalence more difficult. The idea is that 'power' is a medium based in the goal attainment phase of the social process, and compares with money in the sense that it involves binding commitment. Money works because people make binding commitments to surrender goods and services in exchange for it. Power is, for Parsons, power over others, and his concern is to understand how the exchanges among the four phases give some people power over others. For Parsons social scientists have previously taken too narrow a view of power, focusing on only one kind of power relationship, concerned with power in relation to the inequities in its distribution and the conflicts that these engender, but not taking into account the constructive role of power within the social system. The excessively narrow view of power has been in zero-sum terms. If the total amount of power is a fixed quantity divided among people, then any changes in distribution must add up to zero. The overall quantity cannot increase; there can only be redistribution. This means that anyone's gain must be someone else's loss. If A adds three units, then B, or some combination of B, C etc., must lose three units, so the 'plus three' for A added to the 'minus three' for B and C will 'sum' to zero. Such a zero-sum conception suggests that the distribution of power must always be a matter of contest, of struggle, since anyone's increased share of power must be at someone else's expense. Parsons rejects the idea that power is necessarily and generally like this. Not all redistribution of wealth is of the zero-sum kind, for example. Economic growth allows incomes to expand without one person's gain being at someone else's expense. Comparably, the overall amount of power can be increased, again without the necessity for a contest over power.

Further, the zero-sum conception encourages the idea that the struggle over power is an end in itself, sought for its own sake. Parsons' functionalist inclination leads him to ask: what is power for, what can be done with it? Again, the comparison is economic, this time with money. Though people seek to accumulate money they do not seek merely to hold it but to use it. From the point of view of the system, then, power is a resource for getting things done, a mechanism which provides for the availability of effort in collective endeavours, which ensures that those subordinate to power, and subject to binding commitments, will participate in collective activity.

Cybernetic hierarchy

The notion of the 'cybernetic hierarchy' recalls the account of organism, personality, culture and social systems, and provides a way of conceiving long-term social change. Cybernetics is the science of automatic, self-steering systems, such as guided missiles or programmed washing machines. In such systems energy and information stand in inverse relation to control. That is, something which has rich information but little energy can control something which has huge energy but no information. The programmed washing machine requires a lot of electrical energy to rotate the drum but very little current to run the program that turns the drum on and off. This analogy provides, in a way, Parsons' answer to anxieties about idealism on the part of materialist-minded social scientists who reject the possibility that 'ideas', or culture, can have any causal role in social life because they are immaterial phenomena. This rejection is often associated with a supposedly materialistic, scientific world view. Parsons' analogy is drawn from the bona fide and up-to-date scientific discipline of cybernetics. Certainly 'culture' is relatively immaterial but, then, so is the program in a computer and, by analogy, culture, consisting in information, can be considered to be like a 'program' for the social. No one can deny that information, in the form of a program, can have causal efficacy in the material world and, therefore, 'culture' may, too, have an effective causal role. However, though Parsons had always given a central role to ideas in the form of culture, he was never an idealist, for ever since *The Structure of Social Action* he had opposed the idea that reality was simply an emanation of ideas.

The cybernetic hierarchy involves ranking of the four elements – culture, social system, personality and organism – in terms of information and energy, with organism at the bottom of the information scale and at the top in terms of energy. Culture is at the other extreme, high on information but low on energy, with social system and personality ranked in the order of decreasing information and increasing energy. The analogy is with the 'steering' component in many kinds of machines. So, Parsons suggests, just as the program steers the washer through the wash cycle, so does the culture steer the other elements through processes of change by giving general direction to the pattern of change. Culture is, after all, the item which has the greatest longevity on the historical scale. A cultural element can remain unchanged over a long period as, for example, the American constitution has over some 300 years. Social systems, however, tend to undergo restructuring changes in such periods. To stick with the example, American society has gone from a rural to an urban-industrial to, now, a post-industrial society in that time. The life spans of personalities and organisms are nearly coincident and, on the historic scale, pretty short. Thus, any continuity in history, and any constancy in the direction of change, is likely to be provided at the cultural level – for example, the above-mentioned value of 'instrumental activism' has been directive of North American economic dynamism over some centuries.

We have now accumulated all the main elements in Parsons' theoretical scheme, emphasising the change – but also the continuity – between the formation of the outlines of the 'general theory of action' in the early 1950s, and the elaboration of the four-phase model of the social system in the period from then on.

Applying the framework

Although Parsons recognised his own chronic inclination toward abstract theorising, this did not mean that his work and thought were remote from the world, least of all from the social and political issues of his time. Parsons was a participant in collaborative empirical studies, although these did not usually result in reports of researches published under his name. Nonetheless, he wrote numerous essays about empirical topics and contemporary issues. He identified his first collection (Parsons, 1954) as being essays in 'sociological theory, pure and applied', and it is probably fair to say that his most empirically oriented essays were still exercises in sociological theory, but in *applied* sociological theory; that is, exercises in the interpretation of particular phenomena in the terms of his theory. Thus, for example, Parsons saw the steady expansion of professional occupations, with their emphasis on service rather than profit-seeking, as a potentially very significant development in a society which was supposedly devoted to a business ethic and dedicated profit-seeking.

Professional roles: physician–patient relationships

The physician–patient relationship is a leading example of the professional transaction and can be examined in the context of the theory of the social system, that is, as part of the 'social control mechanisms' of the system. Moreover, the form of the transaction between physician and patient could be examined in terms of the pattern variables as organised around the employment of technical knowledge. The study of 'illness', considered sociologically, became in Parsons' hands an examination of 'the sick role'. One's illness might be biological in nature, but how one behaves, and how others react in relation to one's illness, is a socially organised affair. The person with an illness enters a social role, the 'sick role'. Occupants of this role are exempted from the expectations of other roles, and are therefore, in a sense, deviant. But their failure to fulfil the expectations of their other roles is legitimised by temporary occupancy of the sick role. The exemption from the demands of one's other social roles can be a highly gratifying release from life's stresses and tensions, and permanent occupation of the sick role could therefore be a very attractive option, with consequent damage to the social system. Therefore, the sick role itself has expectations attached to it – that the incumbent should seek to exit from that role as expeditiously as possible by making every effort to overcome their illness. Part of their effort to do this involves placing themselves in the hands of those who are most capable of helping them overcome their illness, characteristically the medical profession. Those who occupy the 'sick role' but do not visibly make efforts to get themselves cured will be subjected to negative sanctions, to disapproving and punitive responses. It will, further, be part of the physician's role to act as a representative of the society's interest in the patient's recovery, and to demand the patient's cooperation in whatever treatments are deemed most effective in producing that recovery.

The pattern variables are used to identify the various dimensions of the physician's professional role which are functionally significant. This has especially to do with its effective performance as an application of scientific knowledge in a situation which is not entirely suitable for properly scientific practice, but which ensures that the physician's work will be accepted in the eyes of those being treated as valid applications of a competent authority. Thus, the norms that govern the physician's roles are – in terms of the pattern variables – collectivity-oriented, universal, affectively neutral and specific.

The physician's involvement in the situation cannot be one of self-interest at the expense of the patient. Rather, the physician–patient relationship is to be conducted (ideally) collaboratively, with the two parties 'working together' to achieve the patient's recovery. It is also, as noted earlier, oriented to achieving what 'the society' requires, namely, the transition of the patient from the sick role back into other roles. The physician's role is collectivity oriented. The physician demands 'privileges' that would not normally be available to others who are not intimates of the patient, such as access to 'private' parts of the body, as well as to information about the patient's life and circumstances which would not otherwise be shared even, perhaps, with intimates.

The willingness of the patient and relatives to accord these privileges, and to trust the physician with them, depends upon their acceptance of the nature of the interest the physician will take in these matters. The universalism, neutrality and specificity of the physician's role ensure that they can repose such confident trust in the physician. In respect of universalism, the physician is applying scientifically based technical competence to this patient in the same way as to any other comparable 'case'. The treatment given does not depend in any way upon any particular relationship between the physician and the patient that might interfere with the essential objectivity of the physician's interest in and understanding of the illness. The physician's response to the patient is affectively neutral. The physician's interest in the patient is to be entirely focused on 'the case' and to be of a strictly technical kind; the concern is to diagnose and treat the illness, and not to have moral or emotional reactions toward or against the patient. The 'specificity' of the role follows from this. The physician's interest in the patient strictly as 'a case' contrasts with a 'diffuse' concern with all sorts of things about the patient *qua* individual. The physician should seek to know only that about the patient which is relevant to the technical interest, and which contributes to the identification and treatment of the sickness. It is on this basis that access to private parts and intimate information is granted: that the physician will require this access only for medical purposes and will not use it for any other purposes.

These are, as Parsons points out, all very much 'taken for granted' with respect to the physician–patient relationship but are, nonetheless, essential conditions for its viability.

McCarthyism

Another topic which Parsons explored was that of McCarthyism. This was a movement, led by the notorious United States senator, Joe McCarthy, which in the early years of the Cold War began 'witch-hunting' alleged communists in the US government. Attitudes toward McCarthyism rapidly became a test of political credentials in liberal intellectual circles. McCarthyism was, for Parsons, an unrealistic 'irrational' reaction to genuine 'strains' in American society, ones generated by changes – and resistance to them – in the nature of that society.

American industrialism had been left free to develop without political interference, but in the light of the political, social and economic realities of the period leading into the 1950s when the 'radical right' became influential, state intervention in the organisation of business became more imperative. The problems involved in making such interventions related, in Parsons' view, to tensions within the structure of the elite in the United States, where there had been no traditional aristocracy or elite based in the independent professions to challenge the dominance of the business elite. The latter had, therefore, assumed the main, but not undisputed, role of community leader despite opposition from miscellaneous social sources, such as 'old money' families and military leaders. The dominance of business leadership was being diminished in the post-war period, as a political elite of politicians (who managed public opinion) and of administrators (in the civil and military services) expanded and strengthened its position, and called for the dominance of the public interest over the private one. It was the sectors of American society most attached to 'individualism', and to the pursuit of private interests unfettered by the state, which provided the support for McCarthy's imputations of disloyalty against those social groups aligned with, or who comprised, the new political and administrative elite.

The case of McCarthyism was continuous with Parsons' interest in social change, the way in which social systems differentiate out their social functions (such that political leadership becomes something done by a specialised political and administrative group, increasingly distinct from business leadership), and the ways in which the 'strains' generated by the structural readjustments involved gave rise to alienated responses in some sectors of the system. Such responses sometimes manifested themselves in 'irrational' reactions focusing upon a 'symbolic' (and imagined) threat, such as that of communist infiltration of the political and administrative elite.

These are only two of numerous empirical orientations from which Parsons wrote, including (but by no means exhausted by) ones on the position of women in the American family, the 'Blacks' in the American social structure, the Nazi Party in Germany, the role of religion in American life and the nature of medical education.

Parsons' functionalism and the analysis of social change

This review of a couple of Parsons' applied studies along with earlier comments should dispose of one of the criticisms levelled at functionalism: that it failed to deal with social change. This was often coupled with the further charge that the approach was ideological in its insinuation that actual society is in perfect harmony and that all the institutions and practices of the society are entirely beneficial. As we say, this charge cannot justly be levelled at Parsons, quite apart from whether one disagrees with the value of the theoretical framework he produced.

The allegation is often based on a misunderstanding of the nature of his theory. *For theoretical purposes,* one could entertain the notion of a perfectly integrated society, and seek to specify the conditions under which such an entity could be most closely approximated. However, this should not delude us into thinking that any actual concrete society was, or could be, perfectly harmonious, any more than the use of models of 'friction free' situations in the physical sciences suggests that scientists suppose that there can be actual 'friction free' cases. The extreme case – no friction, no conflict – is a limiting one for simplifying thinking about actual cases.

Much criticism of Parsons was more probably provoked by the suspicion that a functionalist description of contemporary Western society might give a wrong impression of the depth and strength of its cohesion. The objection was that Parsons' theory – unlike, say, Marxism – made no provision for the possibility of lower-class insurrection in industrial societies but allegedly overestimated the extent to which cohesion and civility in these societies was genuine rather than just the hegemonic imposition of false consciousness upon the masses. This criticism, if just, would be empirically rather than theoretically cogent, and Parsons certainly did not share his Marxist and neo-Marxist critics' assessment of the likelihood of a transformative proletarian revolution in modern Western societies, especially the USA. However, doubting that society was not riven by fierce class struggle was not the same as thinking there was an absence of all political tensions. Parsons affirmed that there were possibilities – around gender and ethnicity especially – for significant 'strains' in the social structure of the United States. 'Strains' arose precisely at points in society's organisation where things were poorly integrated as, he argued, were the family and occupational life in the United States of the 1940s, creating dissatisfaction among mainly middle-class women. Such strains would engender changes in society as 'corrective' responses to them were made, and would eventually dissipate the strains themselves; such changes, however, would fall well short of a revolutionary transformation of the whole.

This view contrasts with that of Marx whose theory postulated, as an inherent, inevitable and central feature of any society, social divisions with the potential for the revolutionary transformation of the society. Thus, essential to his analysis was the identification of sources of change internal to the society. If we turn to Parsons' four-phase pattern with its identification of pressures toward 'balance' as inherent to his notion of social change, then this might well suggest that there is no in-built source of change in the social system and, hence, no way of explaining why some social systems do change their overall nature.

This charge is not really just. Parsons' account of the phase structure, and of the pattern of functional interchanges, just like his account of the integration of culture, personality and social system, assumes from the beginning that the harmonious integration of these things is problematical. Integration is not something which can be automatically assured, but is itself the resultant of system organisation and activity, and a large part of the analysis of a social system (or sub-system) must be of the way in which it produces and reproduces its own organisation, responds to, and handles (or fails to) the strains internal to it. However, it must also be remembered that 'social system' in Parsons is an *analytic notion* (recall again Parsons' basic 'analytic realism', meaning that 'the social system' is an abstraction from the actual society or group), and though we may, for shorthand's sake, identify it with a concrete society or group, it actually refers only to that aspect of the group's organisation that has to do with interaction between persons. Many things that are part of the concrete society are *analytically* 'external' to the social system, that is, they belong to the environment of the system rather than to the system itself. Thus, 'technology' is 'external' to the system in that it does not consist in, or engage in, social relationships with members of the society. The social system is comprised purely of social relations between persons. Another society is external to the social system in being a distinct and separate system. The other society is part of the environment for the society of reference. Hence, Parsons does not deny that changing technologies, conflicts with other societies, and so on, are sources of change, but for him many of the important sources that bring about change (which are much more common than revolutionary insurrections) are external to the social system in his sense. Not all sources of change are external, however, for, as noted, there can be systematic strains within the social system which induce change or even system breakdown. But many important sources of change, such as changes in technology, changes in the natural environment, or conquest by other societies are all external to the social system, purely conceived.

Also it is misleading to understand Parsons' notion of the tendency toward equilibrium as suggesting that a system, once in stable pattern, cannot change. This would be the notion of stable equilibrium, in which a given state of affairs is indefinitely perpetuated, but it is not Parsons' notion. His idea is of a 'moving equilibrium'. If our body is not internally integrated we will die, but the fact that our organs are integrated does not mean that we do not change. We do so all the time. We mature, grow and age, and therefore the equilibrium relation between our organs changes, or moves, in response to our maturation. These changes are continuous, not disruptive, involving the development of the body, not its disintegration and reconstitution. And there certainly is, in Parsons' scheme, provision for the possibility of extensive and continuous social change arising within the social system of the kind that involves processes related in moving equilibrium. Thus, for Parsons, many of the major changes in Western society have involved 'upgrading'; that is, building on the existing structures rather than overthrowing them, increasing the capacity of the system to manage its functional requirements by, for example, the highly specialised social division of labour through differentiation of social functions, expanding economic capacity, knowledge base, and general level of education.

Parsons' protégé, Neil Smelser provided just such an account in his *Social Change in the Industrial Revolution* (Smelser, 1959) which treated socio-political disturbances as created by the transition from one equilibrium – in which economic activity in Britain in the eighteenth century was organised around the household and in terms of family structure – to a new equilibrium where economic activity was dissociated from household and located in factories, and where industrial discipline replaced family authority. Smelser also sought, using Parsonian categories, to outline a theory of revolution as an extreme form of collective behaviour, a class of behaviours which included riot, panics and other response to 'strains' in the social system (Smelser, 1962).

So, although we might disagree with Parsons' analysis of social change, it is certainly not the case that he aimed to present a harmonious picture of a perfectly integrated society free of all conflicts and strains. Indeed, and to the contrary, his analysis of the functional prerequisites of the social system was not only to specify, as he saw them, the conditions of stability and integration but, as part of the same exercise, to identify the sources of strain and hence social change. This was a theme developed further by Robert Merton.

Merton's functionalism

We have already mentioned the work of Parsons' contemporary, Robert Merton, who was also sympathetic to functional views, and whose ideas could be said to complement and develop those of Parsons. However, though both agreed that functionalism was a reasonable and useful basis for attempting to develop sociology toward a more scientific level, they were not in entire agreement as to how this should be done. Merton's approach was directed more to facilitating sociological research rather than elaborating highly abstract and general theories of the kind that Parsons sought to build. To realise functionalism's potential more methodological rigour was needed. Indeed, Merton regarded the very concept of function as imprecise and muddled and in great need of clarification. His own recommendation was to be less theoretically ambitious than many earlier functionalists had been, to learn to walk before trying to run, and to restrict the notion of function to the observed consequences of social arrangements which make for the adaptation of a given system. It was also necessary to distinguish between the 'manifest' and 'latent' functions (to a large extent, a distinction between intended and unintended consequences) of practices and institutions. Manifest functions are, as the name suggests, functions whose utility is apparent as, for example, the function of the fire service in putting out fires. Latent functions are those functions that are less apparent, perhaps unknown to those who engage in the practice that has them, but which have benefits for the whole society or particular parts of it, even though they may have no obvious utility. Magico-religious practices are, for Merton, as for Durkheim before him, a clear illustration. Thus, Native Americans engage in 'rain dances' to bring rain. But we know that dancing does not cause rain, so any real value in such a practice cannot reside in its 'manifest' function, that of bringing rain, but must reside in some other, not so manifest (or latent) function such as the production of social solidarity.

It was, however, a matter of being sensitive to the possibility of latent functions, not of taking a rigid, *a priori* view that all institutions and practices *must* have some function. They may not. Indeed, rather than making a 'functional' contribution, they may be 'dysfunctional', that is, have a negative or disruptive effect, and it is only through cautious empirical investigation that an accurate audit of a practice's functional implications can be made.

Merton held, however, as many have before and since, that sociology is often too abstractly theoretical, lacking significant connections between theoretical generalities and empirical findings. Parsons' ambitious, all-embracing multidisciplinary, unrelentingly theoretical scheme would be just what he had in mind in making this criticism. Merton himself was not going to develop any general theory and used functionalism only in a modestly exploratory way. He subscribed to a traditional conception of theory known as the 'hypothetico-deductive' scheme, which sees theory as a hierarchy of propositions, descending in logical, deductive steps from the most abstract and general – desirably universal – to more concrete and quite specific propositions. These lowest-level derivations provide specific empirical predictions, following from the larger generalities of the theory. This is, however, just what sociology commonly fails to do. General sociological theory – like that of Parsons – is too loosely expressed and lacking in empirical content to provide a basis from which logical deduction of specific predictions can begin. Sociological researches, therefore, carry on without regard for the work of the theorist, forming and testing predictions, but conjuring these predictions up *ad hoc*, rather than deriving them from any fully systematic, thoroughly spelled out theory.

Hence, there was, within American sociology, a vast gulf between theory at the 'grand' level Parsons was working at, and research which was marked by not only theories at a low level of generality but theories which were unsystematic and *ad hoc*. What was really needed, argued Merton, was a middle way involving the production of more systematic theory than was usually associated with empirical studies, but theory of more limited ambition and range than was being propounded by Parsons: Merton termed this 'middle range' theory. Thus, it would seek to put forward a set of systematically related theoretical propositions, but covering only a restricted area of social life, such as 'deviance' for example, and would be such that one could derive fairly specific, and testable, empirical propositions from them. However, though seeking to sharpen the character of functionalism he does not lose sight of its basic conceptual framework, but he tends to use it implicitly rather than explicitly. He accepts, for example, the idea of consensus on values and norms, the conception of the social system and the idea that society is a normative arrangement.

A good example of Merton's approach to functionalist theory building is his study, 'Social Structure and Anomie', which draws upon Durkheim's concept of 'anomie' used to describe one form of suicide: that due to a condition of 'normlessness' (in Merton, 1957). He starts from the assumption that in a society there are particular goals which the members of society can hope to attain. Further, there is an expectation that these goals will be sought for by the use of acceptable ways of attaining them. For example, in the United States economic success is highly valued and the legitimate means for attaining this are hard work and application. The combination of the valued goals and the means for attaining them gives rise to the patterns of interaction which constitute the social structure of the society. However, at times there can be a disjuncture between the goals and the means for attaining them. This places structural pressure on the individuals exposed to them to respond in a deviant manner. Lower class children, for example, may well lack the education necessary to obtain high paying jobs and, accordingly, are under some pressure to obtain economic success – money, in short – by illegal means. Although he does not use the terms in his analysis, the theory implies that deviant responses arise when the social system is in 'disequilibrium'. Indeed, Merton's notion of 'dysfunction' implies order, stability and equilibrium through its reference to disruptive elements in the social system and is linked to Durkheim's notion of pathological social facts, that is, those harmful to the society as a whole.

The dissociation between the equally widely distributed imperative to achieve and the uneven distribution of realistic opportunities for success manifests a lack of integration between the cultural values and the stratified social system of United States society. There is, to put it another way, a tension in the lives of individuals between their powerful aspiration to success-through-their-own-effort, and their chances of fulfilling this aspiration. Since they cannot resolve the tension in legitimate ways, some of them are motivated to respond in deviant ways.

To round out the simple summary picture, then, society can exhibit all sorts of organisational discontinuities with associated tensions (or, as Parsons termed them, 'strains') that would press people to deviate from role expectations and to dissent from or withdraw from society. However, the fact that some people were not following expectations would frustrate others, and inspire them to negative, purportedly punitive responses. In short, machineries of 'social control' would be set in motion, which might dissipate the tensions and their source – adjusting the unintegrated bits of the system, motivating the deviant individuals to comply with role expectations, or containing, isolating and/or suppressing them, limiting the effects of their deviant behaviour on the more inclusive system.

The fate of functionalism

For a brief period, the leading American functionalists were confident that they had triumphed and inaugurated a genuinely scientific sociology by establishing a general framework within which there would be a steady accumulation of knowledge, the very hallmark of scientific progress. One of them, Kingsley Davis (1966) went so far as to argue that functionalism was not a distinctive point of view, but simply the general form of all sociological explanation. Moreover, the idea of system if not precisely Parsons' formulation of it, was a popular one at the time and has endured. In political science, for example, as part of what was known as the behavioural movement, David Easton argued the need for the creation of higher order generalisations and turned to the idea of systems to provide a general framework for the understanding of politics (Easton, 1965). Of course, systems thinking itself has its roots outside sociology, particularly in biology, in trying to deal with 'organised complexity'.

However, the pre-eminence of structural-functionalism was, even in its heyday, challenged. Though Davis' claim, mentioned in the previous paragraph, might sound a strong, triumphal one, its plausibility depended upon a very dilute idea of functional analysis. That is, if 'functional analysis' meant using the idea of 'system', then one could indeed hold that the analysis of society as a system was much more widespread in sociology than merely its use among the circle of explicitly functionalist theorists. However, the analysis of society as a system need not carry the kinds of implications about stability, consensus, etc. that many felt were implied by the notion. In any case, there was another way of putting a question mark against the distinctiveness of functional analysis. Was functional analysis really an irreducibly special kind of explanation, or merely a shorthand form of otherwise straightforwardly causal analysis? Does talk about the survival requirements of a system really explain why practices are brought into being, especially since no one wants to suggest that the social system is any kind of agent, actually arranging things so as to bring about the satisfaction of its needs? The whole point about the functionalist form of explanation is that it is drawing attention to the *unintended* consequences of people's actions, the way in which, by going about their activities (though they neither intend this nor are aware of it) they give rise to consequences which perpetuate the system. But cannot all this be stated in causal terms? Critics ask: Could we not just say that people's actions *cause* certain consequences, creating the conditions that cause people again to act in the way they first did? If this were true, then we could either dispense with functionalist terminology altogether and just give causal accounts, or continue to use functionalist terminology, but recognising that it did not provide a special kind of explanation that could be given in no other terms.

Argument about the validity and distinctiveness of functionalism as a form of explanation would erupt again in the late 1970s, this time in an argument over whether or not many of Karl Marx's prominent explanatory strategies were functionalist in character and, if they were, then what form of functional explanation did they use, and, finally, did the fact that it was functionalist in form invalidate that part of Marx's theorising?

The fact that theorists as diverse as the communist Karl Marx and the right wing economist Frederick von Hayek (1899–1992) can reasonably be argued to use functional explanation should suggest then that there is nothing inherently political about functionalism as a form of explanation. The analysis of society as a system with self-stabilising tendencies does not necessarily carry assumptions that societies are naturally and beneficially harmonious – not even in Parsons' scheme. Marx certainly saw historical societies as systems which had self-stabilising tendencies, even though, *in the long term* they would be disrupted by internal tensions. That functional analysis is not inherently conservative does not, however, prevent a particular application of the general strategy from being such, and certainly many readers were suspicious that Parsonian functionalism did have a conservative character, that it was more a form of ideology than it was a true science. In an atmosphere in which the increased politicisation of sociology was being demanded, Parsons was regarded as an obstruction.

Therefore, Parsons' negative legacy to sociology was much greater than his positive one. Whatever the actual merits of Parsons' functionalism, there was an intense and lethal backlash against it. The course of sociology subsequently developed more in opposition to Parsons' theories than on the basis of them. Two main currents of opposition played a major part in shaping the subsequent course of sociology: consensus versus conflict, and structure versus agency.

Beginning in the late 1950s and early 1960s Parsons stood accused of being 'one sided', guilty of unbalanced 'consensus' and 'structure' doctrines. With respect to the opposition between consensus and conflict, the immediate effect of the backlash was simply to reverse Parsons' priorities. Parsons had allegedly given pride of place to harmony and consensus, but at the price of being unable to recognise, let alone deal with, dissensus and conflict. With respect to the structure versus agency relationship, Parsons was charged with 'structural determinism', that is, giving such priority to analysis in terms of 'the system' and its needs that individual actors had virtually lost all significance and figured, at most, as mere puppets of the system entirely manipulated by its requirements and needs. Here, the immediate reaction was the hostility of symbolic interaction and ethnomethodology, as the latter also sought – or seemed to seek – to reverse the priorities to make the individual (or 'subject') prominent to the exclusion of 'the system'. This characterisation does neither Parsons nor his interactionist and ethnomethodological critics any justice. Nonetheless, it has served many other sociologists well, letting them accuse the interactionists and ethnomethodologists of going too far to the other extreme from Parsons. This has allowed them to create the supposed 'structure/agency' problem, which ostensibly requires a third way between the two extremes, one which can recognise and balance both the 'system' and the 'individual' or 'subjective' side of things. The contemporary theoretical work of Anthony Giddens, Pierre Bourdieu and Jürgen Habermas is primarily motivated by the presupposition that the structure versus agency is the main problem to be solved in sociology.

'Conflict theory' was an apt designation for the work of a diversity of sociologists who rejected the primacy of 'consensus' and argued that true social solidarity was at a lower level than that of the society-as-a-whole. Consensus and solidarity were internal to sub-groups within the society: that is, groups such as classes or status groups. These groups were the bearers of distinct values, and the possessors of divergent interests, and were therefore antagonistic to each other. Any unity at the level of society is an appearance only. It reflects not the spontaneous consensus of all society upon the same values, but is likely to reflect and conceal the ascendancy of one stratum over all the others. In essence, then, the critique of Parsons was that he did not make *social stratification* the fundamental element within society, and therefore the basis for analysis of the social whole. This is why, for conflict theory, stratificational groupings, such as classes or status groups, were considered the significant forms of collective organisation. From the failure to give stratification the greatest prominence, all Parsons' other (alleged) failings flowed. In 'conflict theory' Marxist and/or Weberian themes and ideas were being counterposed to Parsonian ones. The key points conflict theory sought to sustain were as follows:

- that society is not essentially conflictual, nor essentially harmonious;
- that the unity of society was only a temporary and unstable outcome of struggles for domination amongst antagonistic social strata and that therefore consensus in society was at the level of appearance only; for
- 'material interests' are more important than values, and the material interests of groups within a stratification system are (virtually by definition) in conflict with each other; and
- manifest dissemination of values was not an authentic consensus but the product of hegemony – effectively, of the imposition of the values of dominant groups upon subordinate strata as a result of the former's control of the institutions of the society, especially education and communications.

As a result, Parsons was also condemned for idealism. This really involves a reiteration of the previous two allegations, namely, that Parsons treated 'consensus' as the cause of social solidarity, and thus regarded the latter as a product of ideas, of cultural elements, so neglecting the extent to which social solidarity and value consensus were not causes but the products of the use of power to achieve domination in a struggle over material interests. Consensus was really only ideology, ideas designed to delude people about their true interests and to blind them to the realities of conflict in their society. Insofar as Parsons tried to project value consensus as the essence of social reality, then Parsons himself was effectively part of the ideological operation itself, rather than the objective social scientist he claimed to be. Such criticisms, as we shall see in Chapter 3, were to be developed by the scholars of the Frankfurt School.

Parsons was, in important respects, being accused of abandoning his own founding principles. It was he, after all, who had criticised idealism for its one-sidedness, and now he was deemed guilty of idealism. The charge rested, of course, upon the emphasis that he gave to 'norms' and 'values' and the key role he gave them in his solution of 'the problem of social order'. However, it is a selective reading of his work that regards him as arguing that social order is entirely produced by cultural elements. The emphasis upon the 'normative' aspect was only a corrective to its neglect by the positivist tradition not at the expense of the 'material' factors but as a complement to them. Parsons did not deviate from this first intention. To suppose that he did is to miss out the importance of his difference between the 'concrete' and the 'analytic', which meant that concrete, observable social situations were *composites* of analytically distinguishable elements. He did not suppose that culture – a realm of ideas – could singularly and unilaterally organise the world of action, but recognised that culture had its effects through the activities of its human bearers, a view akin to, and of course influenced by, Max Weber. Parsons' whole 'Chinese box' construction of systems and sub-systems (and their articulation in the 'cybernetic hierarchy') was designed to show how 'cultural' and 'material' elements were interwoven; how culture was institutionalised in the social system and internalised in the individual personality (which is of course rooted in the entirely material biological organism). Parsons probably said more about the economic aspect of society than his conflict theory critics, co-authoring a book, *Economy and Society*, in which he attempted a sociological reformulation of economic theory (Parsons and Smelser, 1956). The way in which Parsons dealt with 'material' factors in a recast economic theory may not be to one's taste, but it is simply false to treat him as disregarding or minimising these things.

Another significant retreat from the initial position that Parsons was supposed to have made was from his 'voluntarism', from the stipulation that social actors had, effectively, freedom of choice. In taking up the point of view of 'the system' he was, his critics claimed, eradicating all freedom of manoeuvre for individuals. Parsons published *The Social System* about the same time as *Toward a General Theory of Action*, and his own part in that involved a description of the way in which stable social rules and norms could emerge from the interaction of individuals, as well as a long account of the formation of the individual personality. Although Parsons emphasised the degree to which individual personalities have to be in broad conformity with social norms and values if they are not to be chronically alienated from and disruptive of the social order, he recognised that the individual personality is not simply absorbed by socially conventional norms and values. There will always be discrepancies between the demands of individual personalities and those of the the social systems in which they participate. It is one of the problems of social systems to manage this discrepancy between their needs and those created by the personalities of their individual members. The 'social' and 'personality' systems were interdependent, but not identical. In important respects, what else are the 'integrative' and 'latency' phases of the social system about? Again, it is only possible to treat Parsons as one-sidedly prioritising 'system' over 'individual' on the basis of a selective reading, and a distorted account of the aims, strategies and steps of his theorising. The idea that there is a structure/agency problem to be found in Parsons is, we suggest, an illusory one, originating in very partial accounts of his scheme. Parsons' treatment of this issue may not be to one's taste, but it is simply false that he reduced individuals to manipulated puppets of the social system.

Conflict theory as such was relatively short lived, and the role of making sociology a politically radicalised exercise has been handed to European social theory with Michel Foucault (1926–84) and Jürgen Habermas (b. 1929), being, in their very different ways, leading protagonists. This has, for various reasons, had the effect of greatly attenuating sociology's disciplinary identity. Much of what would, thirty years ago, have been done under the umbrella of sociology is now classified as cultural studies, or media studies, or is done in English, history, and language departments, not to mention French, literature and archaeology departments. In that context, and in the embattled effort to sustain a distinct 'sociological theory', Parsons' theories have been reconsidered, and rather more favourable judgements made of them. For a brief period, there was even a neo-functionalist movement (with some of his students prominent in it), in which a basically Parsonian approach was superficially modified to accommodate some of the criticisms made by conflict theory. Recent and continuing revaluation does not lead to wholesale acceptance of Parsons, for these more charitable reviewers have their own reservations about his system, but they do jointly agree that Parsons was hard done by, that many of the supposed criticisms of his work rested on caricatures of it.

We have sought, in passing, to dispose of some of the grossly misplaced criticisms such as those that, by naively mistaking Parsons' abstract theoretical system for an empirical description of actual societies, accused him of making society out as essentially harmonious. The tendency to ask what conditions incline a system toward integration and equilibrium just does not imply the exclusion of all possibility of disintegration and the disturbance of equilibrium from one's scheme, for the identification of the conditions of the first are at the same time the identification of conditions for the latter.

In many ways, the actual disagreement of conflict theory critics was not so much with Parsons' theories, but with his assessment of the condition of American (and, more generally, Western) society. Conflict theorists themselves subscribe to Parsons' theoretical premise that shared values are conducive to social solidarity since they take it for granted that the various 'conflict groups' exhibit internal consensus and solidarity. It was also important to conflict theory to treat subordinate conflict groups as bearers of values, but ones which were distinct from and preferable to those which were dominant in contemporary capitalist society. They could thus argue that there were, immanent within the society, indigenous, alternative (and superior) values to those hegemonically superimposed upon it. An invidious contrast could be made, for example, between the collectivism of the working classes and the anathematised individualism of bourgeois ideology.

The real disagreement between Parsons and those critics was over whether post-1945 Western societies were genuinely comprised of conflict groupings, and whether the potential for revolutionary insurrection actually existed. Parsons obviously did not think that stratification in American society provided any likely basis for collective, revolutionary action. His critics were clearly convinced that such a prospect was conceivable, and Parsons' theory was therefore faulted because it made no provision such a possibility. The fact that a social system had mechanisms that 'automatically' countered disruptive tendencies within the system and sought to contain and dissipate these, did not entail that these mechanisms would be 'successful', that the disruptions could be contained and dispelled. What Parsons' critics were demanding was that an adequate theory should provide for the possibility of revolutionary overthrow as an in-built element of a social system, but Parsons patently did not regard the presence of a revolutionary force or the potential for a revolutionary upturn as part of the *essence* of any society.

For Parsons, whether there was potential for revolution in a given society was an empirical question, and revolutionary transformation was only one (and relatively uncommon) form that social change might take and did not occupy the special place that it held for his critics. The theory could certainly specify conditions under which disruptive tendencies in a social system could overcome the control mechanisms as was attempted by Parsons' protégé Neil Smelser, mentioned earlier, and also by Chalmers Johnson (1964). But revolution was not something that Parsons saw as being 'on the cards' for American society, or Western society more generally, though he did anticipate – as early as the 1940s and 1950s – that gender and ethnicity would become politically problematic issues. Subsequent events have, of course, vindicated Parsons rather more than his critics of the 1950s–70s, and contemporary radical social theorists form their arguments on the assumption that there is no genuine revolutionary potential within the social systems of Western societies.

Whatever its merits, Parsons' was a unique effort within sociology. There was little that was truly original in his basic scheme, which was substantially a work of ingenious synthesis. Parsons' major project, the articulation of the 'theory of social action', was in large part constituted by the convergence he discerned in Durkheim, Weber, Pareto and Marshall. This convergence was not so apparent that others had also noticed it. Latter-day critics have sought to criticise Parsons' identification of this convergence, arguing that it was mainly a product of his own slanted interpretations of the source theories. Parsons not only derived his original project from, especially, Durkheim and Weber, but he continued to incorporate (whether faithfully interpreted or not) ideas and elements from their theories as major elements in his scheme. Not only was the scheme extensively derivative, but, as we have tried to show, the basic ideas were fairly plain and simple ones, which, outside of his synthesis, are largely uncontroversial. Of course, when Parsons sets out to elaborate the Chinese-box relations of system and sub-system, and to articulate the four-phase interchanges amongst them, things get complicated and obscure, and his advanced analyses can be very hard to follow. Nonetheless, the root ideas remain surprisingly simple, given Parsons' reputation as a forbidding writer. Parsons' uniqueness resides in taking fully seriously the idea that a general theory must be thoroughly systematised. His great predecessors may have had general theoretical ideas and approaches, but explicitly and systematically working out their most general conceptions was not their highest priority. Parsons sought to give abstract and general expression to the comprehensive scheme that he saw being formed in the thought of Durkheim, Weber, etc. Its articulation would provide a *balanced* integration of the different strands of the positivistic, utilitarian and idealist approaches that had gone into the formation of sociological theory at the turn of the twentieth century.

Compared to Parsons, his conflict theory critics seem regressive at this level. The idea that social solidarity is achieved primarily through domination and hegemony is in fact a reversion toward Hobbes' conception of social relations as consisting only in force and fraud, in domination and ideological deception. The whole burden of Parsons' argument is that whilst social relations can feature force and fraud, they cannot be founded in them, but this is what would be the case if domination and hegemony were the fundamental concepts of a theoretical scheme. Parsons' critics do not answer his challenge on this point. They simply presuppose what Parsons takes to be the theoretical problem: that there is sufficient social integration for groups to form, sufficient common culture within and between them for the (hegemonic ideological) communications of one group to another to be meaningful, that the members of the conflicting groups will have personality structures 'appropriate' to the groups to which they are affiliated, that there is (more than the Parsonian minimum of) solidarity within the different groups, etc. In other words, those who emphasised domination and hegemony did not have any comparably comprehensive social theory of the kind which Parsons tried to put together, and which sought to provide for the existence of any level of collective life above and beyond that of the individualistic Hobbesian war of all against all. Relations of domination and hegemony are only possible *within* a social order.

Until the recent 'revisionist' consideration of him Parsons has been treated rather as though he were an entirely worthless theorist, with the mere fact that his writings are hard to read virtually being enough to write him off altogether. The contemporary reassessment is much more sympathetic – with Luhmann's scheme being perhaps the most prominent of these (Luhmann, 1995) – but Luhmann is by no means fully converted, let alone uncritical. Parsons' functionalism is like other approaches to sociology, including those of his better critics. It offers the possibility of some interesting and insightful ways of analysing social activities, but is not the answer to all the questions sociology might pose; nor does it even provide definitive answers to the questions it does ask and answer. That this functionalism is judged a reasonable exploratory strategy in sociology does not make it a success even by Parsons' own standards. It should be remembered that Parsons' ambitions for his scheme were hardly modest, for it was to provide a comprehensive and unifying frame of reference for several social sciences, not just one, and a step toward a new level of scientific achievement for sociology. Even taking a generous estimate of Parsons' attainments, these can still be reasonably judged to amount to rather less than a convincingly general and substantial frame of reference for sociology and other social sciences. It may even be argued, as do John Holmwood and Alex Stewart (1991), that Parsons had failed, even against his own objectives, and that this failure marks 'the end of the road' for the approach to general theorising he exemplified. Rather than attribute Parsons' failure to the specifics of his own general theory, it might be argued that this derives from the kind of general theorising Parsons went in for. This was not theorising originating in substantive sociological problems, in puzzles about phenomena and relationships in social life that we do not understand, and which we seek to comprehend by theorising about them. Instead, this originated in a conception of what a properly scientific theory requires – a metatheory, or theory about theories – and then sought to fulfil these specifications. In that case, of course, the theorists who sought to continue within that tradition of general theorising, and to surpass Parsons by repairing the perceived deficiencies of his theory – Giddens, Bourdieu and Habermas most prominent amongst them – would be mistakenly diagnosing why Parsons' project failed, and making consequently fruitless efforts on their own behalf.

CHAPTER TWO SUMMARY

- Early functionalism, in the guise of 'organicism' and evolutionary social theory, was entrenched in American sociology since the late nineteenth century. In British social anthropology functionalism was designed to refocus anthropology toward understanding and explaining the persistence of given social practices, including those of society itself.
- Parsons, in a synthesis of the ideas of Durkheim, Weber, Marshall and Pareto, proposed a theory of action which he later developed in a series of analyses of the social system. For him, functionalism was a second best to his first ambition of building a social theory out of 'unit acts', the focus of his first major works.
- Parsons' use of the notion of a system was intended to provide a means of analysing all the components of society as integrally interconnected arrangements which, if it is to persist, must develop a coherence.
- Merton's adaptation of functionalism involved a move away from the general theory of Parsons in favour of 'middle range theory' which he applied in a number of studies, including the use of Durkheim's notion of anomie in an analysis of deviant responses to disjunctures between social goals and the means to attain them.
- The demise of functionalism had little to do with its own limimitations – of which there were many – and more to do with misreadings by its opponents who wished to emphasise the conflictual nature of social life rather than, as allegedly Parsons wished, the consensual.
- Parsons' work was a unique attempt to develop a comprehensive solution to the initiating problem of sociology: the problem of order.

Select bibliography and further reading

The early writings on functionalism are those of Durkheim, especially *The Elementary Forms of the Religious Life* (Allen and Unwin, 1976). Radcliffe-Brown's study, *The Andaman Islanders* (Free Press, 1922) is an important contribution to social anthropology. His *Structure and Function in Primitive Society* (Cohen and

West, 1952) sets out his functionalism. Malinowski's theories are spelled out in *A Scientific Theory of Culture* (Oxford University Press, 1944) and his *Magic, Science and Religion and Other Essays* (Free Press, 1948). The overstated case for functionalism appears in his article, 'Ethnology and the Study of Society' (*Economica*, 2, 1921).

Collections of relevant papers are to be found in Paul Colomy's collections, *Functionalist Sociology* and *Neofunctionalist Sociology* (Edward Elgar, 1990a, 1990b) and N.J. Demerath and R.A. Peterson's edited reader, *System, Change and Conflict: A Reader on Contemporary Sociological Theory and the Debate over Functionalism* (Free Press, 1967). Cohen's *Modern Social Theory* (Heinemann, 1968) is still a good introductory summary of the main ideas, as is Ryan's more philosophical treatment in *The Philosophy of the Social Sciences* (Macmillan, 1970). Textbooks using the functionalist framework are Davis' *Human Society* (Macmillan, 1966) and Robin Williams' *American Society: A Sociological Interpretation* (Knopf, 1960).

Parsons' work – and he was a very active publisher – is voluminous and a challenging read. *The Structure of Social Action* (The Free Press, 1968; first published in 1937) is certainly large but worth the effort. The development of his systematic structural functionalism is to be found in *The Social System* (Routledge, 1952) and developed further in *Working Papers in the Theory of Action* (Free Press, 1953), the co-edited collection, *Toward a General Theory of Action* (Free Press, 1951), *Social Structure and Personality* (Free Press, 1954b), *Societies: Evolutionary and Comparative Perspectives* (Prentice-Hall, 1964) and *The System of Modern Societies* (Prentice-Hall, 1971). Also worth looking at is the co-authored *Family, Socialization and Interaction Process* (Free Press, 1955). Merton's work is perhaps more accessible than that of Parsons. Many of his seminal contributions to structural functionalism are to be found in his *Social Theory and Social Structure* (Free Press, 1957).

Commentaries on Parsons specifically include Lockwood, 'Some remarks on "The Social System"' (*British Journal of Sociology*, 7, 1956); and Rocher's, *Talcott Parsons and American Sociology* (Nelson, 1972). Max Black's edited collection, *The Social Theories of Talcott Parsons: A Critical Examination* (Prentice-Hall, 1961), is still worth reading.

Applications of the framework include Davis and Moore, 'Some principles of stratification' (*American Sociological Review*, 10, 1945), which sets out its approach to a sociological understanding of stratification. Smelser's application of the framework to social change and to revolution are to be found in his *Social Change in the Industrial Revolution: An Application of the Theory to the Lancashire Cotton Industry, 1770–1840* (Routledge, 1959) and *Theory of Collective Behaviour* (Routledge, 1962). Chalmers Johnson's *Revolution and the Social System* (Stanford University Press, 1964) is also worth reading.

Critiques of functionalism include John Rex, *Key Problems of Sociological Theory* (Routledge, 1961); Rex proposes conflict theory as an alternative. Alvin Gouldner's *The Coming Crisis of Western Sociology* (Basic Books, 1970) set out a vociferous critique of structural functionalism as does his 'Reciprocity and autonomy in functionalist theory', in Gross (ed.) *Symposium on Sociological Theory* (Harper and Row, 1959), pp. 241–70.

A selection of more recent functionalist works is to be found in Paul Colomy's *Neofunctionalist Sociology* (Edward Elgar, 1990), and systems analysis is developed in Niklas Luhmann, *Social Systems* (Stanford University Press, 1995).

The Frankfurt School and Critical Theory

3

BEGINNING CHAPTER THREE

Critical Theory represents a re-emergence of European social theory in response to what was seen as the conservative ideological character of functionalism. It drew upon revisions of Marx and Weber to develop a critical stance against modern society and its social and political thought. The chapter includes discussion of:

- central themes of Critical Theory: alientation, rationalisation and the tragedy of culture;
- capitalism, culture and the nature of social inquiry;
- the critique of the culture of capitalism and modernity;
- the attack on positivism;
- the resurgence of the critique of culture.

The authors who have collectively come to be described as the Frankfurt School were, in fact, a varied collection of intellectuals and researchers whose works covered a wide range of interests. They became known as the Frankfurt School because many of them were associated with the Institute of Social Research at the University of Frankfurt. The Institute, founded in 1923, consisted predominantly of Jewish scholars most of whom went into exile, in 1933, to escape the Nazi regime, spending the following years in the USA and returning to Frankfurt in 1949.

Felix Weil, the son of a wealthy grain merchant, was the founder of the Institute. A radical intellectual, he was convinced that socialist ideals offered both a more practical and a more effective way of organising economic life, and was committed to regenerating Marxism in order to provide a basis for the revolutionary transformation of society. Weil's vision for the Institute was to create a forum for debate, free of the constraints of bourgeois academia as well as those of the Communist Party, in which to analyse the relationship between Marxism and practical political action. Due to its financial independence, the Institute was able to operate with considerable autonomy from its host institution. From the beginning Marxism was made the theoretical basis of the Institute's programme although the Institute had no formal affiliation with any political party. What was centrally taken from Marx for its interdisciplinary research was the importance of the historical context of cultural meaning.

In his Inaugural Address, the Institute's first Director, Carl Grünberg (1861–1940), a Marxist professor of economic history, made plain the Institute's commitment to Marxism and to the materialist conception of history, as well as to a belief that society was in the midst of a transition from capitalism to socialism. But it was with the passing of the directorship to Max Horkheimer (1895–1973), in 1931 on Grünberg's retirement, that the direction of the Institute changed from studies of labour history to the much more theoretical and philosophical path for which the School became best known. Horkheimer was responsible for the development of the Frankfurt School for the next twenty years, most of them spent in exile, and, in important respects, its most productive period. A journal was established, the *Zeitschrift für Sozialforschung* (Journal for Social Research), which had the aim of developing a theory of the social totality, specifically by gaining a greater understanding of the fundamental forces which shape society but which, it was held, are usually obscured from those affected by them by the flow of everyday events.

During Horkheimer's early years as Director many of the scholars who were to play a significant part in the work of the Frankfurt School became members or associates of the Institute. These included economists, such as Leo Lowenthal (1900–93) who worked on a critique of bourgeois ideology and mass culture; Erich Fromm (1900–80), a psychoanalyst interested in combining Marxist and Freudian ideas, particularly in how class influences people's 'psychic structure' and political views; and Friedrich Pollock (1894–1970), another economist, who coined the term and developed the analysis of 'state capitalism'. Apart from Max Horkheimer, two figures stand out as making enduring and decisive contributions to the development and reputation of Frankfurt School thought: Theodor Adorno (1903–69) and Herbert Marcuse (1898–1979).

Adorno's background was in philosophy and music and he was part of the vibrant cultural scene in Berlin in the late 1920s, associating with the likes of the playwright Bertolt Brecht (1898–1956), the composer Kurt Weill (1900–50) and the literary critic and theorist, Walter Benjamin (1892–1940). Benjamin, who killed himself when stranded at the Spanish border while attempting to escape the Nazis, has now become a very influential figure in postmodern thought.

Marcuse originally studied history but later became interested in philosophy, in particular the work of Martin Heidegger (1889–1976). For Marcuse, Heidegger's philosophy, unlike the abstract categories of orthodox Marxism, dealt with the social world in terms of the actual experience of real people and, in doing so, explored how the 'authentic being' of humanity could be realised. Marcuse seized on Heidegger's contention that this authenticity could be attained only by decisive action in the real world. By 1929 he had studied with both Heidegger and his philosophical predecessor, Edmund Husserl (1859–1938) but the decisive moment in his intellectual career came, in 1932, with the publication of Marx's *Paris Manuscripts of 1844*. The initial impact of these was the rediscovery of the earlier 'philosophical' Marx and his analysis of the link between capitalism and alienation. So, like Horkheimer and Adorno, Marcuse was to arrive at a position which required the critique of 'facticity', that is, views which hold that the world, including existing social conditions, is composed of a set of facts which are found to be the way they are through supposedly scientific inquiry. Such views deny the essential nature of humanity and, accordingly, need to be confronted, with the aim of their eventual overthrow.

By the time Marcuse arrived at the Institute in 1933, plans were well advanced for it to leave Frankfurt in the face of the rise of Hitler's Nazis. As a group of predominantly Jewish intellectuals and prominent Marxists, the members of the Institute were in an extremely precarious position. By the time Hitler assumed power, most of the Institute's members had moved to Geneva. This could only be a temporary arrangement and, eventually, they were offered accommodation and affiliation by Columbia University, New York. By 1934 Horkheimer, Fromm, Lowenthal and others had arrived in the United States. Adorno spent three years at Merton College, Oxford, before travelling to America in 1938 to work with Paul F. Lazarsfeld (1901–76), himself an Austrian exile, on the Princeton Radio Research Project, a large-scale study of the effects of popular radio – then a relatively new medium with its origins in the 1920s – on the wider culture. The association with Lazarsfeld's commitment to concrete empirical research was not to prove a congenial affair, and its effect was to confirm Adorno's conviction that positivist empirical research was focused only upon the immediate, most obvious, appearances of social life, thus obscuring the fundamental realities.

The difficulties of exile, compounded by financial problems and personal frictions, led to fragmentation of the Institute's activities. Gradually Horkheimer and Adorno retreated from the commitment to political praxis to concentrate on theoretical and philosophical work, while Marcuse, following war work, retained his political inclinations and remained firmly on the left.

In the post-war period, the authorities in Frankfurt were keen to recapture something of the city's earlier intellectual standing and, after a gap of sixteen years, some members of the Institute returned. In 1949, Horkheimer was reappointed to the Chair of Social Philosophy at the university, and in 1956 Adorno was offered a permanent position after a period as temporary professor. Soon a new generation of German researchers was to emerge, including notably Ralf Dahrendorf (b. 1929) and Jürgen Habermas (b. 1929). The latter – who became Adorno's research assistant in 1956 – was to become one of the most influential of social theorists in the years to come. Horkheimer retired in 1958 and Adorno died in August 1969, and within three years all the younger members of the Institute had left.

It should be evident from this brief review of the development of the Frankfurt School that these were not scholars overmuch concerned with the development of academic sociology. Their aspirations were far wider than sociology and they made influential contributions to economics, politics, history, psychiatry, literature, music, and other fields. Nevertheless, the ideas of the Frankfurt School have had a significant effect on the development of sociological thought, and many of these ideas themselves emerged in response to some of the major works of the 'classic' sociological theorists, notably Marx and Weber. The members of the Frankfurt School, though not narrowly focused on sociology as a discipline, did draw upon its classic thinkers, not only Marx but also Weber, Durkheim and a scholar who, in a different way, had an influence on Erving Goffman, a sociologist discussed in Chapter 5, namely, Georg Simmel (1858–1918). The next section deals with some of the central themes of the Frankfurt theorists, concentrating on connections with the classic thinkers.

Central themes of Critical Theory

Marx and alienation

The sheer variety of the writings of the Frankfurt School is in itself evidence of the enormous influence Marx's ideas had on European thinkers in the early part of the twentieth century. Yet many of them were critical of the orthodox 'materialist' interpretations of Marx which flourished in the years after his death in 1883. Events since that time had severely shaken the confidence of many that the revolutionary transformation which Marx had anticipated was really going to happen. There had been, for example, a period at the end of the nineteenth century and into the twentieth in which both the labour movement and the ideas of socialism appeared to flourish as never before: mass trade unions were founded, and effective political representation of the working class was secured for the first time. Yet on the outbreak of war in 1914, contrary to the expectations of many Marxists, the working classes in Britain, France and Germany were queuing up to fight against each other on behalf of their capitalist masters. Class interests, it seemed, had melted away in the face of appeals to patriotic loyalty. Moreover, it became increasingly apparent in the 1920s that the outcome of the Russian Revolution was not the establishment of a liberated communist society such as Marx had envisaged. Rather, the supposed 'dictatorship of the proletariat' had given way to dictatorship pure and simple in the form of Stalin's tyranny. And when, at the end of the decade, the Wall Street Crash of 1929 plunged international capitalism into its worst ever crisis, the result was not a revolution led by the proletariat, but a prolonged period of economic depression, with millions impoverished and unemployed while the system re-established itself. For all these reasons, then, straightforward interpretations of Marx emphasising the primacy of economic factors, and the historical inevitability of capitalism collapsing through its own contradictions, appeared less and less plausible.

However, many political leaders and serious thinkers remained convinced of the fundamental value of Marx's theoretical insights into the operation of modern capitalist societies. They now saw their task as involving, not the abandonment of Marx's ideas, but their reformulation in the light of these events. The publication, in 1923, of a series of essays called *History and Class Consciousness* by the Hungarian philosopher, Gyorgy Lukács (1885–1971), caused an immediate furore among Communist Party ideologists. Lukács seemed to be questioning the validity of the official communist version of Marxism (which often drew on Engels' interpretations of Marx's thought after the latter's death) and arguing, instead, for a dialectical understanding of society which owed as much to Hegel's idealism as to Marx's materialism. A more long-term effect of Lukács' book, however, was to restore to Marxist thought some of the Hegelian elements which had been suppressed, both by the heavily economistic emphasis of orthodox historical materialism, and by the fact that certain texts which are today regarded as fundamental, notably Marx's *Paris Manuscripts of 1844* and Marx and Engels' *The German Ideology*, had yet to be published.

Lukács' work had a considerable influence on the developing ideas of members of the Frankfurt School who, while radical thinkers, were yet steeped in the Hegelian tradition of German philosophy (Jay, 1973: 44). The belief that a valid understanding of social life (and indeed knowledge itself) could only be obtained on the basis of dialectical analysis rather than positivistic science became, as we shall see, a distinctive and fundamental feature of their approach. Equally important was the way Lukács treated Marx's idea of the 'fetishism of commodities'. Under capitalism, Marx had argued, the production of goods is determined not by their intrinsic usefulness, but by the price they can command on the market – their 'exchange value'. Thus the production process as a whole becomes controlled, not by real people and their actual needs, but by what we now call 'market forces', so that while the 'financial system' as a whole may flourish with the creation of profits, the consequences for increasing numbers of real people can be disastrous. Farming, mining and fishing communities, for example, and their ways of life, as well as those of industrial workers, may be devastated if the price of what they produce falls on the world market. For Marx, then, the result of capitalist production is the loss by human beings of control over their own lives – all must 'obey' the 'laws' of the market, which confront them as objective, impersonal forces even though they are no more than the outcome of the activities of ordinary people. It was in this sense that Marx used the term 'fetishism', suggesting the misplaced worship of objects for their imaginary, often superhuman, powers, because people have lost sight of the fact that it is their activities that actually create these objects.

Lukács echoed this idea, using the term 'reification' to refer to the way in which imaginary entities, or abstract concepts, are treated as if they were real things, which often involves reconceiving conditions that humans have themselves made as if they were the product of impersonal or superhuman forces. For Lukács this was the fundamental aspect of the culture of capitalist societies. Marx had taken the market exchange of economic goods, termed 'commodities' because they were produced for sale in the market, as a prime example of fetishism. The exchange of commodities in the market was treated by people as though it was a law unto itself that human beings cannot, either individually or collectively, control. Under commodity production, he wrote (Lukács, 1971: 83): 'a relation between people takes on the character of a thing and thus acquires a "phantom-objectivity", an autonomy that seems so strictly rational and all-embracing as to conceal every trace of its fundamental nature: the relation between people'.

In developing the idea of reification, and emphasising its importance in understanding the culture of capitalist societies, Lukács was widely taken to have rediscovered the philosophical orientation of Marx's early work. He did this, moreover, by reconstructing those ideas from Marx's later 'economic' writing – in particular *Capital* where these ideas are not directly expressed – rather than through examining Marx's own early texts where such ideas are stated, but which remained unpublished until after Lukács had made his reconstruction. Lukács' notion of reification is in all essential respects similar to the idea of alienation as outlined in Marx's *Paris Manuscripts of 1844*. Through wage-labour in the production of commodities, Marx argued, workers create and reproduce an 'alien' world of things and social relationships which not only seem independent of them, but enforce their subordination. As already pointed out, it is in this context that Marx uses the term 'commodity fetishism' to describe the way in which the objects which are produced by people come to be treated as if they were independent beings with powers of their own. But whereas Marx was mainly concerned to analyse this process in the sphere of economic production, Lukács took it to have a much wider significance:

> Lukács' treatment of fetishism as reification involves the assumption that Marx's concept refers not only to the economy, but to the general form of capitalist social life. As a generalised fetishism, reification is applied to all the characteristic alienations of the human community including such noneconomic institutions as bureaucracy and law. (Feenberg, 1981: 62)

It was this theme, as we shall see, which was to become one of the central concerns of the Frankfurt School.

In essence, their premise was that the condition of *cultural* alienation was characteristic of capitalist societies: that is, in such societies we are confronted with social institutions and patterns of conduct which, although they are created and operated by real people, do not represent or respond to genuine human needs. These seemingly 'objective' social structures and processes have, on the contrary, developed principally as a consequence of the ceaseless drive to maximise the production of 'exchange values' which will yield surplus value, and therefore profits, by making the production process as technically efficient as possible. And just as Marx believed that the alienated condition of wage-workers destroyed their intellectual and emotional capacities, so Lukács pointed to what he saw as the 'subjective' consequences of reification, as the ethos of commodity production, with its emphasis on self-interest and rational calculation, begins to displace genuinely human sentiments. 'Just as the capitalist system', wrote Lukács, 'continually produces and reproduces itself economically on higher and higher levels, the structure of reification progressively sinks more deeply, more fatefully and more definitively into the consciousness of man' (Lukács, 1971: 93).

The result is relentless pressure towards the establishment of an all-pervading cultural system which is 'inauthentic' in that it imposes on people ways of living which are a denial and distortion of genuine human needs. Moreover, it has become, to use Marcuse's later coinage, 'one-dimensional' in that it is almost impossible to express any fundamental criticism of it, or to envisage alternatives. This idea of the ways in which alienated culture degrades the 'subjective' experience of individuals played a major role in Frankfurt School thinking, as when they speak of the 'maimed consciousness' of individuals in modern capitalism, and their 'regression' to a child-like state of dependency which destroys their capacity for original thought or actions. For this reason, members of the School at various times displayed their interest in the ideas of Sigmund Freud and psychoanalysis, and a significant part of their research programme was concerned with examining the ways in which personalities are formed (or deformed) within the 'mass' culture of capitalism.

It was mass culture that was becoming the central barrier to revolutionary consciousness of the sort Marx had envisaged. Increasingly, however, members of the School lost any faith they may have had in Marx's (and Lukács') conviction that the proletariat, in becoming conscious of itself as a class, will ultimately lead a revolution which will bring an end to both capitalism and the alienated condition of humanity. On the contrary: in their view the daily experience of the working masses systematically deprived them of the ability to think radically or critically about their situation, far less take action to change it. In this the mass media played an increasingly important role in providing an ever more impoverished cultural experience. It is a bleak and often deeply pessimistic perspective, but nevertheless one which resonates with the many novelists, poets and cultural critics who have protested against the emptiness and inhumanity of life in the twentieth century. It is also a view which has appealed to many who feel their lives to be ever-more controlled by the pressures of a heartless 'system'.

Weber and rationalisation

In speaking above of the constant pressure under capitalism for the pursuit of economic rationality and technical efficiency in production, we have already indicated a second major theme which runs through the writings of the Frankfurt School, and which provides a strong link between their work and that of Max Weber. This is the concept of rationalisation which, for Weber, had become the predominant and almost irresistible organising principle of modern Western societies. Indeed, in an important sense, rationalisation was for Weber the defining characteristic of modernity in contrast to 'traditional' societies or ways of life in which the guiding principle is to do things in the same way they have been done in the past.

Weber saw human action in all parts of modern societies, and not just in the sphere of economic production, as increasingly organised according to the criteria of economic and scientific rationality, principally that of calculability. Efficiency, as opposed to tradition and customary practice, is the basis upon which all things are relentlessly re-organised. It follows that such societies, in contrast to pre-modern ones, will experience relatively rapid social change, as new technologies are introduced and ever higher rates of profit are pursued. In this context Weber was careful to distinguish between capitalism as a general means of yielding profits – which occurs in various societies at different historical periods – and modern rational capitalism, which was the unique economic system of the West. In conditions of modern rational capitalism, the costs and benefits of activities are constantly measured, and economic and social life are ordered according to the imperatives of predictability and calculability.

Yet while a rationally organised society can enjoy the benefits of unprecedented efficiency in the fields of production and administration, this 'progress' comes at a price. It is true that the citizens of a modern society can exercise their freedom from the irrationalities of religious belief and the tyranny of absolute monarchs but, as Weber argued, the cost of this freedom is twofold.

Firstly, however arbitrary or irrational the old mythologies and religions were, they did at least provide a source of meaning and understanding for members of pre-modern societies. The effect of rationality, however, is to produce what Weber called the 'disenchantment of the world', and create a culture in which not only magic and mystery have disappeared, but life itself may come to seem meaningless.

Secondly, there is a danger that having thrown off the shackles of kings and aristocrats, modern societies have subordinated themselves to a new and equally powerful set of constraints, the source of which is rationality itself, which is made the very apotheosis of Reason. The more that social life is organised according to rational principles, the less individuals can exercise choice, freedom or spontaneity in their lives. The characteristic institutions of modern society are bureaucratic administrative organisations in which there is detailed specification of all aspects of work, and which are established precisely in order to eliminate the discretion of individuals. Indeed, Weber made some gloomy remarks about bureaucracy as a prison for the human spirit. These related ideas – the meaninglessness of social life driven by the forces of rationality, and the rigorous discipline and control by bureaucracy – were also to play a major part in the thinking of the Frankfurt School's members.

A further continuity between Weber and the work of the Frankfurt theorists is evident in their tendency – increasing as time passed – to accept his view that a proletarian revolution of the type envisaged by orthodox Marxism was highly improbable. Again, Weber's arguments for this position were of two kinds. Firstly, he pointed to the tendency of capitalist development to produce a hierarchically differentiated workforce, divided by the sense of status and income difference that their diverse occupations would bring, rather than an homogeneous mass of impoverished wage-slaves unified by intense resentment of their appalling conditions. With the expansion of the middle class, a revolutionary 'class consciousness' which included all workers was unlikely to develop. Moreover, Weber was also concerned to emphasise the importance in any real society of 'status' factors other than those based on occupation – in particular those of religion, ethnicity and nationality – as sources of group identity and personal motivation which could override purely economic interests, and more commonly provided the basis for political action than did class solidarity. These divisive factors would tend to militate against the development of a revolutionary 'class consciousness'.

Weber's second argument against the prospect of proletarian revolution derived from his general rejection of the belief that there was an overall pattern to human history, and in particular the Hegelian idea that a 'dialectical' pattern of historical transformations would ultimately produce an ideal society in which the essential human spirit and social institutions were harmoniously reconciled. Weber denied that there was any such pattern in the unfolding of human history, whether as described by Hegel, or in Marx's notion of movement through social conflict towards a final communist society in which alienation had been overcome. These ideas, too, were echoed by the Frankfurt School, as they lost faith in the capacity of the working class to become a revolutionary force which would overthrow capitalism, and – from a more philosophical perspective – argued against any 'grand theory' which purported to explain the 'pattern' of history.

Doubts about the revolutionary potential of the working class, as we shall see, were often based on the Frankfurt theorists' observation of the ways in which the 'mass' culture of industrialised societies, produced by the 'culture industry' and spread by the mass media, had fundamentally ideological effects, in Marx's sense: that is, they created a cultural environment in which spurious 'needs' were inculcated in people so that they would keep on buying commodities, and through which they were bombarded with escapist fantasies which not only idealised existing social institutions but prevented the development of radical or genuinely critical thought about them. Moreover, these theorists saw the development of modern capitalism as driven above all by the relentless dynamic of rationality, which had long since passed the point at which it was subject to human control. Social changes come about not through the conflict of classes, or the working out of a historical dialectic, but as the often unanticipated consequences of the irresistible force of rationalisation. Whereas Weber suggested – perhaps somewhat despairingly – that we should strive to protect human dignity and autonomy by resisting the relentless pressure towards rationalisation, there is a strong sense in much of the Frankfurt School's work that this is no longer a realistic option, and there are many pessimistic expressions of the belief that modern culture is out of control. Marx was concerned with domination through class, the domination by the few of the many, whereas Weber was concerned with the domination of *all* by the demands of rationality.

Simmel and the 'tragedy of culture'

In this context, the Frankfurt scholars echoed the ideas of Weber's contemporary, Georg Simmel, and in particular his notion of the 'tragedy of culture'. Human social life, for Simmel, depends fundamentally on the production of culture, the public, 'objective' arena, so to speak, with which the unique 'subjectivity' of every individual has to be reconciled, and the way that communication and co-operation between human beings is made possible. In this important sense culture may be said to represent the externalisation or 'objectification' of internal or 'subjective' phenomena, since cultural 'objects' are in the end always the products of human minds. Thus language, to take one example used by Simmel, confronts us as an 'objective' system of words – an idea which not only has strong echoes of Durkheim but, more directly, is the idea upon which Saussure builds his 'structuralist' account of language – which have meanings, and rules by which we connect them in order to make sense to each other. (These ideas are outlined in Chapter 4.) In order to become a competent, fully socialised, member of our society we must learn to accept these meanings and rules, which in effect means that these elements of 'objective' culture in turn become part of our 'subjective' make-up. The 'formula of culture', as Simmel puts it, is thus:

> that subjective and psychological energies attain an objective form which is subsequently independent of the creative life processes and that this form is once again drawn into subjective life processes in a way that will bring its exponent to a well-rounded perfection of his or her central being. (in Frisby and Featherstone, 1997: 68)

Cultural forms, then, 'flow from subjects through objects to subjects' (ibid.). In this respect, Simmel's argument is consistent with that of Durkheim in emphasising, through the idea of the 'internalisation' of social norms, the essentially and inevitably social constitution of individual identities.

However, just as Lukács did in developing the idea of 'reification', Simmel wished to go further. Even language, which is the essential and indispensable basis of any human society, can, he argues, be experienced as 'an alien natural force, which distorts and curtails not only our utterances but also our innermost intentions' (ibid.: 67). In other words, this particular cultural form, although created by humans and vastly beneficial to them, has also, in the process of its 'objectification', become a constraint on the way we think, limiting us to certain concepts, ideas and modes of expression while denying all the alternative possibilities. There is a parallel here with Weber's vision of the 'iron cage' of rationality. There is also an evident similarity between Simmel's view of the 'alien' character of language and Marx's concept of alienation. In fact, Simmel himself made the link explicit:

> The 'fetishistic character' which Marx attributed to economic objects in the epoch of commodity production is *only a particularly modified instance of this general fate of the contents of our culture.* These contents are subject to the paradox – and increasingly so as culture develops – that they are indeed created by human subjects and are meant for human subjects, but follow an immanent developmental logic in the intermediate form of objectivity . . . and thereby become alienated from both their origin and their purpose. (ibid.: 70, emphasis added)

Simmel is here proposing the alienated character of all cultural production, and this for him is the deep and inevitable 'tragedy of culture'. All cultural objects – gods, the state, language, the market, money, and so on – which are created by humans for their own purposes, have the capacity to assume an independent existence, to appear objective and immutable, and ultimately to dominate their creators.

Thus Simmel accepts the implications of Marx's analysis of commodity production, and in fact wrote extensively about the effects on culture of money, which – having begun simply as a means of buying and selling objects – has now, in the form of capital, become a 'commanding social power' which controls the whole process of economic production (Poggi, 1993:163). However, just as Marx had extended the idea of alienation from the sphere of religion to that of the state and political life, and then to capitalist economic production, so the Frankfurt theorists went still further and extended it to culture (to science, art, the media of communication and so forth) which, as a result, is conceived as also developing its own internally driven momentum independent of human control. This is a recurrent theme in the work of the Frankfurt School authors and shows them at their most despairing.

Moreover, the situation is exacerbated in modern societies. Since the process of rationalisation demands constant innovation and the production of new ideas, the result is a huge and ever growing 'stock of objectified cultural elements' which comes to seem overwhelming and threatening to individuals: individuals who are incapable of grasping more than a small part of it, in much the same way that even the scientist nowadays only really understands a very narrow and specialised area of science. An unprecedented array of cultural products is available in such 'rich and overburdened cultures', yet our contact with most of them is fleeting and superficial:

> There thus emerges the typical problematic condition of modern humanity: the feeling of being surrounded by an immense number of cultural elements, which are not meaningless, but not profoundly meaningful to the individual either; elements which have a certain crushing quality as a mass, because an individual cannot inwardly assimilate every individual thing, but cannot simply reject it either, since it belongs potentially, as it were, to the sphere of his or her cultural development. (in Frisby and Featherstone, 1997: 73)

Thus for Simmel the consequence of the 'growth of the objectified mind' is not just the trivialisation and the rootlessness of experience – a theme developed by many twentieth-century thinkers – but a major threat to the individual's sense of inner security. Against this, however, the escape from the limits and constraints of traditional society allowed people to develop aspects of their human potential which were previously impossible (Poggi, 1993: 167ff.). On the 'subjective' side, so to speak, as individuals they could feel that they typically enjoy a much higher degree of personal freedom than before. This was not a view shared by the Frankfurt School, who regarded such 'freedom' as more imaginary than real. The belief in this great freedom was ideological in the sense that it obscured the real state of affairs which was of ever tightening constraint rather than expanding autonomy. On the 'objective' side, Simmel argued that the growth of knowledge itself promotes an unprecedented intellectual understanding of the natural and the social worlds, and in this respect there are continuities between him and the Frankfurt thinkers. In particular, the abandonment of absolute conceptions of truth, and the consequent 'relativising' of knowledge, leads to an understanding that the meaning of things – whether ideas or material objects – is not to be found 'in' them, but depends on how they stand in relation to other things, in the context of particular social institutions. A coin or a banknote, for example, is useless, and meaningless, unless it is placed in the context of an elaborate set of social arrangements that gives it significance, and maintains rules for its proper use. For Simmel the acceptance of the relativity of knowledge was a great gain in human understanding, particularly of the social world, leading to the conclusion that 'reality is not an assemblage of self-standing substances, but results from the innumerable effects exercised upon one another by components, each of which derives its own identity from how it relates to all others' (Poggi, 1993: 173).

It is from the above ideas that members of the Frankfurt School variously drew inspiration for their analyses of aspects of capitalist society and its culture. A crucial element of this analysis was the critique the School mounted against the form of knowledge which characterised capitalist culture, namely, positivism: a form of knowledge which not only infused the natural and the social sciences but lay at the very root of capitalist civilisation. This totalistic critique of capitalist civilisation, its current situation and prospects, was to emerge gradually through the various studies of the School.

Capitalism, culture and social inquiry

The relativity of knowledge espoused by Simmel was very close to the position arrived at by members of the Frankfurt School as they sought to understand particular cultural elements in relation to the totality of which they formed a part, and vice versa. For both Simmel and the School, however, there could be no final, 'objective' knowledge of society as a totality. What the theorist could hope to grasp and convey, however, was 'a snapshot or a fleeting glimpse of some social phenomenon which is, at the same time, also seen to have universal significance or, at least, is taken as an instance of a more general "essential form"' (Frisby, 1981: xi). Such an approach seeks to reflect the experience of individuals as they confront the fragmented and often contradictory culture of modernity and, as Frisby has suggested, has much in common with the artistic movement which came to be called Impressionism (ibid.: 92ff). Moreover while both Simmel and the Frankfurt thinkers took Marx's analysis of commodity production as a fundamental starting point, this perspective on the analysis of social life clearly diverges from orthodox Marxism. The focus has broadened from a preoccupation with economic activities and injustices as fundamental, to a concern with all aspects of contemporary culture, since the analysis of these too, it was held, could reveal much about the nature of modern society. And in rejecting the notion that there could be one objective, all-encompassing, account of social change (or of anything else), they had rejected the idea of historical materialism as a 'grand narrative' – a unified and comprehensive scheme capable of grasping in a single coherent set of terms the whole pattern of historical development.

Within the limits set by the nature of human knowledge, the School set out to offer a radical alternative. Critical Theory was not, we stress, meant to offer just another but different theory. It wanted to offer an altogether different way of thinking. In his later work, especially his *Negative Dialectics*, Adorno would attempt to formulate the contrast as that between the prevailing way of thought – 'identity thinking' – and that offered by the School – 'non-identity thinking' – an improved version of the dialectic as inherited from Hegel. Putting matters crudely, we can say that the fundamental principle of 'identity thinking' is that the gap between thought and reality can ultimately be bridged and that the mind can fully know the nature of reality. The means to this objective is through classification. For identity thinking, to subsume something under a category in a classification is to say what the thing 'really is'. On this view, the whole of reality can eventually be captured when it has been exhaustively classified.

However, dialectical, that is, non-identity thinking cannot accept that thought can ever completely capture reality. There are aspects of reality that remain outside any classificatory efforts. There are, for example, those aspects of something that do not presently exist as such, aspects which are not yet realised but which are, nonetheless, part of the thing's nature as its potential to develop into something other than it now is. It is the task of non-identity thinking to resist the idea that the unity of thought and reality can be attained through thought itself. Thought's development – for reasons shortly to be given – is tied to the development of social reality, and cannot surpass it, and so long, therefore, as social reality itself is divided and riven by contradictions, thought cannot hope to arrive at the thoroughly integrated, contradiction-free state that it aspires to. Thus, there can be no solution through theory alone to this problem. Rather than aiming, as philosophers do, for a contradiction-free philosophical system, the real task should be to create a philosophy (such as that of Critical Theory) that can guide people into overcoming the contradictions that exist in reality and that take the form of antagonistic social relations.

The initial statement of the School's general position was contained in a series of essays by Max Horkheimer written soon after he became Director of the Institute and intended to set out a 'social philosophy' for the School. This was meant to overcome some of the key dualisms that had been at the centre of Western philosophical thought such as those between fact and value, the mental and the material, between thought and reality, subject and object, and between individual and collective.

Fact and value

Max Weber had taken the traditional and dominant view, that there needs to be the sharpest separation between facts and values, between describing how things are and prescribing how they ought to be. Respecting this division involves keeping wholly distinct the responsibilities of the scholar or scientist and those of the activist. To the Frankfurt thinkers, however, it was precisely their refusal to respect this distinction that allowed them to offer a radical alternative, one that would enable them to work toward real and full human liberation, through their theoretical criticism of the ideology of capitalist society. This meant rejecting the dominant strain of philosophical thought. Positivism and empirical science, they argued, meant surrendering the world to the blind force of rationalisation. The aim of Critical Theory was the liberation of humanity from the condition of alienation. They sought neither the disinterested pursuit of knowledge for its own sake, nor the 'scientific' analysis of society, but ethical and political objectives. They aimed to achieve these by revealing the alienated untruth of modern culture, showing that a more fulfilling and authentic social order is possible, a society, that is, which was not dominated by the unstoppable forces of rationalisation but subject to the control of human reason.

Mind and materialism, thought and reality

The School also rejected Descartes' dualistic conception of the mind as a composite of quite distinct mental and physical elements. For them this was a form of idealism involving the misconception that thought could be self-sufficient, taking place independently of involvement in the material world. Also rejected was the contention of idealist thinkers, especially Hegel, that the ultimate reality was the Spirit or Being which had brought the world into existence, and the related belief that history was the process by which the immaterial Spirit and the material world were reunited. Holding, as they did, to the Marx-derived materialist conception of praxis, that thought is integral to and arises from the conduct of practical life, they could not act on the assumption that the mental and material worlds could be separated in that way. Further, Descartes' hugely influential conception of the mind encouraged the view that in order to understand thought it is essential to focus upon the working of the individual mind. However, the School could not accept that mental activity can be understood if it is treated as the product of the isolated 'individual' – who often appears as the fundamental unit in various branches of 'bourgeois' thought – which is really only a fiction, a figment of the bourgeois tradition. Thought, consciousness as it is often called, can only be understood as the product of a collective, social process – praxis – which occurs as human beings collaborate in working on their natural environment so as to sustain themselves in it. Knowledge must therefore be enmeshed in the (contradictory and antagonistic) group relations that make up any real society.

In seeing the production of knowledge and ideas as directly related to the pattern of human activities, the Frankfurt theorists were following the arguments of the early Marx (remarks very much directed against Hegel), who spoke of the ways in which the collective human work necessary for the existence of any society generated the concepts and beliefs which are basic to its culture. In linking physical activity and mental life in this way, Marx was rejecting the idealist concept of a spiritual or intellectual realm which was the essence (and the origin) of humanity, and emphasising instead the material basis of all human life. The implication of this linkage, of course, is that the mental and the material can no longer be considered as two separate realms (just as Simmel talked of the reciprocal relations between the 'subjective' and the 'objective' spheres), since in reality the two are interdependent.

Subject and object

As for the separation of 'subject' and 'object', the one who knows and that which is known, this cannot be sustained in the case of social reality, for the 'subject' of knowledge is the human being, but the 'object' of knowledge is the life of those same human beings; subject and object are one and the same. This notion of reciprocity, of a dialectical interplay between subject and object, the mental and the material, was enormously influential in shaping the Frankfurt theorists' image of the social world as praxis, that is, as perpetually created and sustained through collaborative social action. The social world, therefore, is to be understood as above all dynamic, as a process rather than as a structure or a set of separate 'objects' independent of us. It is a view of society which rejects the familiar dualism of Descartes in favour of a dialectical appreciation of human experience as an indivisible flow of awareness in which 'objective' and 'subjective' elements are indivisible. It is, moreover, a profoundly sociological perspective in that human consciousness and experience are seen as 'historical', in the sense that they are shaped and conditioned by the accumulated activities and ideas which have contributed to the development of a culture at any particular time.

We noted above Simmel's view that meaning is not inherent in objects, but depends on their relationship to other objects within a more general network of social relationships. Two important implications of this idea were to have great significance in the work of the Frankfurt School:

- The meaning of objects is not self-evident, but has to be understood as constituted through social activities.
- As individuals in human society we inevitably experience the world through concepts and modes of thought which are given to us, as it were, by the particular historical context in which we live.

If this is the case, it follows that we cannot step 'outside' the mode of thought which we take for granted in order to arrive at a final, 'objective' understanding. People in different cultures, and in different historical periods, will 'see' the world in different and incompatible ways; and what they perceive will appear to them as an independent, external world of 'objects'. However – and this is the crucial point for the Frankfurt thinkers – this external reality is at the same time a product of human social activity.

Whilst Marx's criticism of Hegel's idealism was accepted, it was equally important to Horkheimer and to other Frankfurt thinkers to retain Hegel's insistence on the dynamic quality of things and the ubiquity of processes of change: any thing (or person) that we observe or experience at a particular moment is inevitably undergoing a process of transformation, of becoming something else – the child becomes the adult, the seed becomes the tree, day becomes night, and so on. Sometimes such transformations were seen as processes in which things turned into their opposite, a notion which had a considerable effect on the thought of the Frankfurt School. For the present, though, the important point is that Horkheimer, along with Marcuse and Adorno, accepted the idea that real understanding was not a matter of isolating facts but of thinking dialectically about processes of transformation; contrasting, for example, the actual state of something with its potential to become something else. This meant developing ways of thinking about the world and human experience which were able to capture their inescapably fluid and dynamic qualities, and which made grasping their potential for further (progressive) change an integral part of understanding their nature.

The claim that Marxism was a comprehensive theory, for example, was not sustainable, not least because it reduced mind to matter and all events to cause and effect relationships. Horkheimer wanted to retain some elements of idealist thought in developing his 'social philosophy'. Just as the 'materialist' emphasis in Marx was intended to counteract the 'idealism' of Hegelian philosophy, so the Frankfurt School aimed to overcome, or 'transcend', the limitations of both idealist and materialist perspectives by developing a 'dialectical' theoretical perspective which could comprehend their dynamic interplay which is the essence of real human experience. As we have noted above, Horkheimer rejected the idea of an opposition between the perceiving 'subject' and the identified 'object', regarding cognition as an active process in which the subject constitutes the object. Thus objects which our senses reveal to us are in fact 'themselves the product of man's actions, although the relationship tends to be masked by reification' (Jay, 1973: 53). As a consequence, Horkheimer argued that the relation between subjects and objects must be understood in a 'dialectical' manner. Dialectics, however, was not to be understood as 'an objective process outside man's control', as some of the Marxists believed; it was, rather, a method of understanding which sought to grasp these sorts of constantly dynamic relationships:

> Dialectics probed the 'force-field' . . . between consciousness and being, subject and object. No facet of social reality could be understood by the observer as final or complete in itself. There were no 'social facts', as the positivists believed . . . Instead there was a constant interplay of particular and universal, moment and totality'. (ibid.: 54)

So, the position which Horkheimer sought to develop involved the rejection of (as he saw them) inadequate versions of both materialism and idealism, with their general theories of history and their claims to ultimate truth. In his view, such truths are unattainable, since human knowledge is always relative and context-bound, and there are 'inevitable limits of the cognition of finite men' (Stirk, 1992: 91). Horkheimer rejected as metaphysical the idea that there was this sort of underlying pattern to history, or that such a pattern – and by implication the whole of human life – could be explained by any one theory.

This 'social philosophy' was meant to begin from Marx's fundamentally materialist approach; that is, from the premise that human beings exist by collectively working on their natural environment. It also sought to build on Marx's view that it is the dynamic of economic activity which 'determines the course, development, and decline of each historical period' (ibid.: 50). Thus, the basic activity of human beings is taken to be the production of the material necessities for survival. What they also produce in the course of doing this (since production is social rather than individual) is what we recognise as the social world of language, beliefs, customs, practices or, in a word, culture.

Underlying all of this there is the assumption that phenomena, as available to immediate, ordinary, everyday perception, present a misleading appearance, and that it requires the right sort of theory to see through them. Critical Theory was meant to be that sort of theory. It took from the tradition of Hegel and Marx the insistence that social phenomena are understood only in relationship to the social whole – the totality – to which they belong. A grasp on the totality of capitalism was not something that was otherwise and readily available within capitalism itself.

The contemporary situation that was to be analysed through this social philosophy was one that had changed a great deal since Marx's time. Three major developments needed to be noted. Firstly, that the nature of capitalism had greatly changed. One idea which greatly influenced both Horkheimer and Adorno was Pollock's claim that 'state capitalism' was developing, that the state was taking over the functions of the capitalist by taking part in managing the economy. Other members of the School disagreed that this was the best formulation of the changes taking place. They were of the view that capitalism was moving to a 'monopoly capitalism' in which there was an increasing concentration of capital in ever larger, but fewer, companies which would eventually come to dominate the whole society. Whatever the case, it was plain that the age of individualistic 'free market capitalism', with many small firms belonging to individual capitalists and competing with each other in the market, was over.

Secondly, these changes would not only affect the economy but would have ramifications for society more generally. There would be an increasing centralisation of power, greater standardisation and less local variation, all in the interests of more efficient planning and operation of economic organisations. The organisation of work and all other activities increasingly comes to be considered in strictly technical terms and, becoming ever more specialised, has the consequence that knowledge of even the production process as a whole is no longer available to any individual: they know only their own specialised part of the process, and have no understanding of the way the system works.

Thirdly, there was the rise of the authoritarian state as exemplified to an extent in the Soviet Union, and even more by the coming to power of Fascism, in particular in Italy, Spain and Germany. The increasingly specialised, technical and concentrated structure of the economy had not done away with the contradictions of capitalism, but there was now doubt whether these contradictions could fatally destabilise the capitalist system. Horkheimer and Adorno considered that the authoritarian state was a means of containing these contradictions, as manifested in the way the Fascists had sought to shatter working class organisation through brutal suppression and through involvement in war.

The thought of the School was taking a more pessimistic turn with respect to the prospects of transcending the alienation and reification of capitalist society. The intellectual tools for such a transcendence were at hand in the School's own doctrine, its Critical Theory. This could be used to expose the fact that the oppressive structures of capitalist society were only the creations of human beings themselves, and not an irresistible necessity imposed by the nature of things. And if people could understand that their own activities had created these oppressive structures then they could recognise that it was also in their power to change them. However, whilst the tools might now be available, the School's thinkers were becoming pessimistic about the possibility of their being taken up. The economic and political developments of the twentieth century had cast doubt on the inclination or capacity of the working class to rise up against capitalism. Rather, the working class had often lined up alongside those who were, from a Marxist point of view, their deadly enemies, right-wing Fascists. The intellectual problem for the School was to understand the complicity of the masses in their own subordination and oppression, and the willingness of some of them to turn their aggression away from their rulers and against those in the same (or even more) subordinate positions as themselves.

Culture against humanity

Horkheimer and Adorno joined forces to write a book called *The Dialectic of Enlightenment* (1997; first published in 1942) to develop Weber's argument about rationalisation. The lesson the School drew from this work was that capitalism was maintained much less by coercion and control than by the progressively thoroughgoing administration of all affairs according to so-called rational principles, often supposedly derived from science. There was, to put it in Weberian terms, a long term trend for the progressive substitution of 'instrumental' rationality for 'value rationality' throughout capitalist society. All activity was becoming dominated by considerations of efficiency, of the most economical means to achieve any given end. But there was diminished concern with whether the ends sought were worth pursuing, no questioning of whether the value of efficiency was the most important, nor whether ever greater efficiency would make human life any better.

To the thinkers of the Enlightenment it had seemed that the development of rationality, particularly through the capacity for control over nature and over social life that the application of the new sciences seemed to promise, would ensure emanicipation from control by arbitrary and irrational authority. The development of science seemed to offer tremendous hope. Social life could be organised on the basis of each individual's use of their natural endowment of the powers of reason: to determine freely – exempt from the dictates of *all* authority – how to conduct their individual and collective affairs. Individual freedom was surely one of the values that capitalism prided itself upon.

However, while there was no denying that it had brought progress, this had been mainly in the form of liberation for the business class. But even in this case, given the concentration of capital, things were getting worse. The equation of reason and freedom that the Enlightenment offered was one that capitalism could use to justify itself, by identifying one form of reason, namely means/ends rationality, with reason generally. *The Dialectic of Enlightenment*, as the title emphasised, was meant to expose the one-sidedness of this view, and to show that whilst reason (in the form of means/ends rationality) did progress with capitalism, this went along with a darker side, as this form of rationality was used to develop ever tighter administrative regulation of individual lives. Reason and authority were not necessarily antithetical in the way the Enlightenment had envisaged, and in modern capitalism, reason was very much the servant of authority. The change from traditional to capitalist society had not meant emancipation from authority, but the exchange of one form of domination for another, with subjection to irrational traditional authority being replaced by 'rationally organised' administratively based authority. The change was also from an overt kind of domination to one that was concealed behind the impression that it enhanced individual freedom but in fact worked manipulatively against this, keeping individuals dependent and acquiescent, unaware of their potential to become truly autonomous.

The Dialectic of Enlightenment thus provided an initial statement of a position on the Enlightenment, authority and reason that is now widely influential in the social sciences and humanities very much as a result of its reinvention in the work of Michel Foucault. The possibility of thinking out the full implications of the ideas of freedom and reason is everywhere being restricted, and the articulation, let alone the realisation, of a critical alternative to the entrenched, capitalism-appropriated concept of the Enlightenment becomes increasingly difficult. Though there may no longer be any prospect of provoking an emancipatory uprising against capitalism, the need remains to develop a critical alternative to the capitalist world view.

Whilst the movement of means/ends rationality into a position of centrality had taken place in modern, capitalist society, its importance in Western culture, and its association there with domination, went back very much further in history, at least to the time of Homer. The role of means/ends rationality was initially that of gaining control of nature so as to manipulate it to suit material needs (as exemplified in the eventual and awesome prominence of the *natural* sciences). However, the development of that kind of rationality was never *simply* a story of domination over nature, for the successful development and application of means/ends rationality required domination over human beings too. Organising human effort to control nature requires disciplined co-operative activity and this demands self-limitation: putting the needs of disciplined thought and activity before one's spontaneous inclinations, denying and suppressing real needs in favour of absorption into whatever organisation is required to achieve technical domination over nature. At most this yields only material betterment. The Enlightenment's effects intensified this long-standing tendency for self-repression. Individuals are not coerced into leading the dull, repetitive, slavish labouring lives that they must lead under, for example, mechanical and bureaucratic production processes, but willingly accept them because of the ways they have already been shaped by the culture of the society; a culture designed to meet the needs of material progress through an apparatus of administrative regulation.

This view of rationality as a means to dominate nature meant both a move further away from Marx, and the intensification of the School's pessimism. Marx had imagined that the alienation of individuals from their true human nature, and from each other, was a product of domination in the relations between human beings. Marx himself had taken the view that nature was there to be exploited for human purposes, a view which the School condemned. For Marx, technology was the means of transforming nature to suit human needs. Here the Frankfurt School separated from Marx, seeing the origin of domination and repression as the reciprocal of the attempt to dominate nature, and as the decades went by they developed a rather religious-sounding conviction that the reconciliation of human beings one with another required a more basic reconciliation of humanity with nature. But, in the dejected assessment of the School, this prospect was already remote and becoming more so, for it required the termination of a very deeply entrenched way of thinking, one built into the very basics of Western civilisation. They rejected Marx's (and Hegel's) belief in history as an ultimately progressive process and, despite the extent of his influence on their thinking, Lukács' view that the class consciousness of the proletariat could come to represent the aspirations of humanity as a whole. Indeed, precisely because of the extent to which all aspects of culture were now permeated by alienated modes of thought, they saw little chance of eventual liberation from the tyranny of the rationalised society.

The Dialectic of Enlightenment therefore argues that Western culture since the Enlightenment was a continuation of the development of human self-suppression in order to dominate nature. It has not been about liberation so much as about the inculcation into individuals of the necessity of suppressing many of their natural inclinations, unpredictable instincts, any disposition toward spontaneous, undisciplined and unruly conduct, in order that they will be susceptible to the discipline, regularity and predictability essential to a rationalised factory system of manufacture. The advance of rationalised capitalism involved the penetration of commodity production into more and more areas of social life, and the growth of the culture industry was one main aspect of that, as people's private and leisure pursuits were increasingly based on things – films, recordings, radio programmes – being made for and sold to them. The advance of capitalism's rationalisation involved, of course, increasing standardisation of the productive process, and of its products, such that it operated most effectively in conditions of *mass* production, providing all consumers with identical items of the product, as was happening in popular music, films, etc.

The critique of positivism

Two important strands in the development of the School's critique of the culture of capitalism were, then, the critique of instrumental reason, especially in respect of the idea that the extension of scientific knowledge throughout all of nature and to social life was intrinsically a progressive move; and, secondly, the critique of the way in which the rationalisation of the whole culture was restricting the capacity for independent thought. The latter gave an important place to the analysis of 'the culture industry'.

Under capitalism, science was primarily a means toward the domination of nature and the self-suppression of humanity. The understanding of nature, and of social life too, was distorted by the fact that the quest for knowledge was interwoven with the desire for control, as expressed in technology that was also meant to regulate and discipline human action. At the level of philosophy, then, the critique of the philosophy associated with science, namely positivism (including its then most up-to-date form, the logical positivism of the Vienna Circle) was required. The attack on positivism was an attack on the very idea of 'knowledge' which permeated capitalist culture and society: a conception of 'knowledge' which was not really knowledge in the sense in which the School invited us to understand it.

In critiquing the positivist idea of science the Frankfurt theorists were carrying on an intellectual tradition that was well established, particularly in Germany. Since the 1890s an earlier generation had initiated a 'revolt against positivism' by challenging the widely held assumption that the rational and scientific modes of thought which had dominated Western discourse since the Enlightenment could be used in the study of social life (H.S. Hughes, 1974: 37). In Germany, there was an intense dispute between those who believed that the established methods of the natural sciences could also be applied in the fields of history and culture, and those who denied this. Unlike atoms or chemical elements, it was argued, humans had consciousness and free will, so social life simply could not be understood in the manner of the empirical scientist; that is, an external observer with no access to people's thoughts or the ideas that motivated their actions. Thus, valid knowledge of the social world depended upon the human capacity for intuition. Others denied the possibility of any kind of 'science' of culture at all, believing that the spiritual essence of humanity could never be captured by empirical methods. Max Weber's writings on the methodology of the social sciences have to be understood in the context of these debates, where he had tried to take a middle road between the two sides by arguing both against the 'superficialities of positivism' and against those idealist thinkers who denied 'the possibilities of scientific work in the field of human culture' (H.S. Hughes, 1974: 302).

However, whereas Weber's aim was the development of a methodological synthesis which would permit valid scientific work in the study of human societies, the members of the Frankfurt School were deeply sceptical of academic sociology, which they regarded as simply another aspect of the emerging bourgeois ideology. The enterprise undertaken by the Frankfurt School, then, was not simply an effort to develop alternative theories to those already established in the human sciences. To repeat, it was nothing less than an attempt to undermine the whole mode of thought which permeated the culture of capitalist societies, and which led to the 'deformed consciousness' of their members. It is in this sense that the Frankfurt School authors came to describe their work as '*Critical* Theory'. Since conventionally accepted theories and concepts inevitably bore the imprint of 'alienated' or 'ideological' ways of thinking, they had to be subjected to rigorous criticism in order to display the discrepancies between the world they purported to describe, and the way things really were. Just as they deplored the tendency of philosophers and scientists to take the world at face value, to identify immediate appearances with the real nature of things, so the Frankfurt thinkers dismissed the accepted view that modern capitalist societies were (or could be) democratic associations of free individuals. Our 'freedoms' are illusory, they argued, and our 'choices' meaningless. The real historical trend of modernity is to create a totalitarian 'mass' society in which the individual is reduced to an insignificant atom, whose life course, lifestyle and even personal experience are increasingly 'administered' through the process of rationalisation.

Rather than being taken at face value by critical thinkers, positivism was to be seen as an intellectual expression of the current realities of capitalist society, and as itself involving the *uncritical* acceptance of the nature of present capitalism as setting the boundaries of its own intellectual horizon. The School could not accept the idealist premise that thought could develop in isolation from social conditions in accord with its own independent necessities. They could not, therefore, accept that knowledge could possibly develop separately from the tensions and struggles within a society. Any proffered understandings of social reality could only be the expression of group interests, understandings which often require that people be misled with respect to their real situation. The ambition of positivism to comprise an objective standpoint, portraying reality from a neutral and universal point of view, could only be a false pretension from the School's point of view. It was a form of self-deception about the actual social roots which nourished the positivist way of thinking, produced in important part by positivism's lack of grasp of the idea of the social totality. Instead, the School sought to develop ways of escape from the constraints which, as they saw it, held back all thinking in capitalist society.

That there can be no kind of final or ultimate knowledge, only perspectives and understandings valid in their time and place, was accepted by the Frankfurt theorists as obviously applying to their own position along with all of established science and philosophy. It meant that their own ideas were conditional, provisional and based on values rather than 'facts'. Horkheimer denied that the natural sciences yielded the 'positive facts' that the positivist philosophers were so concerned with. The positivist notion of fact rested upon the sharp separation of 'fact' from 'value', but this was an entirely false and impossible separation, and not one that could be maintained by positivism in its practice, however much it might insist on the distinction in principle. It was a delusion of positivism that, along with the natural sciences that it sponsored, it was 'value free' and, as a consequence, was neutral with respect to the political conflicts to be found in society. Natural science was supposedly objective, in the sense that it described the facts about the real world in a non-partisan way, such that an understanding of those facts could be used in practical action by anyone, regardless of their political affiliations. The School denied that this was so – it could not be, if facts and values cannot be separated.

As we have already pointed out, having rejected the dualist conception of mind as a composite of distinct mental and physical elements as idealist, the School held to a materialist conception of praxis derived from Marx. Thought can only be understood as the product of collective social process, or praxis, as human beings work together upon nature so as to sustain and reproduce themselves. Knowledge must therefore be enmeshed in the (contradictory and antagonistic) group relations that make up any real society.

Therefore, the School insisted, the results of (even) the natural sciences were suffused with interests, and quite specific ones at that, namely, the interests of commodity-production in developing the rational control of both nature and people.

Positivism was understood by the School as the epistemology of science, and science was the form that knowledge was increasingly taking. In the modern world, Horkheimer had argued, the methods of scientific investigation have come to be accepted as the only valid way in which objective knowledge of reality can be obtained. This was the line of thinking initiated by Descartes in the seventeenth century. Descartes had argued persuasively that neither simple intuition, nor philosophical speculation, nor traditional handed-down wisdom lead us necessarily to the truth. Only the application of the innate power of human reason in properly scientific inquiries involving systematic observations and investigations of the natural world, could possibly work out the truth about the nature of things. It is the acceptance of this idea of natural science as the only source of valid knowledge that has led to the unprecedented expansion of science in the Western world, and the associated development of technologies through which scientific knowledge is applied to the control of the natural environment. Given the success of this project, and the scientific triumphs which have led to the transformation of societies' productive capacities since Descartes' time, it is hardly surprising that 'the scientific method' has come to be taken as a model for any kind of attempt to gain valid knowledge of phenomena.

But such scientific knowledge was mainly only that which was useful for prediction and control. In other words, that which served the purpose of instrumental calculation, conceiving reality as an ensemble of facts which are fixed and immutable, and which need to be captured in mathematical terms.

Facts are considered of use only insofar as they can be manipulated in instrumental ways. It is this doctrine which has shaped the natural sciences and which was proposed as the philosophy of the social sciences.

Positivism was, however, incapable of understanding itself in its own terms, what is nowadays often termed the requirement of reflexivity: that the theory should apply to itself as well as to the rest of its subject matter. It was unable to appreciate why it had become the dominant doctrine of knowledge. It was unwilling to recognise that its aim was not to grasp social reality in its full complexity, but only to concentrate upon those aspects of it that can be reduced to mathematical representations. It was a conception of knowledge relevant to making nature more manageable and controllable – essentially calculable – and therefore more useful in the production process, and that would, when applied to the study of social life, approach that in the same impoverished way. Positivism in social science had reified the social world, and social facts were given an objectified status as though they were subject to their own autonomous laws. Positivism, therefore, reflected and reinforced the reified nature of capitalism, portraying the way the social world currently is as a fixed and immutable fact.

Again, the tendency to think this way does reflect something real, but not something essential and necessary. It reflects the extent to which life under capitalism was becoming increasingly rigid and regulated. However, this is not essential to social relations, merely the form that they were taking in the then current context. But capitalism is only the creation of human beings and their activities, and the point is to reveal and expose this reified character, not to endorse it. In the way that activities had become specialised in the workplace, so that no one any longer has a comprehensive view of the whole – of the totality – so social science of a positivist frame of mind has also been deprived of the concept of totality. This means that it cannot grasp things from the point of view of the whole society, nor can it understand its own relations to that whole. Neither can it contrast the way things actually are with the possibilities that they might allow, the potential that they may contain. For the Marxist-influenced approach of the School, the idea of what something really is must include an understanding of what it is on the way to becoming. It will only be partially and superficially understood by identifying all the features which make it the way that it is now. This is what Adorno condemned as identity thinking. A thorough understanding must also involve those aspects of a thing or phenomenon that have not yet been realised, that will bring about its transformation into something other than itself, those aspects of it that represent its potential to develop beyond its present stage of existence. Positivism thinks that social laws, like natural ones, must be universal and timeless, but social life is not like this, for it has an historical character.

There cannot really be the kind of generalisation about social life that positivism envisages, since understanding must be tied to particular historical periods, and that is why positivism cannot understand itself in the way the School does, that is, as itself a product of this particular phase of capitalism. Nor can it understand the extent to which the way things are constitutes a false situation, not a true expression of human needs and reactions, but a distorted formation of these. Identity thinking is the attempt to impose its categories on reality even though this can never manage to capture its full complexity. By contrast, non-identity thinking seeks to bring out the greater complexity of that reality, with all its internal contradictions, whilst recognising that it cannot, itself, yield a complete and final specification of that complexity. Positivism officially subscribes to the sharp separation of fact and value: science describes only the facts and cannot make a moral judgement condemning an existing situation as humanly unacceptable. However, it does not really honour the separation that it makes, for positivism itself rests upon value, and actually, if tacitly, accepts the values of the existing society. The School does not accept this separation, and makes the evaluation of social order an integral part of its approach.

Further, positivism treats knowledge in a mistakenly individualist way, as though thought was something entirely created by the single, isolated individual mind. For the Critical Theorists, the formation of consciousness and thought is something that goes on collectively, is done in a social context, and through the process of struggle amongst social groups. Positivism, because it does not take into account the collective nature of thought, and thus its connection to the divisions in society, cannot be aware of the essentially contradictory nature of any actual society. Consequently it strives (in a necessarily futile effort) to portray social reality as internally coherent and cannot grasp the contradiction-ridden character of social reality. Positivism does not reflect the truth about social reality, but primarily contributes ideologically to the improvement and perpetuation of instrumental reason.

In this attack on positivism, the now familiar theme of alienation is evident. In this context, though, the Frankfurt theorists argued that conventional discourse and the whole mode of thought that it represented – involving familiar oppositions such as 'individual' and 'society', 'subjective' and 'objective', 'values' and 'facts', and so on – was itself an extension of the 'commodity fetishism' at the heart of capitalist society. In an important sense, what the Frankfurt thinkers attempted was, once again, a development of Marx. Just as he had dismissed the scientific pretensions of the early political economists on the grounds that they assumed the universal validity of concepts – such as 'private property', 'capital', 'profit', and so on – which were really only applicable within the capitalist mode of production, so the members of the Frankfurt School wished to generalise the point, claiming that all established bodies of thought, including science and philosophy, were little more than elaborations of the bourgeois world view. Thus the established procedures of science – such as the identification of 'objects', the formulation and testing of 'hypotheses' to 'explain' their 'behaviour', along with the aim of developing 'laws' with universal applicability – are seen not as objective processes leading to an ultimate knowledge of reality, but as fundamentally compromised in that they depend on, and reproduce, the alienated thought-patterns of bourgeois society. In this respect they are not the embodiment let alone the fulfilment of human reason or values, since they lead to all the material miseries and wretchedness of a world beyond human control, and to the alienated and distorted consciousness of those living in it.

An alternative approach to social science was clearly needed, one that could recognise the inherently conflictual nature of reality and the fact that no abstract account can be given of it as a coherent unity, and one that also recognises the potential, in the present reality, for other realities to develop from and replace it, possibly one that does genuinely enhance human freedom.

However, despite the opposition to positivism in social science, Adorno did become involved in a collaborative study with, among others, the then leading methodologist of the positivist approach, Paul Lazarsfeld on his Radio Research Project. Lazarsfeld wanted to marry Critical Theory with empirical social research and to do so by understanding the appeal of music. Adorno, therefore, seemed an ideal choice of fellow researcher. It was, however, to prove less than an ideal collaboration, due in no small part to Adorno's rather abrasive and arrogant personality. More fruitful was Adorno's collaboration on another study, on the 'authoritarian personality'.

The Authoritarian Personality

The study concerned itself with a theme that had occupied the School as a result of the rise of authoritarian and irrationalist politics in the 1930s. What had led to the acceptance by the masses of such politics? Here we may note the relevance of one of Max Weber's general preoccupations, namely, the degree to which people in society were extensively receptive and obedient to the commands of those in power. Weber had sought to understand this willing compliance through an examination of the different forms of domination and the bases on which power became legitimised as authority. The School, however, was interested in the psychological sources of such obedience. What made people into obedient individuals and what, in particular, made some of them into the kind of people who would persecute Jews and staff the concentration camps?

The School had earlier drawn on the idea that a major source of influence on the individual's psychological development was the family environment of childhood. Horkheimer (in a long essay 'Authority and the Family' (in Horkheimer, 1993)) had offered a materialist answer to the problem of compliance in general: the nature of the family is to be understood in relation to the stages of development of the conditions of economic production within the society. Moreover, it played a major role in stabilising these relationships by instilling appropriate habits of obedience into offspring – at least for a time, until the progressive development of economic conditions inevitably undermined this stability. Horkheimer accepted the canonical account of the bourgeois family set out by Marx's colleague, Engels: that the first source of authority is to be found within the family itself. He saw it as dominated by patriarchal power rooted in the father's position in the economic structure as the then sole source of income for the family. It was the family that first instilled the inclination to accept the authority of the father, which would then become a basis for accepting that of those other authority figures such as the employer and representatives of the bourgeois state. The study of the 'authoritarian personality' inquired into the conditions within the family that gave rise to the specific kind of personality that went to extremes in its acceptance of authority.

The study The study, published in 1950, was in large part inspired by a desire to understand the phenomenon of Nazism and the anti-Semitism that it had encouraged among the German people prior to and during the Second World War. It involved Adorno as a major partner in a cross-disciplinary collaboration with psychoanalytic thinkers as well as researchers with a distinctly positivistic streak. In this respect it was a major departure from the historical and philosophical inquiries in which he and his collaborators usually engaged. This was an empirical study in the more conventional sociological sense, particularly in the use of interviews. The study is often considered a landmark effort in the attempt to make sociology more empirical and quantitative, an effort which, at that time, was guided by the idea that social science needed to develop the means of measuring its explanatory concepts. However, it was also an attempt to bring psychoanalysis into the understanding of social processes.

Sigmund Freud, the founder of psychoanalysis, was, along with Marx and Weber, influential in the early days of the School. The scientific status of Freud's account of the formation of personality has always been contested, and of late there has been a torrent of literature not only questioning the scientific quality of psychoanalytic thought, but much of it casting doubt on Freud's personal intellectual integrity. Nonetheless, early in the century, psychoanalysis came to be widely accepted and had huge influence not least within very different sociological approaches, as we have seen in connection with Parsons' functionalism in Chapter 2, and within French social thought, as is manifested by his presence in Chapter 4 on structuralism.

Freud provided an account of the formation of the individual personality which seemed to fit with the School's arguments about the suppression of the individual's nature under the oppressive social arrangements of capitalism. Capitalism required passive, obedient personalities to staff the rationalised arrangements of society. However, despite the progressively rationalised nature of capitalism, irrational political forces could develop – as testified by the rise of Germany's Nazis – and it was clear that some people must have the kind of personality that would make them receptive to the attractions of dictatorial demagogues. The aim was to understand the formation of this type of personality. The study was, in important ways, a precursor to the later reflections on the culture industry.

Freud's account of personality formation centres upon the early stages of the individual's life, the first few years of childhood, and of the relations within the family, particularly between the child and its parents. The story Freud tells is of the individual's personality being shaped, through interaction with the parents, away from a dependence upon their care towards independence from these significant figures, so that the child will, at full maturity, be able to become a fully fledged and autonomous member of the society.

Freud's might seem a rather conservative story about how the individual comes to psychological fulfilment in conventional society, but this is not entirely true and it was certainly not what the School saw in his teachings. Freud himself thought that civilised social life demanded a price from each individual, namely, the sacrifice of a great part of that individual's instinctive nature to social conformity. In the immediate period following its birth, the infant is driven by indiscriminate needs for the bodily satisfactions of food, warmth and contact (which, in Freud's view, had a very marked sexual component). The role of upbringing was to narrow, focus and restrict the sources of satisfaction that, eventually, the adult would seek and accept. This would typically – because, of course, socialisation does not always succeed – be the conventional outlets, for example and certainly in Freud's time, seeking sexual satisfaction in heterosexual relationships. Whilst the biologically based, indiscriminately pleasure seeking impulses that fill the child's early life can be socially controlled, these impulses are not eliminated but remain part of our biological being. Our social upbringing has, however, made us such that we deny, refuse even to acknowledge, their existence, and it is the suppression of our natural desires that is the price that civilisation makes each of us pay. It was particularly in relation to this latter point, expressed especially in Freud's *Civilisation and its Discontents* (1930), that the School saw something compatible with their basic conviction that the existing social order allowed only a very partial development of the human potential by imposing unnecessary restrictions upon the formation of the personality, and in this way satisfying the needs of industrial production rather than those of individual self-realisation and well-being.

Freud had emphasised the extent to which an individual's feelings are ambivalent, or two sided. It is possible to feel contrary emotions about one and the same person, to feel both love and hatred, admiration and contempt, for someone at the same time; in even more extreme cases, one can love someone but also wish that they would fall ill or die. The fact that there is such ambivalence is not a comfortable situation for the individual, and is often dealt with by suppressing one of those feelings, usually the more inappropriate and disreputable of the two. Thus, the individual effectively denies the ambivalence but it is this ambivalence which was seen as the key to the 'authoritarian personality'.

The *Authoritarian Personality* study itself focused on the possibility of there being a constituency in mass societies available for manipulation by demagogic leaders. What kind of personality would make someone engage in, for example, the intense anti-Semitism that marked Hitler's Germany? What kind of personality would make a person prone to engage in virulent hostility to another group? As the title of the book indicates, a particular kind of personality structure was identified, and its origins located in a certain kind of upbringing.

Concisely, the authoritarian personality is a mixture of servility and resentment involving traits of conventionalism, submissiveness, aggression, intolerance, anti-Semitism, ethnocentrism, intolerance of ambiguity, and conceptions of social relations as power relations, regarding the world as a dangerous and violent place. Its leading characteristic is the desire of the individual to be told what to do, to think that right conduct is fixed by following the commands of those in authority, people who are to be regarded with unquestioning respect. However, this type of individual does not feel only admiration for those in authority – for ambivalence is involved – but also, and at the same time, feels intense resentment against them, but is afraid of expressing this resentment because of the ambivalence and because of fear of punishment. It is these latter feelings which are mostly suppressed. Yet strong but repressed feelings, for Freud, cannot be permanently and entirely bottled up. These feelings will seek expression but for the most part this will have to be in an indirect way. They cannot be released in the form of open hostility to those in authority. If they are released at all, it must be against someone other than those in authority. Vulnerable, socially marginal groups are a good target for such release. It is in this way that the virulent anti-Semitism under the Nazis was to be understood. The policy of anti-Semitism was endorsed by the state authorities, and that fact made it right. The aggression against the Jews could be intensified by the displaced expression of the hostility that was actually felt against the authorities but could not be unleashed against them. More generally, the authoritarian personality is the kind of personality that would be more available to the seductions of demagogic politicians.

The personality type was seen as arising from an upbringing within a family structure where relationships between parents and children were structured in a very hierarchical way, and in which things were done according to strict and stringently enforced rules. Parental love for the child would be doled out conditionally, dependent on the child conforming to the rules. Failure to follow the rules would be punished. This picture of the family structure clearly relates to the picture of a personality dominated by the need to satisfy the demands of authority through rigid conformity with those demands as expressed in commands and conventions, which produced a perpetual anxiety to avoid the punishment that would ensue from infringing the rules.

The *Authoritarian Personality* study itself paid little attention to the structure of the wider society within which personalities of this type were being formed. However, it would be a mistake to suppose that given the orientation of the School it could not have attempted to identify the structural conditions making a constituency available to authoritarian rulers. Such conditions came to be called the 'mass society'. Capitalist society, eventually and ruthlessly, eradicates all that is not essential to the logic of its development. Among these are the 'secondary' groupings, such as the church, the neighbourhood, the occupational group, etc., which stand between the individual and the state and act as a buffer between central authority and the solitary individual. In ruthlessly weeding out these secondary associations, capitalism creates a population that is an undifferentiated mass. Rather than the differentiated structure of secondary associations binding individuals together and collectively mediating their relation to central authorities, society is made up of a vast aggregate of separated individuals exposed to the unfettered power of the state and, through this, the large corporations. Moreover, the attenuation of secondary associations means that the influence they have on forming an individual's outlook is also eliminated. Accordingly, the now isolated individuals can be more exposed to the influences of central authority in the formation of opinion and, dangerously, the propagandistic persuasion of a dictatorial ruler without meeting resistance in the form of attitudes formed by involvement in independent secondary associations.

Thus, the mass of socially isolated individuals were potentially available as a more readily recruited constituency for totalitarian leaders, and there was increasingly in reach of such leaders an ever more powerful means of influence: the mass media. 'Mass communications' as they are often called were becoming the source of meaning for individuals and an important influence on their character and outlook. But this meant that public opinion was prevailingly being formed by, and only by, the mass media. In their analysis and critique of the way in which bourgeois culture had come to dominate Western societies, in *The Dialectic of Enlightenment*, Horkheimer and Adorno gave a central place to an analysis and critique of the 'culture industry'.

The critique of the culture of capitalism

Whilst rooted in the Marxist tradition, in practice the thinkers of the Frankfurt School were close to Weber's ideas about the reduction of life in modern society to existence in an administrative prison for the human soul. If Marx had indeed predicted that capitalist society would be destroyed by a working class revolution as a result of their terrible impoverishment – and it is a matter of scholarly controversy as to whether he did or not – then his prediction had certainly failed and was looking less and less likely ever to come true. In general, the material conditions of the working classes had improved rather than deteriorated with the continuing development of capitalism. By contrast, while recognising that the high and rising material well-being of capitalism was unprecedented in the history of human societies, Weber also noted that this had not led to contentment. Rather, material betterment was accompanied by a deep dissatisfaction: there was indeed impoverishment, but in the spiritual and cultural dimensions of life rather than the material one.

These spiritual and cultural aspects of life were subject to the same pervasive, uncontrollable, and onward-rushing process of rationalisation that Weber believed was the fundamental characteristic of modern Western capitalism. The processes of control, regulation and specialisation that were to be found in economic organisation were paralleled in cultural life, whose products were becoming merely impersonal technical constructions providing superficial pleasures and amusements rather than expressions of and satisfactions for the true needs of the human spirit. Capitalist societies may not be politically totalitarian in any overt way, but they are, through manipulation rather than outright domination, just as oppressive of freedom as any overtly totalitarian regime would be. However, even though capitalism could be seen as culturally limiting, oppressive and inhibiting the possibility for human development and freedom, it did not follow that people necessarily *felt* in any way deprived or, even if they did, that they properly and objectively understood the nature and source of their dissatisfactions. But nonetheless their capacity to think for themselves, to think in terms other than those required for keeping them subject to the illusions of capitalism, was ever more restricted.

The critique of the culture industry

Although the 'culture industry' represented a danger to democracy and the development of a free humanity, it was still open to critical examination and condemnation. In a society in which individuals are being reduced to the members of a mass, their lives will be ever more mediated by mass communications, and these provide a powerful means by which demagogues can recruit and direct their constituency. But even in the routine contexts of everyday life, the media play a powerful role in maintaining domination, in implanting contentment, passivity and obedience into the 'mass'. Novels, films, plays and so on are mass produced according to a formula rather than genuinely created by human inspiration. They are the output of an organisation rather than delivered by creatively gifted individuals, and it is this conception of films and so on as mere products that leads to the conception of the media as part of 'the culture industry'. However, the position of organisations in the cultural industry is comparatively weak in terms of the structure of capitalism. They are, or at least they were, the more dependent and marginal productive entities when compared with the main structures of capitalist industry. Nevertheless, like other industries they were affected by the advance of technology, especially film and photographic technologies. According to Walter Benjamin, an influential associate but never a member of the School, such technologies were increasingly capable of seeming to reflect reality directly. For the Frankfurt School, this was a major illusion and one which, because of the power of these technologies, needed combating urgently. Although the mass media – like positivist science – represented its portrayals of reality as neutral and objective rather than as expressions of ideology, this was precisely their power: to convey ideology in the guise of freedom from ideology.

The emergence of the culture industries was one of the most important developments within capitalist society in the twentieth century. The basic concepts by which Adorno and Horkheimer sought to conceive its operations were intended to bring out its repressive role in effectively creating individuals who deny their own autonomy and potential. It is a process to be understood in terms of the emergence and further development of capitalist rationalisation, pseudo-individualism, standardisation and commodification.

The culture industry had a major part to play in encouraging this 'adjustment' of individuals to a situation which did not satisfy their 'real' needs, but left them, nonetheless, feeling content with – from the School's point of view – grossly inadequate substitutes for real human satisfactions. More specifically, the culture industry did not have the potential to surpass existing social realities in the way that high radical art could; it could only express and reinforce those social realities themselves. Its dependent position within the economic order of capitalist production meant that it was incapable of expressing a view of reality that was other than the orthodox one.

One of the principal orthodoxies mass culture projected was the idea that existence in capitalist society represented the fulfilment of the Enlightenment project. People now enjoyed a free and individualised existence, and nowhere is this more manifest than in the orthodox ideologues of 'free market capitalism' who highlight the autonomy of the individual from the state, the freedom of the individual as consumer to make choices, the individual as free and sovereign. Economic transactions are free transactions, mediated by exchange, between free individuals, and social life more generally will reflect the fact that it is entirely up to the individual to decide what to do. However, from the School's point of view, it is not that the individual cannot make choices, but that these choices are for the most part superficial and restricted. The individual's freedom is largely illusory; an illusion projected and perpetuated through popular culture. Advertising, an important element of popular culture, would seem to present us with a wide array of different kinds of things to consume. There are many different motor manufacturers, for example, and each manufacturer makes several different kinds of automobiles, and each manufacturer's vigorous advertising promotion of its products conveys the impression that the choice of one make and model of car over another is an important matter. But actually, many of the ways in which motor manufacturers differentiate their products involve only fairly marginal and superficial features of their cars, such as, nowadays, the number of seats, the number and kind of doors, the colour, the sound system, badges, styling, colouring and so on. Sometimes, they even promote the fact that the purchaser can select specific features for their make and model of car, presenting this as a way of individualising – 'customising' – the vehicle. But one is still, as far as Adorno and Horkheimer were concerned, buying a mass-produced product which is basically the same as everyone else's.

Indeed, in buying a car one is also buying into a conformist existence – living in the suburbs, going to work every day, shopping at the same supermarkets, and so on – whose gross and basic features are widely shared.

This is the pseudo-individualisation mentioned earlier. The limited choices that are offered are portrayed in the mass media as ways of individualising oneself, of emphasising how different from other people we are, but this is not an individualism that is in creative tension with the basic conformity that capitalist production and social order require. The small differences possible within the basic pattern of conformity are much exaggerated in popular culture. The preoccupation with personal appearance in the contemporary consumer market, the concentration upon clothes and footwear, for instance, and their differentiation through manufacturer logos, are mere marginal differentials rather than representing any essential and functional differences in quality, characteristics and utility.

The School's answer to what they saw as the principles of bourgeois thought was that individuals are not free and autonomous but are extensively manipulated by the culture industry. The kind of individualism available was not that of genuinely independent individuals who go their own way regardless. They were people basically shaped into being conformist who made choices in the purchasing of commodities and in the adoption of lifestyles as defined by commodity consumption. They would never challenge the assumptions of the system and of their lives. Indeed, far from being the kind of individuals who would stand against authority – as envisaged in the Enlightenment conception of individualism – they would tend to identify with authority and, *in extremis*, would readily and unquestioningly accept its dictates.

Art The School's pessimistic analysis of the ubiquitous rationalisation of culture under capitalism brought it close to the paradoxical position in which it was asserting that the very critique in which it was engaged was impossible. In Adorno's view, however, this was not so much a paradox as something that was dangerously close to being true. It was less a matter of expecting Critical Theory to lead to greater emancipation, than a matter of struggling to keep it alive on the periphery of contemporary culture. Rather than engaging with the central political issues, Adorno's later work engaged with matters seemingly remote from politics, namely, philosophy and aesthetics. His *Negative Dialectics* was an attempt to think out the School's relationship to philosophy and the dialectical tradition. His other later major work, *Aesthetic Theory* (1984), developed ideas he used in his treatment of music. Adorno's 'retreat' into philosophy and aesthetics was an expression of his view that the possibility of critical thought had been all but eliminated. What possibilities remained were marginal and outside the scope of the main culture industry.

Much of Adorno's thought was propelled by a deep animus toward the spirit of bourgeois culture as much as toward the economic injustices of capitalism.

His contempt for popular music and film derived from much the same distaste: an aesthetic disdain related to the fact that the popular arts lacked the potential for critique. On the other hand, high art had such a potential even if it could only realise it somewhat precariously. Such art possessed the potential to oppose established reality and to liberate reified consciousness insofar as it could retain the special character that it often possessed in earlier societies, a character that Adorno called 'autonomous art'. Under such conditions the artist could, when free of external influences, such as those of patronage, rise above local and historical limitations to express something close to a universal truth and could give voice to perceptions that differed from those prevailing in the wider society, and were even subversive of them.

The developments of capitalist society were increasingly unfavourable to autonomous art. Instead, the arts were coming to serve the same purpose as everything else, that is, to be products that can be bought and sold. The arts, in the traditional sense, were being displaced by the rise of 'the culture industry'; replaced by what is often called 'mass' or 'popular' culture, but which is, in fact, not an expression of popular needs. Like everything else in modern capitalism, much of art becomes the output of an industry. Autonomous art, given its nature as potentially dissident from and subversive of the dominant culture, is the one last place where one might look for criticism of the society. However, while such art may still be found in capitalist society, the fact that had to be faced was that the arts were becoming marginalised. As a result, the possibility of developing non-identity thinking of the kind attempted by the School was being confined to the very periphery of capitalist society and the reality it produced.

Adorno's project in aesthetics was to provide a method of analysis that would identify the 'objective meaning' of works of art. Works of art unquestionably have *subjective* meaning in that they embody, for example, the vision and purpose of their creator. But they do not *only* have subjective meaning. Walter Benjamin, one of Adorno's early associates, gave his own account of the way in which art had changed with the development of capitalism. Art had initially been integral to and specifically serving of the purposes of ritual, but works of art had then become treated as objects for display and for looking at. Even after being dissociated from ritual, however, works of art had an 'aura', retaining something of a magical authority so long as they were unique and seemingly permanent creations. The arrival of the 'age of mechanical reproduction' involved another change. The fact that works of art could be readily reproduced deprived them of the uniqueness that gave them their aura. Although this loss was a matter of some regret there was a compensating consideration, namely, that popular art could become involved with politics and, accordingly, could serve progressive ends. Thus, Benjamin anticipated that the cinema could help create a revolutionary consciousness even though the cinema industry was dominated by commercial and ideological influences. It could achieve this through its technical capacity to create disruptive effects on the consciousness of the audience and bring them perceptions outside their otherwise limited and everyday ones.

Adorno was not persuaded by Benjamin's view of the progressive potential of the popular 'arts' – indeed, was profoundly contemptuous of popular culture generally – but he was impressed by Benjamin's argument that the meaning of cultural objects could not be traced back, as most Marxists thought, to the economic substructure of society. Rather, cultural objects were in themselves expressions of the social totality at a particular time and place. The idea was that works of art are not just products of individual artists, but of the society as a whole, or 'the social totality' as it is referred to in the jargon of the School. It followed that the analysis of all the elements of a culture, even the most seemingly trivial or fragmentary, could furnish knowledge of the social whole. (As we will see in Chapter 4, it was just this kind of conception held by and central to the Frankfurt School's whole approach that the structuralist Marxist, Louis Althusser, condemned as a complete corruption of Marx's scientific thought.)

On this view, the work of art expresses the nature of the totality from which it derives. The realities of that totality are expressed in the work of art, though they are not purposively injected into it by their creators, nor are they readily recognised by either the creators or their audience. They lack the method, the *dialectical* method, that will yield the understanding of what the work of art 'says' about the society from which it comes, what it gives away about the nature of that society. It is what works of art usually unwittingly express about the social totality that comprises their objective meaning.

The recognition that the individual work of art comes from the totality is the basis for this dialectical method. In this context, the notion of a dialectical method stems from the assumption that a work of art originates in the totality; the dialectical movement is between the whole – the totality – and the part – the work of art. The 'part' is expressive of the whole in the sense that one can, from a part, even a small part, work out the general nature of the whole. Ordinarily, in bourgeois cultures, works of art were understood as individual and isolated artefacts, perhaps referred, for deeper understanding, to the intentions and inclinations of the artist who produced them. That works of art needed to be understood by reference to the 'totality' provided a new way of understanding them, one which explicitly related them to the 'totally organised' society that capitalism had now become. This would give theoretical expression to what were, at best, inchoate and unfocused feelings of disappointment in the more explicit expression of the art work.

Adorno's analysis of music Adorno's major contribution was in working out this project by applying the method to modern music (though he made analyses of literary works too), an art form in which he had no little experience. His was to be no 'scientific' account that could be separated from value judgements on the individual works of art. His theoretical analysis was intended to evaluate works primarily in terms of whether they conformed to, or negated, bourgeois ideology. Adorno was to pioneer a materialist aesthetics.

His efforts were firmly within the lineage of Marx's notion of ideology. Any concrete society – short of the communist utopia – is riven by internal contradictions. In the Hegelian scheme of things, to which Marx's theory of ideology owed much, actual historical periods are marked by contradictions, are both one thing and its opposite. For example, in Marx's terms, capitalism is the form of a society which makes possible the complete and final freedom of all humanity because of its immense economic power. But, at the same time, the capitalist society cannot possibly allow the complete and final freedom of all humanity because its own nature depends upon private property, and all the oppression that goes with this. Thus, the struggle is between the desire to abolish private property (embodied in the working class) and the necessity to retain it (embodied in the ruling, property-owning class). Ideology arises in part because societies cannot openly acknowledge and explicitly address the contradictions which run through them, but they cannot avoid giving expression to them. So, insofar as the work of art expresses the social totality's real nature then it must thereby express the contradictions that mark the totality. But the expression of these contradictions is indirect, involving a kind of fantasising. The contradictions, which are in reality irresolvable, are, instead, represented in thought, in theory, in cultural representation, as if they can be or have been resolved. (Compare this with Lévi-Strauss's similar views about the role of myth in Chapter 4.) The same struggle that goes on in society, between the preservation of its existing order and tendencies which contradict and threaten it, can be found expressed in art.

Adorno's project for the study of art owed much to his interpretation of what two modern composers, Alban Berg and Arnold Schoenberg, had achieved. In Berg's operetta, *Wozzeck*, Adorno had detected a musical logic that, he held, corresponded structurally with a Marxist criticism of capitalist society. But Schoenberg's work went further, for his whole musical project was the replacement of tonality as the organising principle. Tonality was regarded as the expression of the bourgeois conception of music and the rejection of this was, in effect, a critique of bourgeois society. Schoenberg, in his compositions, drove the inner logic of the existing musical form to the point at which it broke down and transmuted into a new form, just as the development of society involved the breakdown of its own inner logic to become something new.

Social reality is never, in this conception, a genuine and harmonious unity, but is always divided, fragmented and marked by contradictions. While culture will sometimes obscure this fact, eventually it will betray this objective truth in artistically radical works expressing it in a demystifying fashion. Thus, Adorno's own work should itself express this same truth through its style as well as the critique of society contained in its arguments. The difficult style of Adorno's writing is, therefore, itself a criticism of capitalist society in that it rejects the misleading impression that social reality is clear and coherent and best expressed through the translucent, accessible style the bourgeois prefer to read (the very style that provoked – in the French context – the extreme antipathy of Roland Barthes, as discussed in Chapter 4).

It has been remarked that Marxist aestheticians – such as Lukács and Lucien Goldmann, as well as Adorno – have been preoccupied with analysing only the most arcane and inaccessible intellectual and art works, ones that will surely not be read by, or have any effect on, the working classes. Adorno's attention and regard were certainly fixed upon what he considered 'serious' or, one might say, unpopular music. He had, as already mentioned, only contempt for 'popular' music. In his view the popularity of a kind of music is no measure of its social importance because the question that really matters is where the potential for the demystification of bourgeois ideology lies. The first need is to break through the illusions created by the culture of capitalism, and it is in the nature of capitalist society that this potential can lie only in works that will be unpopular not least because they violate, if not defy, the commands of bourgeois ideology. From the point of view of Critical Theory, it is the capacity of the work of art to depict the 'negative' aspects of the totality that provides it with its aesthetic value.

While Adorno was interested in the objective meaning of music, this did not imply that the meaning expressed an eternal truth. Music expressed historical rather than eternal truths, truths about the society to which it belonged. In the same way the production of music was also to be understood within its historical context. The composer is confronted by and placed within an existing system for making music, and is constrained by that, regardless of whether the composer's own work is to fall comfortably within or to be disruptive of that tradition. The musical tradition has been formed in and by the society; the composer has to work with materials that the culture provides. Accordingly, the musical problems that the composer wrestles with are also, though not explicitly, problems in the representation of society. Thus, though the artist is strictly concerned with artistic questions, he or she cannot help grappling with the issues involved in expressing the nature of the totality.

Adorno's understanding of the history of Western classical music recapitulates the School's concern with the demolition of individualism. Beethoven's music can be understood as an expression of the ideal of heroic individualism, the self-creating and fully liberated individual: an ideal that is a positive achievement of capitalist society. But Beethoven's music also recognises that this conception is destined for destruction. At the other end of the 300-year development is Schoenberg's music, which rejects the rationalised system of tonality and expresses the extinction of that kind of individualism, offering a musical alternative to that system and conveying the anguish that arises in its absence. In summary form, Adorno's analysis of different composers over the period from Bach to Schoenberg, is concerned to:

- trace the interplay of 'affirmative' and 'critical' elements in the music, and the way in which the capacity for critical elements becomes increasingly restrictive, save in 'unpopular' music;
- trace the way the music interrelates, and sometimes manages to resolve, the opposition between subjective attachment to heroic individualism and the objective diminution and eradication of such individualism in reality, as well as the associated tension between individual and collective interest through the purported reconciliation of these and the equal recognition that they cannot both be accommodated;
- trace the way in which the music is both affected by and reflects the changes in the society, particularly the extension of rationalisation throughout the society as well as in the composition of music itself;
- trace the way in which the technical developments in the tonal tradition both advance and develop that tradition, but also, at times, introduce and explore elements that will not be amenable to successful incorporation into the musical system and will, eventually, when their logic is fully explored, lead to tonality's own overthrow.

These radical developments are, however, confined within music and within Critical Theory. While they express the reality of the total society, there is little room for individual innovation and for the subversion of the prevailing system, for propagating these insights into the mainstream of life. Those who attempt such radical innovations will, likely as not, occupy isolated positions on the margins of the society's culture. Schoenberg's music might be telling people about what was wrong with their society, but they were not listening in any numbers, any more than the masses were reading Adorno's own writings. Criticism was nearly extinct in the administered society. The liberating potential of music, that is, the degree to which it exposed the real nature of the society, was inversely related to the degree to which it could be understood and accepted by ordinary individuals. Music would, almost paradoxically, advance in its liberating potential by becoming more preoccupied with resolving musical problems in radical ways, than by trying to deliver politically propagandist declarations of an overtly critical kind. Schoenberg's revolutionary breakthrough was, however, one which was soon recaptured by bourgeois ways of thinking, being turned by others into a highly regulated mathematical system that was every bit as restrictive on individual autonomy as the calculated regulation of activity in the administrative organisation and the industrial workplace.

Resurgence

Horkheimer and Adorno had concluded that Critical Theory would continue to be marginalized in society and would survive only as a nagging reminder that an alternative to the rampant ideology of capitalism is possible. However, events in the United States gave renewed relevance to their ideas and a rediscovery of the Frankfurt School, making it immeasurably influential on the subsequent development of sociology and many other disciplines. Contemporary prevalence of the idea that sociology should be a critical discipline is in significant part due to the renewed influence of the School.

The rediscovery of the School was at first due to one of its old hands, Herbert Marcuse, who had remained in the USA when Adorno and Horkheimer returned to Frankfurt, and who revitalised interest with the 1964 publication of *One Dimensional Man*. The intellectual climate following the Second World War was a contented one, some would say a complacent one. The doctrine of 'the end of ideology' – holding that the age of extreme ideologies such as Fascism and communism was over, superseded by the post-war economic boom and the arrival of a civil, rather than confrontational politics – quickly became a new orthodoxy. It was argued that the 'mixed economy', a blend of 'capitalist' (privately owned) and 'socialist' (state owned) organisations, had effectively dissolved the tensions between rival economic forms. Post-war society was being increasingly identified as an 'affluent society', to use Galbraith's term (Galbraith, 1960), one in which material prosperity had softened, if not eliminated, the inequalities giving rise to sharp class divisions. A preoccupation with private domestic lives, leisure and consumption was displacing an interest in politics. Sociology (under the leadership of Parsons and Merton) had begun to think of itself as a successfully respectable discipline, holding much the same position as other important professions, such as law and medicine, and sociologists were becoming responsible collaborators with the state and with business in resolving the organisational problems facing modern society. It seemed that Durkheim's dream of a sociological profession had been realised.

The contentment was soon unsettled, however. The Vietnam War, together with parallel and associated cultural developments, through the 1960s created an opposition to the self-satisfied picture, giving rise to what became known as the 'counter-culture'. Marcuse, as a teacher, had influenced some of the key radicals in the protest movements for racial equality and opposition to the Vietnam War. His ideas began to gain prominence as these two movements fused into generalised hostility to the political and economic system of the USA and Europe.

Marcuse effectively updated the School's position to encompass these developments. He did not deny the claims about the 'affluent society' nor the political quiescence which obtained, but provided a different conception of what these changes meant. The true aim of theory, he argued, was not to assist the existing society to administer itself better within its limitations, but to change society and eliminate all inhibitions on freedom. Such theory could not accept the contemporary society as 'the good society' – as a then prominent US sociologist, Seymour Martin Lipset had contemporaneously declared it. Rather it measures society against the potential it contains for further human liberation, and identifies those elements within the society which have the potential to lead it in the direction of further liberation but which are concealed and inhibited by ideology. Far from totalitarianism being obviated by the defeat of the Nazis and the Cold War containment of the Soviet Union, it was creeping up on the 'advanced societies' which, appearances to the contrary, were becoming *totalitarian* themselves: a totalitarianism that had a benign face concealing even 'more effective' forms of control and cohesion.

The societies are totalitarian not in the sense of being brutal regimes that coercively repress their own populations, but in the sense that they assiduously obliterate alternatives to themselves, eliminating resistance to their power at home and imposing themselves on all other societies in the world. All differences between capitalism and oppressive Soviet communism ultimately dissolve. The argument should be familiar: the affluence of contemporary society satisfied the needs of individuals, making them contented. But this was only because these needs were not real ones but needs created by the system and instilled in individuals increasingly by a mass-mediated culture. Political freedom is largely illusory for it is not the case that individuals are free to have and express *their* thoughts and opinions. Society is restrictive in what it will allow and accept as thought and opinion. People are shaped to think only as the society allows.

The society is 'one dimensional' because it allows thought and imagination only within one dimension, namely, that which is needed by, and compatible with, the existing system, and reabsorbs all potentially critical and dissident thought into its own terms:

> Thus emerges a pattern of *one-dimensional thought and behavior* in which ideas, aspirations, and objectives, that, by their content, transcend the established universe of discourse and action are either repelled or reduced to the terms of this universe. They are redefined by the rationality of the given system and of its quantitative extension. (Marcuse, 1991: 12, emphasis in original)

Again the familiar case: the vaunted rationality of the system actually amounted to its very opposite, that is, irrationality. The application of knowledge and science in the management of society's affairs was ever more thoroughgoing and effective, but, for Marcuse, deeply irrational because this way of thinking had no sight of the wider purposes that economic production and politics might serve. After all, did not this 'rational' system produce and threaten the possibility of complete nuclear destruction?

The contentment of post-war capitalism was, then, mere conformism, and the complacency massively reinforced by *repressive tolerance*. The system's further thorough extension of the process of converting everything into commodities, into products for sale, enabled it to neutralise potential dissidence. It did not attempt to directly repress dissidence, but while ostensibly allowing free expression, even dissent, turned these into consumer products – into bestselling books, television discussions, films, theatre, music, etc. Moreover, the 'professionalism' and 'responsibility' of sociology were an expression of its positivist spirit and, as a consequence, its inability to fundamentally question states of affairs. It often worked directly with the state, the military and with organisation in an even more extensive rationalisation of work, administration and political control.

Marcuse became an intellectual mascot to the student radicals of the 1960s not least in their contention that universities were part of the soft underbelly of American capitalism and could, accordingly, be converted into 'red bases' from which revolutionary struggle could be launched. His prominence contributed to the rediscovery of the Frankfurt School and the wider 'Western Marxist' tradition, and to the extensive embracing of the idea that sociology must be critical of society. This was to give the Frankfurt School a powerful influence, both direct and indirect, on the thought of the next generation of social theorists. This revitalised influence – sometimes directly, sometimes indirectly – had an important part to play in the 'revision' of social thought in the direction of 'cultural studies', which have grown inordinately since the 1960s. The School had pioneered the idea that domination in modern society was to be understood not as an overt struggle for control, but as the subtle and largely concealed manipulation of thought, an operation that, increasingly, was carried through by the mass media. It is these ideas, whether inspired by the School or by other sources, that make contemporary social analysis largely the analysis of cultural mediation.

The School's concerns have been carried into the very centre of contemporary social theory by two – actually, fiercely opposed – figures, Jürgen Habermas and Michel Foucault. Habermas, one of the most influential of a handful of leading sociological theorists, in the 1950s studied at the newly returned Frankfurt School but could not accept the School's pessimism about the possibility of emancipation. There were prospects in modern society – through its democratic aspects – for further and more faithful fulfilment of Enlightenment ideas. Habermas began a gigantic effort to rethink the recent history of social thought, including the School's own presuppositions, to bring out the logic of the forces (some of them built into the very nature of human communication itself) as well as the tensions and failures within the system that could facilitate the development of a democratically created rationality. Foucault, perhaps an even more widely influential figure than Habermas, working within French philosophy effectively reinvented the idea of the administered society for himself, later acknowledging that if he had become aware of this earlier it would have saved him a great deal of work. Foucault is, however, rather closer to the pessimism of the School's latter days, and it is his much deeper scepticism about the meaning of Enlightenment ideals in practice, and of the possibility of emancipating people generally from the workings of power, that feeds Habermas' hostility toward him (Ashenden and Owen, 1999). Through a series of studies Foucault sought to show how the human and social would-be sciences were frequently more moralistic than truly scientific enterprises, and played a supportive part in subjecting ever more areas of life to 'rational' control, thus insidiously extending administrative oversight – surveillance – and regulation into the very smallest corners of a whole host of activities. This process smothered all possibility of a full confrontation with power of the kind that Marxists hoped for. The School's influence has been in many ways diffuse but decisive.

CHAPTER THREE SUMMARY

- The Frankfurt School of Critical Theory was a varied group of scholars united by their concern to analyse the relationship between Marxism and practical political action. Most went into exile to the United States with the rise of Nazism in Germany. Two figures stand out: Adorno and Marcuse.
- The central themes of Critical Theory drew upon Marx and alientation, Weber's analysis of rationalisation, and Simmel's notion of the 'tragedy of culture'. The School's aim was to present an analysis of the changed nature of capitalism and the new forms of oppression that had arisen. Although capitalism was not overtly totalitarian, its culture served to limit and constrain the possibility of human development and freedom. The contentment of post-war capitalism was mere conformism reinforced by repressive tolerance.
- In its analyses of the culture of capitalism and the culture industry, the School contributed much to the development of contemporary cultural studies.
- Though committed to the idea of critique, the School became increasingly pessimistic about the possibilities of ending the oppression of capitalist culture though Habermas, who had studied at Frankfurt when a member of the group, attempted to formulate the conditions of emancipation.

Select bibliography and further reading

Since much of the work of the School involves a close reworking of themes originating with Marx and Weber, reading the expositions of both these scholars in Hughes et al., *Understanding Classical Theory* (Sage, 1995) will provide more than useful background. Lukács' important contribution to Marxist theory was his *History and Class Consciousness: Studies in Marxist Dialectics* (Merlin Press, 1971), originally published in 1923. H. Stuart Hughes, *Consciousness and Society:*

The Reorientation of European Social Thought, 1890–1930 (MacGibbon and Kee, 1959) is still a good account of many of the intellectual contexts out of which the Frankfurt School emerged. Dave Frisby and Mike Featherstone's edited *Simmel on Culture: Selected Writings* (Sage, 1997) is useful.

On the Frankfurt School itself T.B. Bottomore, *The Frankfurt School* (Ellis Harewood, 1984) is useful. Also Jay's, *The Dialectical Imagination: A History of the Frankfurt School and the Institute of Social Research* (Little Brown, 1973) has endured as one of the standard texts. Rolf Wiggergaus, *The Frankfurt School: Its History, Theories and Political Significance* (Polity, 1994) is both recent and extensive. David Held's *Introduction to Critical Theory: Horkheimer to Habermas* (Hutchinson, 1980) discusses the Frankfurt School, Marcuse and Habermas. Jay Bernstein's *The Frankfurt School: Critical Assessments* (Routledge, 1994) is a six-volume collection of commentary and criticism. Paul Connerton, *The Tragedy of Enlightenment: An Essay on the Frankfurt School* (Cambridge University Press, 1980) is a fine reflective essay. Two edited collections by Axel Honneth, *Cultural-political Interventions in the Unfinished Project of Enlightenment* (MIT Press, 1991), and *Philosophical Interventions in the Unfinished Project of Enlightenment* (MIT Press, 1992) contain recent papers discussing the history and state of the Critical Theory tradition.

Adorno's *Negative Dialectics* (Routledge, 1973; original German publication, 1966), can be tough going but is essential nonetheless. Prior to this work is that with Horkheimer, *The Dialectic of Enlightenment* (Verso, 1997; first published in 1942), which set out the critique of Enlightenment thought. Adorno's ideas on the 'culture industry' are to be found in a collection, *The Culture Industry: Selected Essays on Mass Culture* (Routledge, 1991). His thoughts on music are to be found in his *Philosophy of Modern Music* (Sheed and Ward, 1987) and he has a large and difficult book on *Aesthetic Theory* first published in 1970 (Routledge, 1984). Adorno et al., *The Authoritarian Personality* (Harper, 1950) is a large report on a large study. Among commentaries on Adorno's work, Jarvis' *Adorno: A Critical Introduction* (Polity, 1998) is worth looking at as is *The Adorno Reader* (Blackwell, 2000) edited by Brian O'Connor, a convenient and apt selection of his writings. Most of Max Horkheimer's independent writings are not easily available, but see his *Eclipse of Reason* (Seabury Press, 1974; first published in 1947) and his collection, *Critical Theory: Selected Essays* (Continuum, 1995). Horkheimer's *Aspects of Sociology* (Heinemann, 1973) was published under the authorship of the Institut für Sozialforschung. Some of his early writings are available in *Between Philosophy and Social Science: Selected Early Writings* (MIT Press, 1993).

Marcuse's early work includes *Reason and Revolution: Hegel and the Rise of Social Theory* (Beacon Press, 1960; first published in 1941) and his attempt to fuse Marxist and Freudian approaches, *Eros and Civilisation: A Philosophical Inquiry into Freud* (Beacon Press, 1966). The book that provoked much of the resistance to the critical 'complacency' of advanced industrial societies, largely restating the School's view for application to 1950s America, *One Dimensional*

Man: Studies in the Ideology of Advanced Industrial Society (Routledge, 1991) was first published by the Beacon Press in 1964.

Daniel Bell's reprint of his original 1960 book, *The End of Ideology: On the Exhaustion of Political Ideas in the Fifties* (Harvard University Press, 2000) has an added retrospective 'The resumption of history in the new century'. Chaim Waxman's edited collection, *The End of Ideology Debate* (Funk and Wagnalls, 1968) is worth dipping into. Seymour Martin Lipset's *The First New Nation* (Heinemann, 1964) contains an account of the United States as the 'good society'. J.K. Galbraith's *The Affluent Society* (Riverside Press, 1960) is also relevant.

The idea of the mass society is not unique to the School even though its thinkers did much to develop it. William Kornhauser's, *The Politics of Mass Society* (Free Press, 1964) is a classic statement of the idea. The edited collection by Philip Olsen, *America as a Mass Society: Changing Community and Identity* (Free Press, 1963) contains readings from various traditions other than that of Critical Theory. David Reisman, *The Lonely Crowd: A Study of the Changing American Character* (Yale University Press, 1950) and W.H. Whyte, *The Organization Man* (Cape, 1957) are early presentiments of the idea of mass society.

On more recent thinkers within the Frankfurt tradition Thomas McCarthy's *The Critical Theory of Jürgen Habermas* (Hutchinson, 1978) is a substantial account of Habermas' earlier work. David Rasmussen, *Reading Habermas* (Basil Blackwell, 1990) is a concise and accessible introduction to Habermas. Also Rasmussen's *Handbook of Critical Theory* (Basil Blackwell, 1996) contains a discussion of issues arising from Critical Theory. Raymond Geuss, *The Idea of a Critical Theory: Habermas and the Frankfurt School* (Cambridge University Press, 1981) is a short, very elegant discussion of the notion of ideology in the Critical Theory tradition. Richard Wolin, *The Terms of Cultural Criticism: The Frankfurt School, Existentialism, Poststructuralism* (Columbia University Press, 1992) connects Critical Theory to recent developments in social thought. Samantha Ashenden and David Owen's edited, *Foucault contra Habermas* (Sage, 1999) contains useful discussions of the differences between Habermas and Foucault.

Structuralism 4

BEGINNING CHAPTER FOUR

Structuralism sought to implement linguistics as the model for the social sciences, a linguistics based on the structural linguistics of Saussure. Claude Lévi-Strauss' work in anthropology and the analysis of myth was massively influential. The chapter includes discussion of:

- the contribution of Claude Lévi-Strauss;
- Roland Barthes and the 'oppression of culture';
- Jacques Lacan and the return to Freud;
- Louis Althusser and the resurrection of Marx;
- the move to post-structuralism.

The rise of the school of structuralism in French, especially Parisian, intellectual life was a key transition in modern social theory even though its prominence was relatively brief. For a moment it seemed as though the dream of a sociological science was to be realised and, though its ideas were seen as a radical departure from those which had dominated Anglo-American sociology, structuralism drew impressed attention which ensured that, thereafter, a much more deferential note would be taken of European (especially French) social thought, even to the extent of following its every vagary. The expectation of a scientific breakthrough was high but short lived as structuralism collapsed in upon itself, transmuting into 'post-structuralism' and, in doing so, turning against the whole ambition for science. Here we are concerned with structuralism's flowering, though we will trace out, in the concluding section, some of the reasons for its implosion.

Although, as we have said, regarded in some quarters as a radical shift in social theory, in significant respects structuralism was a reworking of the ideas of Marx and Freud, sometimes filtered through the ideas of the linguist, Ferdinand de Saussure (1857–1913). Louis Althusser (1918–90) saw himself as rescuing the 'true' Marx from many of his commentators and followers: the Marx who had made the decisive shift from ideology to science. Jacques Lacan (1901–81), similarly, took Freud's notion of the unconscious, connecting it to language through the claim that the unconscious was structured like a language, a language conceived in structuralist terms. Connections were also made to the work of Durkheim through the ideas of the anthropologist, Claude Lévi-Strauss (b. 1908), who founded structuralism in anthropology, and whose work was influential for Parisian structuralism generally. Lévi-Strauss claimed inspiration from 'structural linguistics', a school of thought originating in Prague in the 1920s and 1930s, itself indebted to the linguistics developed around the time of the First World War by Saussure who was, in turn, influenced by Durkheim.

There are four key but assorted scholars in the structuralist story, three of whom have already been mentioned: Claude Lévi-Strauss (anthropologist), Jacques Lacan (psychoanalyst), and Louis Althusser (philosopher). The other is Roland Barthes (a literary critic/sociologist). However, it would be misleading to present these as unified in their thinking. Indeed, there is really only the most superficial of resemblance among them. Lacan, it is true, was influenced by Lévi-Strauss – though the latter complained he could not understand what Lacan wrote – and Lacan was an important influence on Althusser but mainly as a means of drawing attention to his own work. The points of mutual influence were, really, more general and orientational than close and specific. Lévi-Strauss' patient, focused and sustained analysis of mythical thought had little to do with Barthes' tortured, tortuous, and constantly reconstructed reflections on literature and ideology, and both were equally remote from the back-to-basics revisionist efforts of Lacan and Althusser to restore, respectively, the *true* teachings of Freud and Marx. The model of what structuralism involved – cutting edge research of some technical sophistication linked to, and matching, what was seen as the leading 'human science', linguistics – actually concealed the fact that much of the substance of structuralism was reworked Marx and Freud. Its attainments would only count as achievements to the extent that one unquestioningly accepted Marx and/or Freud as the starting point.

The debt to Marx, Freud and Saussure

Two dominating figures in French intellectual life since before the mid-century were Karl Marx and Sigmund Freud, and for much the same reason. Marx's influence, however, in the context of structuralism (and, as we have seen, in Critical Theory) was due less to his analyses of capitalism, the role of social classes or the formulation of revolutionary politics, than to his contribution to the idea of how society and social activities were to be explained. He and Freud together, though not entirely alone, played a central part in forming the idea that social activities are the product of unconscious forces.

The power of this idea, and the force of its influence upon French intellectual life, may perhaps be understood as a consequence of the strong 'Cartesian' elements in that culture. René Descartes (1596–1650), the greatest French philosopher and an immense figure within modern thought, had regarded the mind as unproblematically knowable, as transparent to itself. The one thing about which we cannot possibly be mistaken is the content of our own mind (or consciousness since, for Descartes, mind was pretty much the same as consciousness): we know our thought directly. Marx and Freud, albeit in different ways, shook the foundations of Cartesianism by arguing that the mind did not consist solely in consciousness and that direct access to our consciousness did not ensure access to the full or main truth about our own thoughts. The true nature of our mind, and its role in our conduct, awaited discovery by science and could not be revealed through self-reflection. The mind does not know itself, and can only achieve this by the same means that any phenomenon can be known, that is, by means of a properly scientific theory. Thus, the role of mind and ideas in explaining human actions was in need of re-examination. The contents of people's consciousness, the things of which they were aware, were not those that actually explained why they acted as they did. Nor, furthermore, did the extent to which they were aware of their own conscious thoughts mean that they truly understood their nature. The idea that people's conduct was driven by forces of which they were unaware was an astonishing not to say shocking idea. It was also one which proved to be very attractive.

Though united by the idea that human behaviour could be explained as resulting from forces or drives of which people were unaware, Marx and Freud formulated their ideas of these 'unconscious' forces very differently. Marx developed the notion in terms of social forces working specifically through the concept of 'ideology'; that is, systems of socially spawned, disseminated and functional assemblages of distorted and false beliefs. By contrast, Freud sought them in part of the individual mind, the unconscious, a source of psychological energy which fuelled many of the conscious thoughts and actions of individuals despite the fact that – by definition – they were unaware of what these forces were. In addition to these, respectively, sociological and psychological contributions to the idea of unconscious forces we can add the contribution from linguistics, especially from the work of Ferdinand de Saussure, whose formulation of linguistics as the science of 'the sign' was drawn upon in the formation of structuralism.

In many respects, structuralism reflected the 'turn to language' which was to come to prominence across the whole of Western thought after the 1950s, and taken, perhaps, to its extreme extent in the 'post-structuralist' period of the present. For the structuralists what became known as structural linguistics was the most developed of the human sciences. Its aim was to study the unconscious structure of language; that is, the relations *between* the units of language rather than the units themselves. Largely because of the influence of Durkheim, European linguists had shifted their attention from individual language behaviour to that of the group or collective. Ferdinand de Saussure applied Durkheim's notion of the 'collective consciousness' to structural linguistics. He divided language into two different parts, *la parole*, individual speech acts, and *la langue*, the rules of language. Language itself consisted of individual speech acts plus the rules of language. Following Durkheim, Saussure regarded *la langue* as a social fact in being general throughout the community and constraining upon individuals' speech practices. However, the important step was to argue that linguistics ought to deal only with *la langue*, studying the common patterns shared by all the speakers of a language. He held that *la langue* was a stable set of relations among linguistic entities, an abstract system independent of, and distinct from, speech. The system, *la langue*, is something that operates in and through the human mind, but it is not consciously operated by the mind: when we speak we unconsciously apply the rules of the language system that we have learned.

Saussure's crucial bequest to the structuralist tradition, and to the further developments in French thought which fuelled the transition to 'post-structuralism', was the idea of language as a self-contained system; a system whose elements were 'signs', the identity of which was determined relationally from within the system. Saussure had in mind a more general science (to be called semiology) which would encompass all the various sign systems employed by humankind. Although language was by far the most important of these systems, semiology would have a wider compass to include, for example, gestures, food, clothes and music among many others. Accordingly, if language was to be considered as a system of signification, a structure of signs along with other such systems, then the word on its own could not be treated as the constituent element of language. After all, semaphore as a system of signification uses flags rather than words. The 'sign' is a notion that can include words as well as other kinds of meaningful units in non-linguistic systems.

The idea of words as 'signs' might seem to fit with the idea that words stand for things, a view that would be congenial to the idea that language is essentially a system of names for things in the world. However, whilst 'signs' did stand for something, in Saussure's view it was not for things in the world. Saussure did not deny that many words do function as names, but argued that even words which do name things in the world have only an arbitrary relationship to the things they name. 'Dog' might be the name of a certain kind of animal, but there is no necessary connection between that particular word and that kind of animal. Some other word could equally well name that kind of animal as, indeed, is the case in other languages. In French the word 'chien' performs much the same function as the word 'dog' in English. From the point of view of studying the language system, then, the connection between words and the things that those words are used to name and otherwise talk about is inessential. The nature of the sign, in language 'words', is to be understood internally to the language system not in relation to anything outside itself, that is, not by virtue of its relation to whatever it might 'stand for'.

According to Saussure, each sign is a composite of two elements, the 'signifier' and 'the signified'. In this way Saussure seeks to fuse two elements whose relation has been a perennial and root problem for modern thought, namely, 'matter' and 'mind'. The signifier is the material element, such as the sound waves or the inscription on paper that carries the word, and the signified is the mental element, the idea, or 'concept', which is invoked by this sound or inscription. In Saussure's scheme, it is the 'concept' (or 'thought') that the sign really stands for, and that might then be associated with some object, as the sound/inscription 'dog' is inextricably associated, for us, with the thought, the idea, of a certain kind of animal, which is then associated with an actual animal. The signified is the idea of dogs, not dogs themselves. Though Saussure makes the sign a composite of two constituent elements – the sound and the thought – these elements are thoroughly fused. They are connected, he famously says, as are the two sides of a sheet of paper, distinct but inseparable. The arbitrariness of the sign is to be understood as a result of the fact that signs are elements in the language system and, as such, discrete. They are the materials out of which signs are fashioned and those of sound and thought are themselves continuous. If they are continuous, then by definition, there are no natural breaks in them, and if they are to be subdivided, their subdivision into elements must have an arbitrary character. One can cut a single sheet of paper in innumerable different ways since the paper itself does not dictate any single way in which it must be cut. This means, of course, that the shape of the bits of paper into which the sheet is cut will be related to each other – when we cut one bit we also shape the next one. Thus, in Saussure's idea of the language system, signs are compositions from interrelated subdivisions of the sound and thought continua – when we shape one we also shape the other – and, of course, one could divide up the sound continuum differently than we have, or the thought continuum similarly. There must be an arbitrariness in the way one divides up a sheet of paper. A different idea could be associated with the sound 'dog' than the one which we associate with it. Once these two elements are fused, however, within the language system then they are compulsory for us as speakers of the language. The combination has, from the point of view of us as individuals, the status of a social fact.

However, and this is the important consequence of the idea of the subdivision of continua, the identity of the individual items is given only relationally *within the system of language*. It is not that a set of pre-defined elements has been brought together and organised into a system, for there are no elements independently of the system: they gain their identity entirely from the system. We have mentioned how the cutting up of a strip of paper means that the way in which we cut out one piece shapes the adjoining pieces. This is the key – and most consequential – idea of structuralism, namely, that the identity of elements in a system is determined by the relationships among those elements. What makes the element what it is, is not some characteristic it holds in its own right, but the way in which its characteristics are different from those of other elements. In other words, an element has no identity on its own, but only *in relation* to other elements. Its identity is not given by any characteristic intrinsic to the element.

On this view, the system is not a composite of elements but of relationships, for the elements are only derivatively identified in terms of those relationships. *La langue* – the language system – is, for Saussure, a system of relationships in which the elements are determined differentially: it is a system of contrasts. This will be explained further, and more concretely, when we consider the influence of the Prague School of linguistics on Lévi-Strauss. However, nothing could be plainer than this idea that the relationships within a system have primacy over the elements making up the system which is in close harmony with the anti-individualism of Durkheim's views or, with the view sloganised as 'anti-humanism' in structuralism and in its successor, post-structuralism.

Taken together, then, the emphasis upon the extent to which minds are saturated with ideology, driven by unconscious psychological forces and regulated by the language system seems to leave the conscious mind with a relatively small role in the direction of human action. That role seems even smaller if it is recognised that Marx's and Freud's arguments do not merely emphasise the role of forces of which individuals are not conscious, but also maintain that these forces distort consciousness itself. The content of our conscious thought is not at all as transparent as Descartes supposed. For Marx, our conscious thoughts are largely constituted by ideological convictions that are imposed upon our minds and that give a false picture of social realities. They are foisted on us through the ideology-inducing mechanisms of society. For Freud, the contents of our conscious thoughts are shaped by, and often express, our unconscious wishes but can appear in our consciousness only in a way that conceals and disguises the true nature of these unconscious wishes. Indeed, if our conscious mind recognised these unconscious wishes for what they are – such as a desire to kill one's father – we would be repelled by them. So when such thoughts arise in our minds we have to disguise them from ourselves.

The operations of the conscious mind are, in the terms just outlined, more a species of rationalisation – a matter of providing people with a more acceptable and agreeable presentation of the things they believe, want and wish for, even where these things are really quite unpleasant – than of true explanation. True explanations have to be sought elsewhere, that is, in the structures or systems of society, in the unconscious mind and in the culture, for in these lie the forces, the structures, which really regulate human conduct.

It is these considerations which form what structuralism counts as a crowning achievement of social thought, and one which has become *de rigueur* in much contemporary thought, namely, the 'decentring' of the individual. Though the basis and form of such 'decentring' varies across structuralist and 'post-structuralist' thinking, the essential point is the abandonment of the notion that human activities are to be understood and explained in terms of the intentions and purposes of individuals where these are seen as the expression of a single, unified mind. The mind is, rather, divided against itself, split between the conscious and the unconscious parts. Further, the mind is not an autonomous force initiating the individual's conduct. It is not 'the centre' in the sense of being that which directs what an individual does, for the individual is actually propelled by those unconscious forces – the unconscious itself, the structure of language and the deeper-lying social forces – of which the individual is unaware and does not even recognise. Durkheim's campaign against individualism is finally triumphant. The individual's intentions and purposes explain nothing or, if that seems too strong, have very little significance. These intentions and purposes are what need explaining, for they are produced out of the interaction of systems of organisation which the individual neither knows nor understands, but which operate through the individual and which must, therefore, operate unconsciously.

The contribution of Claude Lévi-Strauss

In anthropology, the structural-functionalist tradition of Radcliffe-Brown, Malinowski and Evans-Pritchard had focused upon institutionalised social relationships rather than upon culture as a phenomenon in its own right. To the extent to which anthropology saw itself as a science it clung to an empiricist, positivistic conception of science concerned with mechanism and function. Religion, for example, was explained by the needs of society or reduced to an ideological mirror of the social structure. Despite the fact that the virtually mandatory fieldwork involved learning a language, language itself as a system of meaning was of little theoretical interest.

Lévi-Strauss' interests were distinctive although they did not emerge all at once but developed as his work progressed. Nevertheless, he does speak of the strong unity in his work, namely, that of formulating the basic structural laws of human consciousness (Lévi-Strauss, 1970: 9–10). For him this was an examination of the mental structures that show that the seeming arbitrariness and variety of cultures to be found among the peoples of the world in fact rest upon a common foundation of logical organisation. To this end, though after a long period of fieldwork, in Brazil during the 1930s, had been completed, Lévi-Strauss began to work out the possible links between anthropology and linguistics. Eventually, after some struggles, he came to define anthropology itself as a semiotic (linguistic) discipline, that is, relating to the study of patterns of communication as signs and symbols. And in this he drew upon Saussure for inspiration. Anthropology should be absorbed by semiology and direct its attention to language, economics and kinship, the three most fundamental sign-systems (Lévi-Strauss, 1967). If these social phenomena could be reduced to unconscious laws, then it could be shown that they were products of the same basic nature and laws.

The overriding concern for Lévi-Strauss was one which frequently emerges in the history of anthropology: the question of the common nature of humankind. The issue was not so much about the biological commonality of human beings as about whether, or the extent to which, human social and cultural variety was the product of a common human nature. Quite what this 'human nature' might consist in was one of the key issues in the debate but, in essence, it was about the constitution of the mind. Is the human mind universally the same, or does it vary from time to time and place to place? An important dimension to the question arose when comparing so-called 'simpler people' with ourselves. Is it possible for them to think in the same way that we do? Are they capable of logical reasoning, for example, or do they have a different way of thinking, one which is 'prelogical'? Arguments about this break out sporadically for there are, of course, many implications stemming from the claim that their thought may not be as sophisticated, as rational, as our own, not least the implication of inferiority and, furthermore, the charge that disciplines which assert such intellectual claims are unscientific.

The structure of the human mind

Lévi-Strauss was eventually to make the culture, especially the mythology, of the tribes of the American continent, especially those of South America, his lifelong study. He took the view that the human mind was everywhere basically the same. He was also inclined to the view that the ways and beliefs of 'simpler' peoples were morally preferable to our own and, moreover, given his opposition to racism (he wrote a pamphlet against it for the United Nations) much of his work is a systematic effort to show that so-called 'primitive' peoples possessed equivalent logical powers to those who pride themselves on living in 'advanced' societies. He justified the claim that the mind was structured in the same way universally by insisting that the human mind is based in the brain and the brain must operate in the same way in all human beings.

Basically, the operating process of the brain is similar to that of computers, that is, according to a binary logic. Both the brain and the computer operate by controlling the flows of electrical charges. In the case of the computer, information processing operations – though this can often be a misleading way of putting it – are encoded as binary sequences of 0 and 1 which are equivalent to turning the electric current 'off' and 'on'. As far as Lévi-Strauss was concerned, the mechanics of the brain are much the same as the computer. This means that the basic structure of human thought must also be basically binary (to be processed through the brain). This kind of positive/negative opposition can, in addition, be seen as the very basis of logical thought itself. Given the way in which logical thought is underpinned by the organic structure of the brain, it cannot be the case that people differ in respect of their possession of logical powers.

However, it was some time after his fieldwork that Lévi-Strauss began to formulate a more coherent conception of his position. We can begin our account of Lévi-Strauss' ideas with his differences with Durkheim. The disagreement was over the direction of causality between 'the mind', on the one hand, and 'society' on the other. In his last great work, *The Elementary Forms of the Religious Life* (1976), Durkheim had tried to show that, contrary to Immanuel Kant's view that the fundamental categories of thought (such as those of 'space' and 'time') were built into the human mind, these were, in fact, variable from society to society and from one person to another. For Durkheim, even the basic categories of thought, those of space and time, were derived from socially given models, such as the layout of a residential community or the annual cycle of group activities. In other words, the very categories with which we think are socially derived rather than innate. Lévi-Strauss, convinced that the underlying forms of human thought are everywhere the same, could not concur with Durkheim. Instead, he took a direction which Durkheim thought that he had closed off, that of 'intellectualism'. In his study of religion, Durkheim was critical of treating religious conceptions as intellectual products; that is, as attempts at understanding problems posed by, for example, natural phenomena, such as thunderstorms, drought, seasons, and so on. In short, as attempts to work out the nature of things. Given his programmatic assumption that the explanation of religion must be social, then the explanation of the categories of thought and of religion must reflect 'social facts'. They were the symbolic expression of forms of collective life and imposed by social structures, and as such, a contribution to the reinforcement of social solidarity rather than intellectual constructions intended to assuage the puzzlement of the members of society.

By contrast, Lévi-Strauss was of the view that efforts at intellectual explanations had some point in the explanation of cultural categories but not in any simple way. Durkheim and Lévi-Strauss agreed that there is cultural variety, and that this is socially regulated, but the latter is not prepared to accept that, therefore, the basic organisation of the mind originates from this socially regulated cultural variation. Cultural variation can be seen to result from the application, in different contexts, of the general principles of the mind's operations to recurrent problems in understanding human existence, including social life but also the relationship of human beings to nature and the universe.

Lévi-Strauss' first major published work was *The Elementary Structures of Kinship* (1969) with its obvious allusion to the writings of his great predecessor, Durkheim. Though a major achievement in anthropology, the greater part of this study is of mainly technical interest to anthropologists rather than relevant to those who wish to know about Lévi-Strauss' structuralism. It involves an attempt to provide an understanding of various complex systems of marriage rules, mainly found among Australian Aboriginal groupings and, through that, to understand the cultural ubiquity of the incest taboo, which is the restriction upon sexual relations with one's closest kin. The problems of understanding the incest taboo and of finding a coherent 'logic' to the prohibitions and prescriptions bearing on the issue of who can marry whom were long-standing for anthropology. Lévi-Strauss' proposal was bold and original though it remains controversial.

Taking the view that culture is a set of communication processes, he treats marriage rules as a means of communication; that is, as a means of sending 'messages' between social groups of men, the means of communication being the exchange of women. In other words, these Aboriginal groups were composed essentially of their male members, and the relations between them were defined in terms of who marries whose women. Did the marriage rules of group A prescribe that its women should be married to men from group B? If so, then the men of groups A and B stand to each other as, respectively, 'wife givers' and 'wife takers': a relationship which is often key to understanding the organisation of myth in Lévi-Strauss' subsequent work. The problem was to understand the marriage rules as systems for the circulation of women amongst groups of men as a stable process: it must be one of exchange. Clearly, if social groups are to be perpetuated, then the circulation of women could not all be one way, but must involve reciprocity. Thus, the incest taboo, rather than having a biological character, has a social role as a means of ensuring that social groups 'marry out' so that women cannot be retained as sexual partners within the group which contains their family.

However, the prohibitions on marriage within the group must be matched by prescriptions on marriage to women from other groups which will ensure that a balanced circulation of women will take place amongst all the groups involved within that set of marriage rules. The marriage systems, far from being disorderly and confusing, can now begin to seem impeccably logical in their structure as they work out one or other of the possible variations on the ways of achieving the balanced circulation of women. For example, one possible, and prominent actual form, is that in which 'wife givers' and 'wife takers' do not stand in reciprocal relation to each other; instead, members of group A are 'wife givers' to members of group B who, in their turn, give wives to group C, who give wives to group D, who give wives to group A – an arrangement Lévi-Strauss terms 'generalised exchange'. The system ensures that all groups receive as well as give wives, so weaving the respective groups into a network of dependence based on the women they 'gift' to each other.

In the treatment of kinship there was a manifestation of one of the main concerns of Lévi-Strauss' lifework, namely, working out the general logic underlying the customary practices of the tribal peoples who were the main focus of anthropological interest. The study of kinship exhibited his disdain for 'the empiricism' and consequent superficiality of so much of anthropology and social thought more generally. Because of this empiricism, social scientists had failed to recognise that the real structures producing phenomena were never directly manifested in observable occurrences. The real structures were at a level much deeper than the surface facts, and can only be properly identified at a much higher level of abstract generality than those at which social scientists are wont to operate. Thus, Lévi-Strauss had reconstructed the problem of incest by relating it to the general problem of social solidarity between otherwise discrete social groups rather than relating it just to a kinship connection between males and females that would make it unseemly for marriage to take place between them. The problem had been turned around. It was no longer about attempting to understand why men should be denied sexual connection with their close kin, but about seeing the necessity of making women available to other social groups by entering them into a process of circulation, the consequence of which is that they are denied sexual relations with their own kin.

The conception of science and the attack on empiricism

Lévi-Strauss stressed that scientific explanation reduces one type of reality to another, as in Marxism and psychoanalysis which seek, in their own distinctive ways, to show that the world we ordinarily experience, one type of reality, is in fact merely an appearance of the operation of 'real' forces of which we are unaware. His structuralism is the search for the deepest and most fundamental properties that generalise across the whole range of the phenomena, and is therefore necessarily very abstract and not intended to give an exhaustive account of the details of each and every case of the phenomena. It is intended to identify the essential properties of the phenomenon in general. This is one reason why so-called primitive forms of social organisation are of value to him: because the logical structures built by the unconscious are more evident (Lévi-Strauss, 1969: 269). In a debate with Jean-Paul Sartre (1905–80), Lévi-Strauss made the point that the distinction between explanation in the physical and human sciences was no different. Science's objects of investigation are not the reality of the human subject, that is, the world as it is experienced by human beings in their everyday lives. Indeed, the point of focusing on the unconscious is that at this level the subject is eliminated. Science must decompose the empirical and reconstitute it at a truer level. (In passing we can note here at least an analogy with Parsons' 'analytic realism', discussed in Chapter 2, as well as the arguments of the Frankfurt School, the topic of Chapter 3.) This was the lesson, as Lévi-Strauss saw it, of Marx and Freud. When human beings reflect upon their own meaning they always arrive at meanings which are false and it is structuralism's achievement to award the social sciences the status of the natural sciences by unveiling the objects that a true science requires. Human beings should be studied as if they were ants (Lévi-Strauss, 1962: 246). Indeed, the ultimate goal of the human sciences is not to understand man but to dissolve him.

Totemism

This conception of science in Lévi-Strauss is clearly manifest in his next, small, but crucial book, *Totemism* (1973b). Here is the very topic on which Durkheim's

The Elementary Forms of the Religious Life had focused, and which had bedevilled anthropological thought before and since that work was published. Lévi-Strauss' contribution to this discussion is to do away with the phenomenon altogether. Of course, he does not deny that Aboriginal groups have special relationships with totems, that is, with natural phenomena which, in effect, comprise the 'badges' of those groups. Instead, he wants to erase the problem of totemism by arguing that it is but one aspect of a much more general problem. Those who wrestle with the 'problem of totemism' are imprisoned by empiricist thinking and seek to explain the practice in terms of something observably special about totemism itself and therefore miss the extent to which totemism is but one way in which a general culture problem is 'solved'. For Lévi-Strauss, the empiricists are not thinking generally or abstractly enough. Of course there are things which are specific and distinctive about totemism, but these will only be properly understood if they are set in a comparative context.

In totemic systems social groups are matched with, and identified by, some natural phenomenon, such as a species of animal or a feature of the landscape. As such it seems an alien institution when compared with our own culture. On the face of it, totemism seems to set such peoples apart from ourselves, to separate a primitive mind from the civilised one. But is totemism the only case in which human beings order things by making a match between natural and social phenomena? By no means. There are many such cases: consider the names of sporting teams. In Rugby League, for example, following the practice of American football and baseball, these days there are 'Bulls', 'Broncos', 'Bears' and 'Rhinos'. For Lévi-Strauss totemism is not a distinct phenomenon at all and that it has been treated as such is due to the prejudice and incomprehension of too empirically minded ethnographers. In fact, totemism is one manifestation of a much more general phenomenon of associating social groups with some natural phenomenon. To consider totemism on its own cannot result in a proper understanding of the phenomenon it is because it will not reveal the general principles which are in operation and which determine its form. Had Isaac Newton just studied apples falling from trees, as a thoroughgoing empiricist might, he would not have formulated the law of gravity and been the great scientist that he was. It was only by treating apples falling from trees as a single instance of the general problem of motion that he attained his far-reaching results. In the same way, studying totemism as a distinct, free standing topic, rather than as an instance of the interplay of *socio-cultural* and *natural* categories cannot engender true understanding. Totemism will only be properly, scientifically understood, according to Lévi-Strauss, when it is treated as one of many forms in which the general principles governing the interconnection of natural and social categories can be systematically worked out.

Lévi-Strauss thinks it helpful to consider totemism in comparison with another mode of social organisation: caste. The prevailing strategy in the social sciences would have been to note the differences between totemism and caste – which are numerous – but this would be, for Lévi-Strauss, precisely the kind of empiricist superficiality of which he complains. The point for him, and as we shall see more fully later, is to regard these as two possible variants on the ways in which the relationship between natural and social categories can be worked out, each being seen as a manifestation of the phenomenon of making statements about social relations through the use of animal, or floral, or climatic or other natural conditions. A system of natural discriminations is being used as a coding device to make statements of social significance.

So, for Lévi-Strauss, the problem's true character is abstract in nature, having to do with the various ways in which categories from different sets of discriminations – in this case, the natural and social – can be matched and permutated. It is the possibilities for matching and permutation which matter, not the specific nature of the content of the natural or social categories themselves. Thus, totemism is anthropology's illusion, because it has failed to recognise that all four of these combinations are both possible and actual full-blown variants on the same basic pattern; anthropologists have noted only the first two because these occur, respectively, in the Australian and North American forms of totemism.

	1	2	3	4
NATURAL	Category	Category	Particular	Particular
CULTURE	Group	Person	Person	Group

For Lévi-Strauss, the point about these four arrangements is that they represent all the logically possible ways in which natural and social categories can be related – many to many, many to one – and a proper understanding of totemism must, in the first instance, begin by locating it within this 'logical space'. Understanding why people have totemism ceases to be a matter of trying to identify a set of causes which give rise to the specific practice of binding, say, a group of people in association to a species of animals, making the latter the totem of the former, as previous anthropologists tried to do. Rather, it is one of seeking to understand why one of these sets of possibilities should be preferred to any of the others. This amounts to understanding the ways in which these various possibilities differ from each other.

Lévi-Strauss picks up the argument from *Totemism* again in *The Savage Mind* (1962). This is clearly not a title to be taken literally in English. In the original French the idea of 'sauvage' is akin to that of 'wild' in the sense of 'spontaneously blossoming' as we might say of a 'wild flower'; it is to be contrasted with 'deliberately cultivated', and applies to the way the minds of tribal peoples work.

The Savage Mind

In this later book, Lévi-Strauss works out the argument about the relation of totemism to caste, an argument which also connects with the 'exchange of women' and the theme of his first major work. Totemism and caste are both ways in which societies internally differentiate themselves into separate groups. In a caste system differentiation is on the basis of occupational specialisation whereas in the totemic system differentiation is by the totemic species or object. Being separated from each other, groups which are part of the same society must have some way of integrating with each other otherwise they cannot be of the same society. This is done, in these two cases, by exchange. In the caste system, the groups are distinguished by occupational function through a specialist division of labour, and they must, therefore, exchange goods and services. But the totemic groups are not differentiated by their place in the division of labour or in any other way except that of belonging to different totemic groups. These groups do not differ culturally or occupationally, so they exchange with, and therefore integrate with, each other through the exchange of women. Castes, on the other hand, are 'endogamous', which means they take marriage partners from within their respective groups and do not exchange them.

It is important to remember that Lévi-Strauss is seeking to plumb the logic, the structure of the thought, which underpins, in this case, totemism. The totemic group and the caste system are two ways of thinking about social differentiation and about the relationship between 'nature' and 'culture'. The totemic groups are groups whose members all lead much the same kind of lives based on the same mode of economic acquisition, namely, hunting and gathering. The groups are, of course, of the kind Lévi-Strauss had written about in his book on kinship rules, and these groups relate to each other through the 'exchange of women', that is, they marry out. The groups are distinguished by their totems, by whatever species or phenomenon they are related to, often believing that they are specially responsible for the well-being and proliferation of the animal species which stands as their totem. By contrast with totemic groups, caste is a system of groups which are socially closed to each other. They do not exchange women, for the groups making up the caste system are 'endogamous' in requiring marriage from within their own number. The groups are differentiated by economic specialism, for specific kinds of occupations belong to particular castes and are inherited within the respective caste membership. The two systems are plainly very different and we need to find a systematic basis for this difference. For Lévi-Strauss this needs to be sought in the fact of social differentiation itself not in the observable features which happen to characterise the two types of differentiated social groups.

Analysis needs to begin by seeing how social differentiation presents a problem for the thought of the members of the respective groups. For too long, he argues, ethnographers have neglected primitive man's search for knowledge. Indeed, it is difficult to understand, for example, the Neolithic revolution in agriculture and the domestication of animals unless we allow that such peoples were capable of patient observation and experimentation (Lévi-Strauss, 1962, 13ff.). If we follow this advice, he argues, then we will see that the two systems are ways of solving the same problem: a problem which has general importance for Lévi-Strauss' work and profound significance for all human thought. This is the problem of the relationship between 'the natural' and 'the cultural'.

Considered as a natural species human beings are as one in having the same biological make-up. Yet they are differentiated into social groups; differentiations that have no basis in their biological nature. There is no significant biological difference between the members of one totemic group and another, any more than there is between one caste group and another. Yet, we draw lines around, socially separate, these biologically alike beings. The differentiation of people into groups is not itself a natural, but a cultural, division. Thus, culture requires us to treat people who are naturally alike as though they were really very different. Human beings, then, are both the same as and different from each other. But if they are both the same and different, in what respects are they the same, and in what different? And what is the importance for social organisation that follows from the facts of similarity and difference?

For Lévi-Strauss there are only two bases in reality upon which the notion of socio-cultural differentiation can possibly be modelled in the minds of the members of the society. The separation of people into distinct groupings can be analogous to the diversity of animal species; as a differentiation amongst creatures with distinct natures as reflected in the fact that there is no natural complementarity or collaboration among them, nor can they interbreed. The other basis is that of the functional differentiation of human beings in terms of their role in a division of labour. However, this is precisely a notion which entails complementarity and collaboration, for a division of labour makes its members interdependent. The two models are, themselves, classifiable in terms of the natural/cultural dichotomy. The diversity of species is a natural phenomenon, the division of labour is a matter of cultural differentiation. However, the 'exchange of women' sits uncomfortably between the 'natural' and the 'social', and it is as an attempt to work out a systematic solution to this relationship between the 'natural' and the 'social', and their respective weightings, in connection with women that Lévi-Strauss pitches his comparison of totem and caste.

With caste there is true cultural differentiation to its organisation in that the castes are distinguished from each other through occupational specialisation. The castes, being functionally distinguished in occupational terms, can achieve social integration into a single community through the exchange of goods and services, that is, the exchange of culturally created products. Hence, there is no need for the exchange of women to secure integration amongst the different castes: their economic interdependence does that. How, then, is endogamy to be understood as a socio-cultural necessity except as an attempted balancing of nature against culture? It is, claims Lévi-Strauss, understood within the caste system in *natural terms*; that is, on the basis of the above-mentioned model of the natural differentiation of species. Caste differentiates in a way which means that the fact of cultural differentiation outweighs that of biological alikeness. The women of culturally differentiated caste groups are conceived as being too different from each other to be exchanged: a parallel is with the natural phenomenon of the diversity of species and the impossibility of breeding between them. Therefore, the women of different castes are regarded as different from each other in the way that the females of different natural species are, and so no 'exchange' is possible. Accordingly women within the caste system are both naturally *and* culturally differentiated.

With totemism the cultural differentiation of people into different social groupings has no true cultural basis for, recall, the only real cultural basis for differentiation is the division of labour. But this does not exist amongst the totemic groups which are self-subsistent. There is, then, no true basis, either natural or social, for the fact of socio-cultural differentiation in totemic groups. Since the integration of these culturally differentiated groups cannot be achieved by the exchange of culturally produced means, such as the results of economic activity, it is brought about by the exchange of a natural product, namely, women. This time, biological similarity is deemed to outweigh cultural difference: women are only culturally and not biologically diversified. Though the totemic groups have no differentiation of economic function, they nonetheless envisage themselves as having such. They have created an imaginary division of labour to explain their differentiation through the totemic system, thereby using a *natural* phenomenon as the putative basis of, and explanation for, their *cultural* heterogeneity. That is, the totemic system, representing the differentiation of groups through relations to animals of different species, represents its cultural diversity in terms of the natural diversity of species. Insofar as the model of the diversity of natural species is drawn upon, so also can be the idea that the association between a totemic group and a natural species is the basis for a functional, that is, a cultural one. Each totemic group is 'responsible' for the well-being and proliferation of the species associated with it, thus making its 'specialist' and reciprocated contribution to the general material well-being of all the groups via its ritual respect for the totemic species and promoting a thriving collective ecology.

Thus, Lévi-Strauss tries to show how two culturally and geographically remote ways of life involve, nonetheless, attempts to solve the same intellectual problem about the relation between the natural and cultural nature of human beings. Though they adopt different solutions to these problems they define the two solutions in terms of a common set of possibilities. For example, the fact of cultural differentiation of women as members of different groups is more or less important than the fact of their common biological structure and capacity.

Let us be clear, once again, about the level at which Lévi-Strauss is operating. He is not analysing totemism and caste as concrete group phenomena, but as *thought systems*. The overriding fact about human thought, primitive or civilised, for Lévi-Strauss is that it seeks logical order, seeks to work things out systematically. Human intellect means that everything can acquire significance. Even when confronted with things which, in reality, cannot be reconciled, and which create insuperable contradictions for thought, thought will still attempt to fashion a logically coherent system. This was, indeed, an important aspect of Marx's theory of ideology, namely, that it results from the attempt to resolve, through thought, through imaginative creations, the contradictions in society, presenting them as though they have been solved even though, in reality, they persist. Thus, if human beings cannot find satisfactory logical coherence in the organisation of their social existence, they will attempt to produce the illusion of such coherence. Totemism, despite being based on an imaginary division of labour, and in this sense an ideological construction, is based on the same logic that underlies our own thought. There is no need for ethnographers to postulate strange connections between social groups and animal species. Its real nature is as a coding device to make statements of social significance. In this case, nature provides the human mind with materials – animal species in the case of totemism – to think with (Lévi-Strauss, 1973b: 162).

The linguistic model

Earlier we drew attention to Lévi-Strauss' idea that a properly scientific human science ought to be built around linguistics; a linguistics as set out by Saussure who, himself, had been influenced by the Prague School of linguistics. They had proposed a method for analysing the sound structure of any language in terms of a simple number of basic features.

The basic tool of this analysis has already been referred to in connection with Lévi-Strauss' analysis of the binary character of totemic structures, namely, '+' or '–', or 'presence' or 'absence' of, in the case of languages, a particular characteristic. Accordingly, different languages could be compared in terms of a small set of characteristics by noting the presence or the absence of each characteristic.

This means of differentiation in terms of the presence or the absence of some characteristics had great generality and was capable of representing all kinds of binary, or paired, values – 'has–lacks', 'is–is not', 'does–does not', 'true–false', 'on–off', etc. These kinds of contrastive pairings, these binary oppositions, provide one of the basic tools of logic: a tool which is not only a simple but effective way of mapping the sound, or phonological, structures of a diversity of languages but, for Saussure, also applicable to the 'meaning' of words in a language. Saussure's key idea was that the meaningful elements in a language – for all practical purposes, words – do not have meaning 'in themselves' but only and entirely by virtue of their belonging to a system. We have already mentioned Saussure's emphasis upon 'the language system' rather than speech as the object of scientific understanding, but not the way in which he had proposed that meaning should therefore depend upon the contrastive relations between them. For a simple example, consider the colour words: red, blue, green, etc. Rather than trying to say what 'red' means by identifying the colour to which it refers, we should, according to Saussure, understand its meaning in terms of its relation to other words. Thus, meaning is not a matter of a word 'standing for' something in the world, but due to its place within a system of words. Accordingly, the meaning of 'red' depends upon its differences from, its contrasts with, other words.

Lévi-Strauss' idea that anthropology should be a semiological science meant that meaning should be central, though it was to take some years for his own treatment of this idea to mature (Lévi-Strauss, 1964: 364). What attracted him to Saussure's idea was that it seemed to offer a means of moving from elements which themselves have no meaning – the phonemes, or sounds, of a language – to things which do, namely, the semantics of the language. Thus, the binary structure identified by the Prague School was a pattern that, embedded as it was in the mind, would also characterise the structure of language and, ultimately, the culture. Accordingly, the diversity of cultures was the reflection of a finite code or structure. For Lévi-Strauss meaning is reducible and rests upon structures which themselves do not contain meaning. From the laws of thought the human mind is capable of creating meaning.

The discussion of totem and caste in *The Savage Mind* was a preparing of the ground for this mode of analysis. The main aim of *The Savage Mind* was to deal with the fact that 'our' (modern, Western) ways of thought, our culture, are very different from those of so-called 'primitive' or 'simpler' peoples. Lévi-Strauss' objective, as stressed earlier, was not only to understand the differences between the two kinds of culture but also to show that they did not reflect a difference in underlying mental capacity. Thus, the contrast of totem and caste (one of which is a 'primitive' set of social arrangements, the other associated with a complex and highly sophisticated civilisation) had sought to show how remote and very different systems of organisation could be the product of similar deep structures of thought. The difference between 'the savage' and 'the civilised' mind was, from the point of view of logical capacities, superficial. The differences between the two kinds of culture are, according to Lévi-Strauss, due to the exigencies of their respective environmental circumstances and histories rather than to any differences in essential capacities for rationality. Myths have been displaced, in our civilisation, by the growth of science. Insofar as myth persists in our civilisation, it belongs to the realms of music and literature. Our science, mathematics and formal logic, often taken as testimony to our superior intelligence and rationality are, for Lévi-Strauss, but a set of specialised tools for the exercise of logical thought rather than distinctively manifesting the presence of logical thought itself. The contrast between 'savage' and 'civilised' thought is a difference, then, in the kinds of tools available to each. Human beings have always thought equally well. 'Savage' thought, whether manifested in magic, in myth or in totemism, is founded on the same demand for logical order as is modern science.

Bricolage

However, there is an important difference between the 'savage' and 'civilised' mentality. While the savage has the same desire for logical order as the civilised, his attention is directed more to the concrete. The difference between 'savage' and 'civilised' is akin to that between the *bricoleur* – the French term for handyman – and the professional car mechanic. The latter possesses all kinds of tools which are specific to the specialised work of fixing cars, whilst the *bricoleur* is a kind of all-purpose handyman without any specialist tools, having only a collection of things and materials which comprise a kind of *ad hoc* assemblage that is ready to hand and must be made to do for any of the variety of work that the handyman may be called upon to perform. If the *bricoleur* is called upon to fix a car, then this will mean finding some way of making use of whatever materials are to hand, often adapting tools which are not designed for the particular purpose of mending cars. The *bricoleur* is no less intelligent or proficient at fixing things, no less logical in approach to tasks than the car mechanic, but the nature of the problem he faces is different, and the ingenuity that the former expends is on turning things to a purpose they were not made for, whilst that required of the car mechanic involves making use of a set of specially prepared tools.

Inquiries into nature can be at two levels. Our science operates at an abstract level, whereas the 'savage' builds a 'science of the concrete' out of sensory qualities and concrete objects. Our science creates events out of theoretical systems while the savage constructs structures out of events. He is a *bricoleur* with no special tools for thinking with but must construct systems of thought out of 'odds and ends'. Mathematics and logic represent specific tools for working on logical problems, but they are not essential to engaging in logical thought. If, however, the society has not developed those tools, and logical thought is to be engaged in, then other resources – whatever is available to hand – will have to be used. What the tribal peoples have is their rich body of empirical knowledge of the world which surrounds them, of the flora and fauna of their environment, the observable patterns of the heavens, and the routines and cycles of social life, working much in the manner of the *bricoleur*. As, in solving algebraic equations, we use the expressions *a*, *b*, *c*, =, and so on, to represent various values and operations for calculating, no less must the 'savage mind'. But since it has no such symbols or their equivalent, it makes use of, for example, the lynx, the coyote, the sloth and the eagle as its expressions, and must state relations and solve problems by manipulating these expressions. Thus, just as *a* can stand, in an equation, for many different numbers, so can the lynx, the coyote etc., in the 'equations' of 'primitive thought' stand for other things. In the latter, the manipulation of the expressions does not take the form of their arrangement into equations but their combination *into stories*. The logical thought of 'the savage mind' finds its fullest expression in the mythological tales whose telling and retelling is such a major part of their social life, and it is thus that Lévi-Strauss' major work (a huge, four-volume opus of more than 3,000 pages with later shorter attachments) has as its collective title *Mythologiques*, the logic of myths.

The analysis of myth

Lévi-Strauss had a subject matter and a method. The method is derived from linguistics, for myths are, of course, themselves linguistic phenomena. They are stories told in words. More than this, though, they are especially appropriate for revealing mental laws since, in myth, the mind converses with itself (Crick, 1976: 49). However, in 1955 Lévi-Strauss argued that the study of myth was akin to the state of linguistics before it achieved scientific status (Lévi-Strauss, 1962: 207). Myths are diverse and yet, suggests Lévi-Strauss, certain patterns are widespread and can be brought out by analysis of their logical structure. Myths are stories. They narrate a series of events. But their significance for Lévi-Strauss can only be revealed by bringing out their underlying atemporal structure. His attitude that the true nature of things is not to be grasped through their superficial manifestations means decomposing their narrative structure so as to reach the underlying code. Later, Lévi-Strauss was to compare this code to the harmonic structure of a musical composition. Like a musical score, myths must be read both vertically and horizontally (Lévi-Strauss, 1970: 15–16).

The process of decomposing the myths involved reducing the text to sentences, or 'mythemes'. Each of these mythemes is a relation and has to be combined with others to produce 'bundles' of relations which will show up the patterns of logical connection and transformation. The means of decomposing them is, in the first instance, the notion of 'binary opposition', the linguistic technique of identifying things in terms of their contrastive values, such as 'has/does not have', 'up–down', and so on. Myths are layered. A single myth states a message several times in different ways.

Lévi-Strauss' initial task was to reduce the hundreds of South American myths to a coding scheme by which one myth could be transformed into another. His aim was to construct a 'mythological syntax' to show how, for example, empirical categories like 'raw' and cooked' could be combined as logical signs to form abstract propositions to show that underneath the diversity of myths were logical rules (Lévi-Strauss, 1970: 10). Even the titles of the four volumes of *Mythologiques* suggest the nature of such a monumental enterprise. *The Raw and the Cooked* (1970) identifies two contrasting terms which comprise, respectively, natural and cultural states. Cooking is a cultural activity. It is an activity which changes something, namely, that which is inedible (–) into something which is edible (+). *From Honey to Ashes* (1973a) contrasts something (honey) which can be taken from nature and consumed raw, and tobacco, which requires cultural preparation for its consumption. Its consumption transforms its nature yet again, releasing smoke and producing ashes. *The Origin of Table Manners* (1978) pertains to the difference between those who eat in a natural way like animals, and those who eat in a 'civilised' fashion, that is, in a way that is culturally regulated. This contrast can further serve to contrast animals and humans, but can also draw a line between different human beings, such as those who behave like animals – are beastly – and those who behave like proper 'civilised' human beings. *The Naked Man* (1981) alludes to the importance of dress and adornments as cultural characteristics of human beings, contrasting them with humans in their naked and 'natural' state.

The topics identified by the titles reflect the extent to which these subjects appear in the myths, with the emphasis upon food, its preparation and consumption being very prominent, featuring explicitly, after all, in three of the four titles and, indirectly, in all of the four. In the fourth volume the emphasis switches from the examination mainly of the myths of the South American tribes to those of the North American peoples. This switch is not merely a shift of his interest but involves, Lévi-Strauss argues, corresponding switches in the way things are represented and, for his argument, new data with which to develop his claims about the logic of myth. The North American myths do not deal with the same subjects as the South American ones. Nonetheless, below this level of superficial difference the same logical structure is at work. The idea of people as 'naked' or 'dressed' in these Northern myths, is, he argues, the equivalent of the ideas of 'raw' and 'cooked' in the Southern ones. So, there is still an allusion to 'cooking' as, according to Lévi-Strauss, standing for the 'cultural' as opposed to the 'natural'. Although transformed in the respective myths of the Southern American and Northern American peoples, the underlying logic is the same.

Lévi-Strauss is tracing out the way in which the 'savage mind' reasons about the relationship of nature and culture and its meaning for human life. The four volumes, examining some 800 myths and taking eight years to write, contain a unified, but roundabout argument, one which Lévi-Strauss himself says involves an interlinking series of circular arguments which, as they accumulate, progressively broaden the range of the discussion: a discussion which extends from, at the beginning, one single myth to, at the end, a contention that the mythical thought of the American continents is all connected in one 'transformation set'. That is, they are all versions of each other in the way that mathematical equations are variants of versions of more general formulae.

Illustration: 'the reference myth'

Myths are, for so-called 'primitive peoples', ways of thinking that exercise the same logic of thought as science and mathematics. They are ways of thinking about the nature of the world and the place of human beings within it. That the world is as it is, and that it is a divided and diversified world, is something that needs to be understood. Why is there a division between down here on earth and up above, in the sky? Why are human beings and animals divided into different groups and kinds? How did that division come about? How did human beings come by their characteristics and lifestyles? How did they acquire the crafts that are so vital to their existence? These are just some of the kinds of questions that the mythical stories consider in their diverse and indirect ways.

Lévi-Strauss takes as his point of departure, his 'reference myth', a story about a 'bird nester', someone who, in attempting to climb up a cliff to acquire birds' eggs, becomes stranded halfway up.

The general importance of Lévi-Strauss was due not to his subject matter, but to his method. His way of analysing myths as combinations of logical elements seemed to offer the prospect of a general method for the analysis of all cultural phenomena. This method was a painstaking and laborious one, often seeming perhaps arbitrary, of working out the 'semantic' value of the constituent elements of myth, and of figuring out the relationship between them. What does somebody stranded halfway up a cliff stand for in this story? The method, remember, supposes that things are organised around oppositions, around contrasts. Accordingly, the location itself is something which provides a contrast, for a cliff has an 'above' and a 'below'. The stranded bird nester was seeking to move from 'below' to 'above' but has been unable to complete the transition and now stands midway between 'above' and 'below'. The movement from 'below' to 'above' is, again in this case, a movement from a human (cultural) habitat, toward an animal (natural) habitat. Though the opposition, or contrast, is the basis for the operation, the two oppositional values are not the only ones available to mythic thought, for there can be values which stand between oppositions, which are midway between (as being halfway up the cliff is between above and below) or which are closer to one extreme than another. 'Above' and 'below' can serve as a contrast between earthly and celestial realms. The attempt to move from the below to the above can raise the question of the connection of above and below, the relation of earth to heaven.

Lévi-Strauss elaborates this myth into one about the origin of cooking fire. As noted, cooking is a crucial notion in mythical thought, and the origin of cooking fire is a most prominent and persistent theme in the four volumes. The similarity between fire in the sky, that is, the sun, and fire on the earth means that the cooking fire is taken as an identity. The same thing occurs in both places, and it is therefore the same thing. If the same thing exists in two places that are cut off from each other, then how could it be that it exists in both of them? One answer is that these things which are now separated, the above and the below, were once united, such that fire could pass from one place to the other. Thus, fire is conceived as something which has come to earth (the 'below') from above, the celestial realm, the abode of the gods. Cooking fire is accordingly something which has been obtained from the gods but which has been obtained *at the price of* an interruption of the communication which once existed between earth and sky. Through their separation Lévi-Strauss, later in the argument, develops this 'cosmological' theme into what he terms a 'sociological' one, an explanation, in terms of myth's logic, of why it is that the women do the cooking. The separation of men as 'givers' and 'takers' of wives is a discontinuous relation between them, as is that between the earth and the sky. So, if fire is something which passes between, which mediates, the relationship of earth and sky, so women pass between, mediate the relations of, separated groups of men, and it is this which connects women to fire and thus places them in charge of the cooking oven.

Myths show the *bricoleur* at work. The construction of myths is achieved by taking whatever is 'to hand' to address some of the fundamental questions of human existence. Yet, through the codes that they embody the myths can be transformed one into another as instances of the same logical structure. Mythical thought, no less than our own philosophy, for example, is directed toward the great problems of the meaning of life and the nature of things, and it deals with these at all levels of generality, from myths which explain quite specific aspects of a given group's way of life, or feature of its habitat, to ones which concern the origin of all things.

The whole argument closes with the notion that the fundamental driving force of myth is the bleak sense of the disparity of the importance of our lives to us and the indifference of the universe toward them. Lévi-Strauss' own gloomy *envoi* remarks reflect that his – and by implication those of any human being – 'hopes and his works will be as if they never existed, since no consciousness will survive to even preserve the memory of these ephemeral phenomena, only a few features of which, soon to be erased from the impassive face of the earth will remain as already cancelled evidence that they once were, and were as nothing' (Lévi-Strauss, 1981: 695, first published 1971). The world existed before human beings and will continue to exist when human beings cease to be. Physical laws indicate that ultimately the human creation of culture must revert to the natural world. Thus, anthropology is 'entropology', the science of the running down of things.

It is difficult to summarise Lévi-Strauss' work since nowhere is the semiological framework used for his analysis of myth clearly set out. Yet despite its deficiencies, it is perhaps the most substantial and impressive achievement of structuralism. It is an attempt, taking over a lifetime of scholarship, to work through the implications of a point of view with a rare and tenacious thoroughness. However, two of the main structuralist thinkers, Lacan and Althusser, show only superficial resemblances to the linguistic model that Lévi-Strauss was developing. Barthes, on the other hand, has a much greater kinship with him, certainly in his determination to turn social science into semiology.

Roland Barthes: the oppression of culture

Barthes was both sociologist and literary critic, and his overwhelming preoccupation was with language in the form of writing, especially with literary writing, and with literature as a social institution. His deepest conviction was that culture is a matter of convention; a convention that is restrictive and oppressive, imposing conformity upon the individual and inhibiting the capacity for free expression. Barthes himself was deeply oppressed by the thought, noted above, that the operation of social conventions and of the unconscious forces of the mind gave only the most restricted space for the independent thought and action of the individual. The recognition that culture is a matter of convention and, what is more, composed of signs, meant that one of the ways in which convention oppressed was by concealing its own conventional nature and presenting itself as a manifestation of the immutable and unchangeable nature of things.

Initially coming from a broadly Marxist point of view, and thus critical of the dominance of the French bourgeoisie and their culture, Barthes tried to improve the fairly standard Marxist critique of ideology's capacity to mislead by giving it a new twist that would show how ideology actually works in detail. This involved using the resources of semiology to reveal the specific manner and extent to which culture was passing itself off as a reflection of natural realities rather than as something that is really only constituted through the conventional system of signs.

As Saussure had set out, there is no connection between the nature of things and the organisation of the system of signs: the relation of the latter to the former being an arbitrary one. Barthes was later to write a book about Japan, a society that had captivated him because it was itself fascinated with signs for their own sake. The contrast was therefore between a Japan, *The Empire of Signs* (Barthes, 1983), which was much more 'up front' about the artificial, conventional character of its cultural traditions, and his French homeland, where bourgeois ideology infiltrated sign systems and treated these – mistreated or exploited would be better, from Barthes' point of view – as if they were reflections of a natural reality.

These concerns of Barthes were expressed, though not exclusively, in a preoccupation with writing, especially in the context of literature as a social institution, and the possibility of free and creative expression. The conventions of literature were one set of restraints upon truly individual expression. The unknown workings of the writer's unconscious provided another limitation. Complementary concerns were also pursued in respect of popular culture. Barthes was to become a key figure in the development of modern 'cultural studies' with a variety of capsule studies of media output, and a sustained study of the semiological structure and ideological presuppositions of fashion writing in the French fashion magazines of the 1950s (Barthes, 1972).

One of Barthes' most influential works collected some short, journalistic pieces which criticised the 'mythologies' perpetuated by French middle class society, and which analysed several instances from popular culture such as all-in wrestling, eating steak and chips, and Tour de France bicycle racing. The point was to show that our experience of things is never of the things themselves but is mediated through our culture. Thus, the wrestling bout or the bicycle race are not things which are ingested 'raw', but are presented to us in culturally stylised ways. The Tour de France was presented by the mass media in terms of traditional literary devices, in this case the epic. The all-in wrestling match is an entirely stylised encounter in which all the 'signs' of violent encounter – blows, kicks, strangleholds, aggressive yells, and cries of pain – are present but do not actually function as signs of the things they represent. The violence is all pretence, the 'signs' of violence are make-believe, and everyone knows that they are.

Barthes was operating on two basic principles: firstly, that the sign system is organised according to a 'code' which structures the sequences of signs and which, therefore, shapes our experience; secondly, that all aspects of culture can be analysed as manifestations of a sign system, as a means of sending messages or making statements. For example, again among the *Mythologies* articles, Barthes examines the way in which the consumption of steak and chips and wine operate not merely as means of satiating one's hunger or thirst, but as ways of making statements about oneself, about one's masculine nature or one's national character. Steak and chips is a manly meal, a taste for wine the mark of a civilised person, and the ability to hold one's drink a proud national trait of the French. In these cases, natural processes such as eating and drinking are endowed with cultural meaning.

Barthes tried to give more systematic exposition of the technical structure of the framework for the analysis of sign systems in *Elements of Semiology*, and an equally systematic instance of the application of such a mode of analysis in *The Fashion System* (Barthes, 1967, 1985). Clothing serves the practical purpose of covering our body, keeping it warm and dry, but it does so in a culturally coded way. The different kinds and items of clothing comprise the equivalent of the 'language system' and provide a collection of elements and their rules of combination – bowler hat goes with pinstripe suit, grey tie, black shoes, and so forth. The particular clothing ensemble that an individual wears is like a statement in that language. The clothes one wears make statements about oneself, say that one is, for simple example, a formal and official person or an informal one. The systematic aspect of *The Fashion System* examines the way in which fashion magazines write about clothes. Barthes took the view that each sign system had its own science, its semiology, with linguistics dealing with just one of those systems, namely, natural language. Other sign systems are interwoven with language, and linguistics is, therefore, the master scheme. This idea premises his analysis of fashion journalists' writing rather than the clothes themselves: the cultural meaning of clothing is tied up with language, not something distinct from it. Thus, Barthes sought to analyse the underlying structure of the written discourse, decomposing it into the basic elements which were then recombined in the statements fashion magazines make. For example, using linguistic-like techniques, he noted the ways in which items of clothing could be characterised in the categories of 'object' (O), 'support' (S) and 'variant' (V). A cardigan, the object, has a characteristic such as a collar, which is the support. The collar may be 'variant' in that it can be either open or closed and, in fashion, the difference between the collar open or closed is a difference between the cardigan as 'sporty' or 'dressy'. Working this out rather elaborately, Barthes then tried to show how fashion writing creates and recreates 'the world of fashion' as we know it. It is very much a social world in which the important times are 'the evening', 'the weekend', and 'the vacation'; the important events 'the party', 'the concert', and so on. It also conveys an ideology about the place of young women – at the time when Barthes wrote, young women did not have serious jobs, work was always shown as incidental to their lives, and so on, all traits reflected in the fashion writing of the time.

However, though Barthes analysed popular culture his abiding interest was in literary writing, an interest powered by his opposition to the French treatment of literature as regulated by strong, virtually official, conventions, much more so than, for example and according to Barthes, English literature. There were two prominent aspects to this. The first was the insistence that literature was not to be considered as a means of representing anything outside of itself. Accordingly, 'realism', which masqueraded as an attempt to capture reality, is an illusion. Thus Honoré de Balzac (1799–1850), the grand master of French literary realism, was, in Barthes' terms, 'exposed'. The second was the attempt to revalue the relationship between writer and reader. Literature should not embody such a thick condensation of convention as to restrict the reader's options for interpretation. This revaluation was intended to turn reading into a kind of writing and place criticism on the same level of creativity as authorship, moves that were immensely successful if the way in which these ideas have been absorbed into literary studies, often causing disruption and reconstitution there, is taken into account.

The 'death of the author'

Barthes is notorious as a protagonist of the idea of 'the death of the author'. One of Barthes' major works is *S/Z* (1975), the analysis of a novella, *Sarrasine*, by Honoré de Balzac, a major representative in French literature of the idea that literature should report upon the world. This tale is about a man, Sarrasine, who conceives a passion for an opera singer, La Zambinella, but who discovers that this singer is a eunuch, not a woman at all. This misconception, based on sexual stereotypes, results in Sarrasine's death, and is, for Barthes, thus a demonstration of the destructive role of convention – in the form of stereotypes – in our lives. The investigation of the story has various purposes, but one of them is to demonstrate that the substance of this story does not directly derive from any transcription of reality itself but is a highly conventionalised product, drawing upon several codes. These codes – there are five of them – endow things with meanings and make the text intelligible to the reader. All the 'lexia' (an element of narrative or 'units of reading' in the novella that Barthes is analysing) fall under one of these codes. The codes are, in our own words, as follows:

- the hermeneutic code which has to do with creating those things that the text invites us to interpret such as ambiguity and mystery which create the suspense of the story;

- the semic code to do with the capacity of terms in the story to make reference to things: a place or person for example. Such references often participate in the following;
- the symbolic code where references in the semic code gain a richer resonance as, for example, the name 'Los Alamos' evokes a connection with the creation of the nuclear age;
- the proairetic code, which has to do with the ways in which the actions of the character in the story are sequenced;
- the cultural code actualised by the plot, which invokes the shared understandings that the readers can draw upon to decide the plausibility of the story in terms of 'what they know to be believable'.

The 'death of the author' refers to a downgrading of the position of 'author' within literature, and a restructuring of the relationship between writer and reader. Congruent with his other structuralist contemporaries, Barthes seeks to subvert the idea that the individual should occupy a central place in the attempt to understand cultural activities. Even in the supposedly 'creative' ones, such as literature, the consciousness of the individual is not the sole, or even main, source of meaning. The individual author is operating within – at least – the pre-given complex of codes of the kind just described in connection with Balzac, as well as subject to the workings of the unconscious. Therefore, much of what the author writes is not consciously produced by the individual author, let alone to be understood, in any properly scientific analysis of the text, by reference to the author's intention. A traditional idea had been that literature is to be understood by focusing overwhelmingly upon 'the author', and that the main business of literary criticism was to identify what the author intended. This procedure is to be displaced by a more scientific and, therefore, systematic examination of what is written without depending on reference to the author. The one who writes a book – as structuralists commonly maintain – is not then the source of its meaning, any more than someone who chooses a particular outfit of clothes is the source of the meanings that the outfit can convey. The potential for meaning derives from the system, whose underlying code is one of which the individual is unaware, and this is true both of the fashion system and the literary tradition. Certainly someone must write, but 'the author' is an overrated figure in our culture. Recall, again, the assumption that the individual mind has little space between convention and the unconscious in which to move, and that, therefore, what the author does as a conscious being must make little contribution to the text that flows from the pen or from the keyboard. Compare our fêting of the one who does the writing with the anonymity of those who tell myths of the sort that Lévi-Strauss analyses. Why should 'the author' matter more in the understanding of literature than this figure does in the analysis of myth?

Barthes proposes that we should think of 'the author' in more old-fashioned terms, as in the middle ages, when the writer was deemed a much more lowly figure, a mere 'scriptor', or one whose job it was to copy down things. For the development of structuralist, semiological ideas the notion of 'the author' is not a useful one. This would redirect the character of literary critical activity by involving it in a transition in the treatment of writings from considering them as 'works' (i.e. the creations of an author) to considering them as 'texts' (i.e. free-standing sequences of signs). The effect of this would be to dispense with anything 'outside the text', from a need to concentrate on – from his point of view – 'extraneous matter' such as the life and opinions of the writer; instead attention could be paid exclusively to the writings as *language*, as text. Rather than being preoccupied with writings insofar as they were related to each other through the figure of their author, one could, instead, consider the connections which writings have with other writings, regardless of whether these are by the same author.

The 'death of the author' means, then, the elimination of the role of 'the author' as this has developed in and is now understood by our culture. The move was intended as a liberating one by Barthes, one which would diminish the oppressiveness of reading literature in the rigid, conformist tradition of French writing. The exaggeration of the importance which attaches to the figure who puts words on paper is to be drastically reduced by transforming the relationship of the reader to what is read, making the reader more *participant* in the creation of the meaning of what is read. The traditional treatment of a sole 'author' of the work's entire meaning has placed 'the reader' in a passive position, as one who has merely to receive, through reading, the meaning that the author intends.

Barthes played a major part in opening up a popular line of development – which many others nonetheless deplore – in departments of literary study. The literary critic is as important to, and as creative in respect of, literature as are the 'authors' – scriptors – who turn out the books they comment on. Barthes puts the idea in terms of a contrast of two types of texts, the 'readerly' and the 'writerly'. The former is written in such a way as to strongly determine its own meaning, to be so dense with prescribed meanings as to virtually dictate the sense that the reader can make of it. The airport bestseller would be a clear example of this kind of text. The 'writerly' text preferred and promoted by Barthes is that which presents the reader with maximum opportunity to determine what it means, as exemplified by those experimental novels in which the clues as to meaning are few and scattered, and where the reader is provided with many possible ways of interpreting its meanings. The reader assumes a creative role, participatory in producing meaning from the text. In respect of literary criticism, this meant that the activity of the critic in reading literary works was being placed on a creative par with the writing of them, an idea which has been embraced widely in the US academy. It is also an idea which has received fierce denunciation for displacing the trained sensitivity of literary appreciation from the centre of critical activity.

However, if Barthes had been enthusiastic about the structuralist idea of a comprehensive semiology for the systematic analysis of cultural meaning systems, especially literature, then he began to cool toward this idea, even by the time of writing *S/Z*. Though this book draws heavily on the seemingly systematic idea of 'codes' it does not itself consist in a terribly systematic analysis of the novella, but is, in various ways, arbitrary and whimsical.

Barthes was always somewhat ambivalent about the value of scientific systems, and was probably uncomfortable even with those he himself was involved in trying to create. After all, they too, if successful, would become highly conventionalised, rigidly imposed *conventions*, and, as noted, Barthes was unsympathetic to convention. Why, given that he always had doubts about such constructions, did he undertake to build these would-be scientific schemes? Perhaps because of their utility as means of exposing the ideologies coded into the culture. Having undertaken them, Barthes did recognise that these schemes demanded to be put together systematically, something he attempted to do in the essay 'Myth today' in *The Fashion System*. He tried to show how the level of cultural analysis needed to be layered on to the underpinning level of linguistic analysis, and how – in the example of writing about fashion – the method of analysis could be thoroughly worked out for a particular case. However, Barthes began to ask himself what the point of such schemes actually was, whether they were reductionist with respect to the phenomena they sought to understand, looking for formal similarities between things – especially works of literature – at the expense of their specificity and spontaneity. Certainly he decided that he would no longer do such things, that he would give up the quest to identify scientifically defined fixed structures and expressing himself in terms of theoretical systems; instead he would adopt a way of writing that was much more personalised and wayward than literary or scientific convention allowed. Barthes thereafter moved toward post-structuralism.

Jacques Lacan: the return to Freud

For both Lacan and Althusser, it was a given that Freud and Marx had founded successful sciences; the problem was to ascertain just what their achievements consisted in. Lacan, particularly, was a singularly defiant individual and very much a law unto himself, out to attack the psychoanalytic establishment in its claim to perpetuate Freud's thought. As his commentators have noted, Lacan's 'true' Freud holds rather different views than any expressed by the actual Freud. As David Macey (1988), a sympathetic commentator on Lacan, notes, Lacan's borrowing from other disciplines, such as linguistics and mathematics, is cavalier in its treatment of the original sources.

As far as Lacan was concerned, the corruption which had afflicted the development of psychoanalysis since Freud's death was especially exemplified in tendencies in the American arm of that discipline. Psychoanalysis was the clinical application of Freud's psychological theory about the structure of the individual personality, diagnosing the sources and nature of mental illness in terms of the conflicts within that structure. Freud's admirers frequently see his development of the notion of 'the unconscious' as the key to his achievements. The 'unconscious' is the source of our psychic energy, what sets us into motion, for it is where the drives, the demands for gratification which govern our lives, reside – demands for food, for sex (construing 'sex' very broadly, not merely as genital relations) and where we attempt to imprison forbidden thoughts and wishes. For human beings to live along with others, their biological urges need to be tamed or controlled. Such urges are blind and indiscriminate in their greed for satiation and if allowed a free rein would ultimately destroy the organism which houses them. Individuals have to learn to adjust their demands for satisfaction to those that are realistic and socially acceptable. They have to develop a capacity for conscious thought which can take account of what reality is like and what society will permit, and which can shape and direct biologically given urges.

However, conscious thought is powered by the unconscious drives but is only aware of them in terms of their promptings for satisfaction. Nevertheless, the conscious mind must regulate and impose limits on the unconscious drives. The unconscious drives do not care about reality or about society. Indeed, they engender thoughts which the conscious mind cannot entertain with equanimity and which it tries to exclude from its awareness by keeping them captive in the unconscious. These 'prisoners' in the unconscious try to escape the constraint of the conscious mind, often adopting the method of the true prisoner, that of disguise. Massively simplifying as we must, we can say that it is the ongoing struggle between the unconscious' attempts to escape and evade the conscious mind's efforts to keep it captive that create the symptoms of mental illness. Such symptoms are aspects of our behaviour that express the contents of the unconscious that have managed to escape the control that the conscious mind attempts to impose. Thus, and for example, the content of dreams may be seen as expressing the unconscious, for dreams occur in sleep, when the conscious mind is less alert.

Psychoanalysis is in the business of penetrating the disguises of the unconscious. By bringing to awareness the unresolved tensions between the conscious and the unconscious, psychoanalysis proposes to alleviate mental illnesses. It offers a 'talking cure': that is, through the talk between the psychoanalytic therapist and the patient, the latter can discover for him/herself what has caused the need to consign certain thoughts to the unconscious and, moreover, caused the need for their indirect expression in the form of 'symptoms'. Once aware of the true nature of the problem the patient can consciously come to terms with it.

According to Lacan, in the United States psychiatry had become a way of reconciling the individual's needs with the requirements of society, in a word or two, a means of domesticating individuals. This, again for Lacan, was entirely the wrong lesson from Freud. It was not an approach designed to help individuals understand themselves by merely making them picture themselves as conventional. To prove that this kind of psychoanalysis had taken a wrong turn Lacan called for a new determination of what Freud really meant. The kind of psychoanalysis provoking Lacan's rethink was known as 'ego' psychology, and it was upon its alleged misunderstanding of Freud's lesson about the ego that Lacan's attack was focused.

The linguistic structure of the unconscious

In this context, two aspects of Lacan's thought need attention. Lacan has a complicated, and evolving, story to tell about the mind-according-to-psychoanalysis which is difficult to relate in the space available. However, crucial to his story is the notion of the 'mirror stage' and the idea that the unconscious is structured like a language.

For Lacan, the truth which Freud tells is that the subject, the individual mind, is divided. The conscious mind is not the whole of the mind, nor is it the part of the mind which understands what we really are. The 'ego' (using that expression loosely as the equivalent of the conscious mind) itself lives under an illusion about the extent to which it is unified. There is an irreducible degree to which we live an illusion, one that is laid down early in childhood, and this is a product of 'the mirror stage'. This stage is initially formative of the individual's ego, and ensures that the latter is thereafter built upon the illusion that it creates. The illusion is the ego's self-delusion: it imagines a greater wholeness and integrity than it actually possesses. It is as if the immature child, which yet lacks complete control and coordination over its body, its gratifications and urges, for the first time sees and recognises itself in a mirror before it has any really unified control. There, in the reflection, it sees itself as a single, unified-looking entity, and from this reflection draws the false conclusion that it already is such a thing. Thus, the ego originates in a false sense of its own unity, the falsity of which has been exposed by Freud's theories. Since, in the Freudian scheme of things, the occurrences of childhood substantially determine the individual's subsequent psychological development, the misapprehension of the actual disunity persists into adult life.

Lacan's reinvocation of Freud, with its emphasis upon the disunity of the individual's psychological organisation and the role of the 'unconscious', complements Lévi-Strauss' emphasis on the unconscious operation of the underlying laws of thought, and reinforces the scepticism about the extent to which someone's consciousness is capable of truly directing, let alone understanding, the sources of their patterns of behaviour.

As we have already seen, Lévi-Strauss's first major work had been about the 'incest taboo' which was also a major preoccupation of psychoanalytic thinking. It had brought psychoanalysis close to anthropology. The Oedipal stage (named after the Greek tragedy *Oedipus* in which the principal character under a misapprehension married his mother) was, according to Freud, an indispensable phase in the development of the male personality. The growing male is sexually drawn to his mother, but such sexual feelings are in violation of the incest taboo, and a classic example of the kinds of things which are not acceptable to society, and which must, therefore, be denied and exiled to the unconscious. In the successfully resolved Oedipal transition, then, the small boy will renounce sexual desire for the mother so as, later in life, to direct that desire to women outside the circle of kinship. But was the Oedipal stage truly a general stage in male development? What about societies in which kinship arrangements are different to our own? This issue had drawn psychoanalysis into controversy with anthropologists, and even into anthropological studies of their own. Lévi-Strauss' own emphasis upon the ubiquity of the incest taboo would therefore attract Lacan, and interest him in his method.

Accordingly, Lacan's back-to-basics account of Freud took a linguistic turn. Psychoanalysis was in the business of the 'talking cure', alleviating mental symptoms by getting sufferers to bring to consciousness the thoughts that were causing their psychic tensions. This was achieved by talking to the therapist. The aim of the exercise was to get the patient to *verbalise* the contents of the unconscious. However, if the contents of the unconscious can be put into words, then it must be that they are organised in such a way that they can take linguistic shape: they must have a form that can be captured and represented in language. Accordingly, there must be a similarity between the unconscious and language; the unconscious must be structured like a language. Naturally enough, in a Parisian setting, where the prestige of Saussure-inspired approaches to linguistics was high, Lacan turned to such linguistic models for the further development of his thought, though in ways that often exhibited only a casual fidelity to them.

Turning to linguistic structuralism for his analysis of language, Lacan proposes a revision of the concept of 'the sign', one of the key elements in that approach. In the classic Saussurean conception, the sign is made up of two essentially inseparable components, the signifier and the signified, or, in plain words, the acoustic or graphical vehicle – the written or spoken word, primarily – and the idea or concept which is associated with that vehicle. Thus, the sound 'tree' is connected with our idea of a tree in a single, unified thing: the sign. Signifier and signified, in Saussure's oft-cited metaphor, are like the back and front sides of a sheet of paper. Lacan modifies this by talking about the 'primacy of the signifier', since a signifier, the sound vehicle, can be associated with any signified, not merely the one with which it is conventionally associated. This connects to Freud, according to Lacan, through two crucial psychological mechanisms identified by Freud: condensation and displacement which operate in the same way as the linguistic devices of metaphor and metonymy. 'Condensation' is a way in which the unconscious seeks to express itself by attaching meanings to something – such as an image in a dream, a piece of behaviour – other than those conventionally attached to it. 'Displacement' is using one thing to stand for another very different thing. When using a metaphor we give a word a meaning other than that which it conventionally has. Thus, the 'head' of the table represents a place at the table using an expression we should normally associate with the body, so saying something about the importance of that place at the table. In metonymy, the part of something can be used to represent the whole – as 'wheels' can be used to refer to the whole vehicle, or 'a pair of hands' the whole worker.

Lacan seeks to fuse psychoanalysis with social and cultural analysis by giving language a prominent place in his reconstruction. Language is a social and collective phenomenon, and its meanings are, therefore, those which are common to those who share the language. Language brings us together in the sense that we can make connections with other people, can form and conduct relationships using it, but it is, at the same time, something which both divides us against ourselves, and sets us apart from each other. First of all, the language divides the individual's own psychological structure. The child's 'entry into language' is a momentous event and it is with the acquisition of language that the unconscious comes into being. Thus, it is that language 'divides the subject', separating the unconscious from the conscious. The subject is comprised in large part of the unconscious, but this is excluded from the direct communication between individuals. Hence, although people can be engaged in social relationships communicating with each other through language, the relationship between the subjects is only indirect. The parties to the linguistic exchange are not the full experiencing subjects but only their egos – that imaginary construction which is comprised, in significant part, of what other people and social convention demand that a person must be. The illusion of unity created by the 'mirror phase' also conveys an image of how the child looks to others. Moreover, the acquisition of language not only forms a common, conventional structure, it also creates division within the individual. The individual is substantially 'alienated' in language, made into something which is separate from its true self, and which exists for public consumption external to its true nature.

These ideas give a better idea of the deep reason for Lacan's revisionism in psychoanalysis. The 'ego psychology', which had developed in the United States, sought to assist individuals in adjusting to the demands that reality made upon them. It assumed that mental illness involved the maladjustment of a person's relationship to reality which needed correction. For Lacan this would not help people better to become what they are, but would alienate them further by making them more into creatures of social convention, not helping them to become what they truly (unconsciously) are seeking to be.

Since language excludes the individual's unconscious, it cannot truly bring individuals together, only keep them apart. Yet, it is through the alienating medium of language that subjects are represented to each other. For Lacan, a signifier represents the subject for another signifier. That is, what people say in language is what they are for other people. The problem for psychoanalytic treatment involves getting the patient to express him or herself other than through conventionalised means which have been emptied of their actual individuality; to replace the 'empty speech' in which the individual addresses the therapist, but which says nothing about the unconscious. With 'full speech', in which the patient will express their unconscious, the therapist is directly addressed, rather than carrying on a conversation by way of the conventionalised ego and the conventional language.

Structuralism represented a fateful development for the humanities and social studies, one that triggered a reconfiguration of disciplinary relations and boundaries which continues today. Lacan's treatment of psychoanalysis in linguistic terms was to encourage its affiliation with social and, more emphatically, cultural studies. Before Lacan the understanding of the unconscious was as an essentially organic phenomenon involving the biological drives of hunger, thirst and, for Freud, most importantly sex. This suggested that the basic affinity of psychoanalysis would be with the natural sciences, especially biology, and with medicine. By using those parts of Freud's writings which emphasised the importance of language, and the linguistic nature of the therapeutic transaction, Lacan's revisionism held that much more attention would be given to anthropology, linguistics and other forms of cultural investigation. For Lacan, such a shift would bring out what Freud had meant all along.

Lacan, in his turn, was influential upon Louis Althusser, the philosopher, who also sought to renovate an intellectual approach by way of an attempted return to the original and essential teachings of the founder. In Althusser's case, Marxism. Althusser also borrowed elements of his method and some explanatory ideas from Freud, via Lacan.

Louis Althusser: the return to Marx

For Althusser it was the heirs of Marx who had taken his thought along the wrong road and it needed bringing back to the right track. Althusser's career had its own vicissitudes, and his position would change much over his career. At one stage he took the same view as Lacan, that Freud was the founder of an authentic science, but later changed his mind on this point. In the first instance, however, he insisted that Marx, too, was the founder of a science, but that the nature of his achievement was widely misunderstood. The science was there to be found in Marx's writings, but it needed to be brought out. Though Marx had provided the science, he had not developed the necessary philosophy to go along with it, and this was Althusser's own task. Marx had propounded the scientific doctrine – historical materialism – and now Althusser would elaborate the complementary philosophical one – dialectical materialism.

There were two very basic ways in which, in the twentieth century, Marx had been misinterpreted. Firstly, he had been treated as a crude 'economic determinist'. In Althusser's view, Marx *was* an economic determinist, but certainly not a crude one. Secondly, he had been mainly interpreted on the basis of his early writings which, in Althusser's view, Marx had to break with in order to establish a science. The true Marx was not to be found in the early writings even though they had achieved popularity and prominence. What was called for was a re-reading of Marx, one which sought to locate the point at which Marx made the move – the 'epistemological break' – from ideology to science.

Marx had written extensively, and variously, over his career, and the Althusserian task was to re-periodise Marx's intellectual career, and explain what the difference was between Marx the true scientist and his pre-scientific work. Althusser's pivotal contribution – made in conjunction with a group of colleagues – was found in two books, *For Marx* (1969), in which he explains where the 'epistemological break' resides, and *Reading Capital* (1970).

Marx's break with ideology and the move to science

The important break is between science and ideology. For Althusser's part, the trouble with Marx's early writings was that they are full of ideology. They are formed out of ideological preconceptions that his fully developed thought, his actual *science*, would later reject. The progressive movement is from ideology to science, and Marx had made this momentous advance. However, his readers, including those who were more than sympathetic to his ideas, disregarded this crucial shift in his thinking and construed Marx's whole thought on the basis of the ideology he had actually abandoned. However, we cannot just sit down and read Marx and expect to make the right discriminations. We need to be taught how to read Marx. We need the right method, one which Marx himself had taught us, the method by which he was able to critically read his predecessors. For Althusser this method had close parallels with the manner in which the psychoanalyst attends to the speech of the patient. What is required is a 'symptomatic reading' in which we are attentive not merely to the things that are said but also, so to speak, to 'the silences', to the things which go unsaid. What is not said can be as significant as the things that are stated. But, importantly, like the psychoanalytic patient, Marx must not be presumed to know the full significance of what he himself is saying. Althusser thus licenses himself to read Marx against the grain.

Not only does the reading of Marx require a Marx-originated method of reading, but it also requires a Marx-derived theory of science and it was important for Althusser that he could develop such a Marxist conception. In this Althusser had debts to some French scholars of the history of science, particularly Canguilhem and Bachelard, who had pioneered the idea that rather than by steady progression the sciences develop by radical discontinuities in their ideas, and from whom Althusser gained the idea which was to prove crucial in his re-reading of Marx, that of the 'epistemological break'.

Marx regarded the human essence as labour in the activity of production, and the business of science must therefore be understood in the same terms: theoretical activity must be a form of productive activity. The topic is not 'theory' but 'theoretical practice'. The process of labour involves raw materials, the transformation of those raw materials through the productive work itself, and a final product. How does this idea apply to science? In Althusser's terms, by way of Generalities I, II and III.

Contrary to received wisdom, Althusser insisted that science does not work directly on nature itself, as though the scientist could face nature and start thinking without any preconceptions at all. The scientist starts to think about things through the thought and ideas of his or her predecessors, on the basis of ideas already available. Thus, the 'raw materials' of scientific thought are not provided by nature itself but by prior thought about nature. The 'raw materials' of science are, in fact, the set of prior general ideas about the nature of the phenomena which have been accumulated up to now. Marx, it should be remembered, did the greatest part of his research and the development of his science in library reading rooms, working out his economic theories on the basis of reading his predecessors in economic theory, such as Adam Smith and David Ricardo. The materials on which Marx's thought worked were the theories (the Generalities I) of these earlier economists. Marx developed ways of reading these theorists – his own kind of 'symptomatic reading' – so that he could essentially rework those ideas. He devised, therefore, his own procedures (Generalities II) for operating on these 'raw materials' so as to generate his own theory, his own general economic scheme (Generalities III) as the final output. Marx's own theories of capitalism were, then, produced by his reconstruction of ideas found in his intellectual predecessors, not by examining capitalism in itself.

The transformation of Generalities I, by means of Generalities II, into, finally, Generalities III, is the general pattern of theoretical work. But not all theoretical work eventuates in science. There has to be a point at which a science is founded. Prior to the creation of that science, there is, as far as its domain of phenomena is concerned, only ideology. Thus, there must, if there is to be a science, be a transition from ideology to science – this is the moment of the 'epistemological break'. However, if a science is to come into being, then its raw materials cannot be prior scientific work, for as yet there is no science. The production of a science must begin with ideological raw materials. Marx had to start his career with only ideological materials available, and had to work on them to get a science out of them, but the production of the science means breaking with the ideology being used to get started. The mistake of those who have read Marx's thought as a more or less continuous whole is that they have not understood the fact and nature of this break. They are, thus, reading Marx's scientific work in the light of the ideological 'raw materials'. In this sense, they are going back on Marx's own great achievement, and reading the ideological raw materials of his science as though it already contained the essence of that science. Hence, the need to radically review the conventional periodisation of Marx's writings. As we have said, Marx himself, starting with only ideological raw materials to work with, and having to think through those – for what else could he think with? – must have been, at first, himself mainly engaged in ideological thought. Thus, in making 'the break' from ideology to science Marx was not only breaking with the ideologies from which he had extracted his ideas, but breaking with the ideological content of his own earlier works.

The transition in Marx's thought is protracted, and Althusser proposes the following scheme of division:

1840–44 – Early Works
1845 – The Works of the Break
1845–57 – The Transitional Works
1857–83 – The Mature Works

One of the troubles with reading Marx in the wrong way, particularly placing emphasis upon the early works, which most directly manifested the inheritance of Hegel's philosophy, is that Marx's scientific writings will be read in terms of those conceptions with which they are meant to break. The result is that the true nature of Marx's economic determinism will be seriously misunderstood.

The early Marx reflects two ideological legacies of Hegel which are displaced in his later works. Both need to be purged from the reading of Marx. It is Marx's mature writings that contain his authentic science, which is why reading *Capital*, Marx's major work of the mature period, is the recommended task for the Marxist who would understand the science that resulted from the break. The two ideological legacies are those of 'the organic totality' and 'humanism'.

The legacy of the organic totality

The idea of an 'organic totality' is particularly irritating to Althusser since it is conducive to the treatment of Marx as a crude 'economic determinist'. Hegel is a prime bearer of the idea of society as an 'organic totality': the view that the whole society is pervaded by the same thematic elements. The notion is that there is some dominant principle which defines a society at a particular stage in its history, a principle which is reflected in each aspect of its existence. Whatever principle it is runs throughout the society, is reproduced at each and every point of the society's life. One can see that this – for Althusser an utterly misguided conception – is the very idea of which the Frankfurt School made much, as we saw in Chapter 3; that the structure of contradictions of the whole society will be manifest in any single part of its culture. Accordingly, if the notion of the 'organic totality' is read into Marx's conception of society divided into an 'economic base' and a social-ideological 'superstructure', with the 'economic base' as the causal determinant of the 'superstructure', then it will be supposed that the former determines everything about the latter. But this is wrong. The idea that the economic base determines *everything* about the superstructure is false. Not every aspect of a society's life develops according to the dictates of its economic structure. Hence, if Marxism is an authentic and sound science, it cannot give prominent place to such a patently false thesis.

However, the base/superstructure model is not entirely abandoned. Instead, it is to be given a more complex and moderate interpretation. Religious institutions, for example, must develop to an important extent according to the fact that they are *religious* institutions – or, as Althusser refers to them, practices – and not economic or political institutions.

This is not to say that political institutions will be unaffected by the economy but that their character will also have much to do with the fact that they are involved in the business of controlling and regulating the society rather than delivering economic goods and services. It is also obvious that not everything in society changes together. There might be, say, a fairly rapid change in political institutions with not much change in the religious ones, or educational practices might remain fairly constant across political and religious upheavals.

The way in which religious institutions develop is affected by their interaction with other institutions in the society, or even with those in other societies, but there is a substantial extent to which the course of their development will simply be the product of their own internal organisation rather than of any external influence. Thus, the development of any one institution has a degree of autonomy from other institutions. It is not, however, *absolute* autonomy, as though an institution developed free of any influence at all from another institution. There is only a degree, a relative level of autonomy on the part of any given institution, and it is this notion of 'relative autonomy' that is counterposed to that of 'organic totality'.

But if the notion of 'organic totality' goes, then so also must an oversimplified idea of the role of 'contradiction' in Marx's social thought, in favour of the idea of an 'overdetermination' of contradictions as the cause of any actual revolution. The concept of 'overdetermination' is taken from Freud's conception of the cause of psychiatric symptoms, and the way in which a single symptom might manifest and be condensed within a whole diversity of psychic tensions. Marx's idea of contradiction – of the insoluble tensions built into the structure – as precipitating revolutionary transformation suggests that the same kind of single contradiction which splits the whole society runs through all its conflicts. Since the society is not – at least in Althusser's account – an organic totality, then the different parts of the same society will not be at the same level of development, nor afflicted by the same contradictions. If there is a revolution in society, it will not result from a single, fundamental conflict that pervades the whole society, but will be the consequence of a number of different kinds of conflict, along with the specific circumstances which make it possible for those contradictions to have a cumulative revolutionary effect. The Russian Revolution, for example, occurred because there were all kinds of conflicts in Russian society, some resulting from the fact that it was entering the age of capitalist organisation, others reflecting the fact that in other respects the society was barely out of the middle ages, and class conflicts between all sorts of class elements:

> the exacerbation of class struggles throughout the country, not only between exploiter and exploited, but even within the ruling classes themselves (the great feudal proprietors supporting autocratic, militaristic police Tsarism; the lesser nobility involved in constant conspiracy; the big bourgeoisie and the liberal bourgeoisie opposed to the Tsar; the petty bourgeoisie oscillating between conformism and anarchistic 'leftism'). (Althusser, 1969: 96)

There is no formulaic way of working out the patterns of reciprocal effect between parts of the society, or the conjuncture of contradictions. The postulation of 'relative autonomy' means that the 'social formation' (or the whole complex of parts and their interrelationships) is a complex, differentiated and only partly integrated structure.

However, though there is no rigid, mechanical, determination of the rest of society by the economic 'base', Althusser is not letting go of the Marxist supposition entirely. He resorts, rather, to an expression coined by Engels, of 'determination in the last instance' of the other structures of the society by the economic base. The limit on the 'relative autonomy' of the development of any other part of the society is set by the nature of the economic 'base'. It is this which, not immediately but only 'in the last instance', fixes the organisation of the rest of the society.

It would, on Althusser's terms, be foolish to read Marx as saying that the organisation of a society is necessarily dominated by the economy. In any given society, it is likely that one element will be dominant over the rest and will exercise prevailing power within the society. It might be the political structure, run as an autocratic dictatorship, for example, or it might be religion that prevails over everything else. Although the social formation is composed of 'relatively autonomous' parts, they are not all equally influential in any given society. Hence, the formation is a structure-in-dominance, a complex with one part – to borrow the way the dominance of the British Prime Minister over the rest of the Cabinet is characterised – the 'first among equals'. The fact that one part is dominant does not inhibit the relative autonomy of the other parts. Though it prevails over them it does not dictate their every aspect and feature. It is only in *some* societies, such as our own contemporary one, that the economy will be dominant in this sense. But it does not follow that the economy is only occasionally the 'determinant in the last instance' of the shape of the overall structure of the social complex. Even when the economy is *not* the dominant structure, it is nonetheless the causal determinant of the broad form of the larger social formation to which it belongs. Which part of the social whole will be the dominant structure is something that depends upon the nature of the economy itself. The economy provides the general framework within which the other constituent structures will, through their own interconnections and their relative autonomy, develop specific relations with each other. The economy forces the general outline of the social formation rather than the specific arrangements.

The legacy of humanism

The legacy of 'humanism' is another of the ways in which Marx is misread. As we saw in connection with Lévi-Strauss, one of the persistent themes of structuralism is its rejection of humanistic influences on the notion of science. Science is impersonal and objective, giving no special place in the scheme of things to the lives, thoughts and consciousness of human beings. 'Humanism' places humans at the centre of things, and treats developments in the world as if they were primarily, even essentially, about them. Thus, Hegel had sought to give a general and coherent account of the whole of history by making the story one about the development of the human mind or 'spirit', a story about the fulfilment of human essence. This was certainly a strong influence on Marx's early writing but abandoned in his mature work in which, instead, he sees history as the development of the structures of social formations and their constituent practices. Human beings are not placed, as they were in the Hegelian tale, at the centre of the story, but feature rather more as a supporting cast. They are not the sources of history, its dynamics and change, but are more like place-fillers in the structure of society.

The point of view of the human individual is one which places the individual at the centre of things, in the sense that we experience the world as radiating outward from our personal here and now. There is no other way in which we could live and experience our lives – which is consequential for Althusser's conception of ideology, as will soon be seen. But there is no reason why a scientific account should preserve that particular perception. 'Humanism' is ideology and, therefore, something which should be dispensed with in a scientific account, especially one which registers the reality of capitalist society. It is human reality which has made human beings into mere occupants of places in the systems of production and social life. The capitalist system is a system of positions and relationships between those positions, and from the point of view of that system, human beings figure as mere occupants of those positions. The capitalist system needs X million workers, whoever they may be, and does not call the roll from a list of identified individuals. From the point of view of capitalism, one pair of hands is pretty much the same as another, so long as it can do the appropriate work, and the importance of 'the individual' is part of capitalism's ideology rather than its essence. It would surely be wrong for a key constituent of capitalist ideology, 'the individual', to be given any part in a Marxist science that was critical, root and branch, of the whole capitalist system.

Overall, Althusser is arguing for the analysis of 'the social formation', that is, the society as a complex structure composed of other structures – a structure of structures, in his slogan – which stand in relationships of relative autonomy to one another. All are interdependent and mutually affecting, but not rigorously integrated into anything approaching an organic totality, though structured in such a way that one structure, at any one time, prevails over the others. The form of the configuration, the fixing of the structure in dominance, being, *in the last analysis*, determined by the structure of productive relations. The American sociologist Alvin Gouldner (1959) had argued, more concisely, something very similar with respect to the balance of 'reciprocity' and 'autonomy' in functional theory, accusing the functionalists, as Althusser accused the Hegelianising Marxists, of exaggerating the degree of integration of institutions within a system, again suggesting that there is no reason to anathematise functionalism as inherently a vehicle of conservative politics.

Science and ideology

Science and ideology are rigorously opposed in Althusser's thought, but not because they are rival occupants for the same space as the orthodox view would have it. In this conception, ideology is seen as a form of understanding which awaits displacement by a true scientific understanding. But, in Althusser's scheme, this cannot be. Science views the world from an impersonal point of view, and hence cannot be substituted for the individual's personalised relationship to the world: the former has no space for the latter. In an important sense individuals have to represent their own relationship to the world through the imaginary forms provided by ideology. Ideology is indispensable to human existence, not to be eradicated with the arrival of true science. The 'individual' is, in any case, the creation of ideology. Ideology enables people to think of themselves as the specific and distinctive beings that they imagine themselves to be. Ideology 'interpellates' – meaning 'hails' or 'calls up' – in the individual human being a particular conception of themselves. Thus, though the individual is an ideological illusion, and dispensable from science, it is indispensable to real human existence.

The final element in Althusser's argument is to provide an analysis of the role of ideology in the structures of capitalist society. Ideology may be what creates the individual, but it does not exist for that purpose but, rather, for the purpose of maintaining control over the society. The need is for a depiction of the organisation which generates, installs and disseminates ideology in society, for the prevailing form of control over the society is not that of physical coercion, but that of mental domination. Developing this was mainly a matter of elaborating ideas of what a proper Marxist account of the state might involve. While acknowledging that the state is, in important respects, a 'body of armed men' – the police and army – prepared to exercise repressive force against potentially revolutionary forces, it is, more importantly, as Antonio Gramsci (1891–1937), the Italian Marxist theorist had recognised, a matter of inhibiting the disposition of people to have revolutionary ideas by instilling in them the kind of outlook that makes them compliant to capitalism's needs. The state combines a repressive with an ideological apparatus. The state ideological apparatus contains such things as the education system and the family. Including the family in an ideological *state* apparatus may seem perverse, since the 'family' is usually considered a 'private' matter detached from the state. But Althusser insists that this simply reproduces what is a bourgeois ideology, namely, the distinction between and ostensible separation of the spheres of the state and of private life, which is not one that a true Marxist theory, rejecting bourgeois ideology, need respect. The family and the state's educational apparatus in modern society collaborate in preparing the young for, and making them compliant with, the need for capitalism's reproduction of itself.

Althusser was later to deny that he had ever been a structuralist, and with some justification. His position was that of 'structural Marxism' and had no particularly significant use for the linguistic model that was of such importance in Lévi-Strauss, Barthes, and even Lacan. He was later to withdraw his certification of Freud as the founder of a science, and to mount a rigorous criticism of many of his own former ideas, but by that stage his work had already had tremendous effects in reorienting sociology, but no longer had the influence it had once possessed only a little while before. The argument had moved on.

The aftermath and the move to post-structuralism

Even as the structuralist movement was becoming the focus of international enthusiasm, back home in Paris it was already under criticism for not being intellectually radical enough. There was disappointment, too, with the failure of structuralists, especially Althusser, to give leadership in the student disturbances in Paris during May 1968. However, the criticisms did not entirely abrogate the structuralist programme but sought, rather, to recast it. The common way of characterising this transition is as one from structuralism to post-structuralism, but it is not entirely implausible to treat the same transition, as Dosse does (1997), as one from a first to a second phase of structuralism. The label 'post-structuralist' is likewise intended to emphasise the combination of continuity and discontinuity involved in this succession.

The political and intellectual disturbances of the 1960s were interwoven, as we indicated in Chapter 1, with a condemnation of social scientists for compliance with 'the military industrial complex' which led to a deep and spreading distaste for structuralism's ambition to be a science. Structuralism had placed great emphasis upon the scientific character of the exercise, and the critical development into post-structuralism or, if preferred, Structuralism II, was to turn against scientific aspirations. Eventually this move was to give wide currency to the demand for 'reflexivity'; that is, to the requirement that one's form of supposedly scientific analysis should be applied to one's own activities in just the same way that they are applied to the conduct of others. Greatly oversimplifying, we can say that post-structuralism was stimulated by consideration of the consequences – and the difficulties – involved in applying structuralist methods to structuralism itself. As mentioned, Roland Barthes, provoked by critical discussion with Michel Foucault and Jacques Derrida, had himself moved out of structuralism, arguing that the attempt to give a scientific account of literature was a reductionist one.

Foucault and Derrida are two of the key names associated with the post-structuralist phase. Foucault has unquestionably become the most influential social thinker of all during the period since the 1960s. Derrida was an innovator of the 'deconstructionist' approach, the title of which – though not normally used in the way he intended – has now become the equivalent of a household word in intellectual circles. The issues in their work, and that of other less prominent participants in the reaction against structuralism, retain at least the continuity with the structuralist precursors by a preoccupation with language and a firm anti-humanist stance.

Outside of Paris, and in Anglo-American thinking, the rise of structuralism contributed to the breakdown of prejudice against 'continental' social thought. Althusser's rehabilitation of Marx was crucial. In the period since the 1960s much of the initiative in social thought has shifted to European thought, and much of the change in Anglo-American social theory comes from developments there.

Structuralism initially caught the attention because of its scientific pretensions. It offered an alternative conception of science to that which was on offer from thinkers such as Parsons and Merton, who were still attempting to model social science on the natural sciences. The structuralist adoption of a social, or at least a human, science, namely linguistics, as the exemplary model was a refreshing move, and offered the possibility of a science which could be mathematical in character, but which would be a formal rather than a quantitative discipline. Without giving up the aspiration to be a science, there could be a radical readjustment in the conception of what this would entail. This readjustment also offered resistance to two unsettling developments which had put pressure upon the received picture of social science: firstly, the emphasis upon social phenomena as *meaningful* ones and, secondly, the development of individualist/phenomenological alternatives to the failings of system thinking of the kind exemplified in Parsons' functionalism.

The idea that social phenomena are meaningful, and that understanding them is a matter of understanding the meaning that they have for the individual member of society was, in the 1960s, gaining ground, especially when expressed in the terms of symbolic interactionism and ethnomethodology, discussed in Chapter 5. These approaches provided materials for serious criticism of the dominant theoretical and methodological ambitions, such as those of Parsons and Merton. However, the criticism was not simply directed at these two doyens of American sociological theory, but at all thinking which regarded society as any kind of system, whether functionalist or characterised in terms of conflict. Such thinking was a form of illicit reification. Symbolic interactionism and ethnomethodology, often seen as 'phenomenological' since, in the eyes of some critics, they held that social reality existed only the consciousness of individuals, were frequently accused of the most rampant subjectivism. Phenomenology was one of the main targets of structuralist denigration – especially from its 'structuralist Marxist' brand. Structuralism of course accepted that social phenomena, being cultural, were also meaningful, and concurred with a central idea of both symbolic interactionism and ethnomethodology that language was the critical bearer of meaning in social life. However, it drew a very different conclusion. The need was to understand not individual consciousness of meaning, not the 'subjective' dimension of meaning, but objective systems of meaning and to see that individual consciousness and individual expressions of meaning derived from these objective systems.

Structuralism was seen as a way of containing the threat of subjectivity in sociology, though the issue of the relation between 'objective' and 'subjective' aspects of social life had not been resolved. Dubbed 'the structure/agency' problem, it rumbles on today. Althusser's combination of an insistence upon the pre-eminence of objective structures with an equal insistence upon the scientific status of Marx's later thought greatly assisted in defending system-type thinking against what were seen as the encroachments of 'subjectivism', and, given the right political twist, furnished credibility to Marxist ideas and politics which had, only a handful of years before, been declared scientifically irrelevant and discredited. If the enthusiasm for Althusser was not universal, it was certainly vigorous and provocative, and if it did not establish Althusser's version of Marx as authoritative, it did much – as did the thought of Herbert Marcuse (as discussed in Chapter 3) – to make Marx's thought very much an issue and draw much greater attention to a wide range of European thinkers who, during the twentieth century, had made efforts to reinterpret Marx's doctrines.

No less importantly, Lévi-Strauss, Barthes and Lacan made a decisive contribution to the formation of what is now known as 'cultural studies'. They had provided seminal ideas about the ways in which the putative science of semiology could be applied to the analysis of cultural forms, with Barthes bringing both popular culture and literary materials under its purview. Moreover, the way that Marxist and/or Freudian presuppositions were interwoven into their ideas enabled this analysis to be given the kind of critical dimension that was increasingly deemed necessary for any respectable mode of social thought.

CHAPTER FOUR SUMMARY

- In significant respects, structuralism was a reworking of the ideas of Marx and Freud filtered through structural linguistics. The basic idea was of language as a self-contained system whose elements are 'signs', the identity of which is determined relationally within the system. The aim was to extend this beyond language to encompass other facets of social life.

- A crowning achievement of structuralism was seen to be the 'decentring' of the individual; that is, the abandonment of the idea that human activities are to be understood and explained as the expression of a single, unified mind. Individual intentions and purposes are themselves produced out of systems of organisation – culture, the mind, the society, language, fashion, gesture, etc. – which the individual neither knows nor understands. The system of organisation has to be revealed through structural, or semiotic, analysis.
- Post-structuralism emerged as a reaction against the scientific pretensions of structuralism. The demand for 'reflexivity' – that structuralism should apply to itself – and difficulties of doing so, eventually led to its transformation into post-structuralism. Nevertheless, it had offered a significant alternative to the attempt to model the social sciences on the natural sciences.

Select bibliography and further reading

Good accounts of Saussure's linguistic ideas can be found in Crick, *Explorations in Language and Meaning: Toward a Semantic Anthropology* (Malaby Press, 1976). Roy Harris, *Saussure and his Interpreters* (Edinburgh University Press, 2001) is also a more than useful account of Saussure's ideas.

Short and accessible introductions to structuralism and post-structuralism include Donald Palmer, *Structuralism and Post-structuralism for Beginners* (Writers and Readers, 1997 – in strip cartoon form), Terence Hawkes, *Structuralism and Semiotics* (Methuen, 1977), Peter Caws, *Structuralism: the Art of the Intelligible* (Humanities Press, 1988), John Sturrock, *Structuralism*, 2nd edn (Fontana, 1993), and Richard Harland, *Superstructuralism: the Philosophy of Structuralism and Post-structuralism* (Routledge, 1991). J.G. Merquior's *From Prague to Paris: a Critique of Structuralism and Post-structuralism* (Verso, 1986) is a very scholarly, but highly readable book which tries both to explain structuralist ideas clearly and to criticise them severely. Michael Lane, *Structuralism: a Reader* (Cape, 1970) offers a selection of source readings. Ino Rossi's *The Logic of Culture: Advances in Structural Theory and Methods* (Tavistock, 1981) shows some of the applications of structuralism in the social sciences and Jonathan Culler's *Structuralist Poetics* (Routledge, 1975) provides a clear explanation of how structuralism can be applied in literary studies, and thereby shows how it was able to catch on outside of the social sciences, beginning the transformation of literary studies and other areas of the humanities into pursuits that are nowadays much more like the social sciences.

Somewhat more advanced guides and discussions are Eve Tavor Bannet, *Structuralism and the Logic of Dissent: Barthes, Derrida, Foucault, and Lacan* (Macmillan, 1989), Miriam Glucksmann, *Structuralist Analysis in Contemporary Social Thought* (Routledge, 1974) and Edith Kurzweil, *The Age of Structuralism: Lévi-Strauss to Foucault* (Columbia University Press, 1980), which deal with structuralism more generally, whilst Simon Clarke's *The Foundations of Structuralism* (Harvester Press, 1981) and Christopher Badcock's *Lévi-Strauss: Structuralism and Sociological Theory* (Hutchinson, 1975), are mainly concerned with its impact on sociology. Annete Lavers focuses on *Roland Barthes: Structuralism and After* (Methuen, 1982), and Ted Benton's *The Rise and Fall of Structuralist Marxism: Althusser and His Influence* (Macmillan, 1984) is about – as its subtitle indicates – Althusser and his influence. An extensive history of structuralism is François Dosse's two-volume, *History of Structuralism* (University of Minnesota Press, 1997).

Lévi-Strauss' corpus is extensive. His *The Savage Mind* (Weidenfeld, 1962) is a good place to start, as is his *The Scope of Anthropology* (Cape, 1967). *Structural Anthropology* (Basic Books, 1964) sets out the structuralist principles underlying his conception of what anthropology should be about. *Totemism* (Penguin, 1973) contains his attack on existing anthropological theories of totemism. *The Raw and the Cooked: Introduction to a Science of Mythology* (Harper and Row, 1970), *From Honey to Ashes* (Cape, 1973), *The Origin of Table Manners* (Cape, 1978) and *The Naked Man* (Cape, 1981) make up his *Mythologiques*. Edmund Leech's *Lévi-Strauss*, in the Fontana Modern Masters Series (Fontana, 1974, rev. edn) is a good introduction.

Barthes, too, has been a prolific writer. His *Elements of Semiology* (Noonday Press, 1967) sets out his ambitions for semiology. As might be expected, *The Fashion System* (Cape, 1985) contains his semiological analysis of fashion. *Mythologies* (Cape, 1972) contains journalistic pieces analysing aspects of bourgeois culture. *The Empire of Signs* (Cape, 1983) analyses Japanese culture from a semiotic point of view. *S/Z* (Cape, 1975) is the reference for Barthes' thoughts on writing and authorship.

Althusser is not easy reading. His most famous work is *For Marx* (Penguin, 1969). But see also Althusser and Balibar *Reading Capital* (New Left Books, 1970). Lacan, like Althusser, can be tough going. See his *The Four Fundamental Concepts of Psycho-Analysis* (Hogarth Press, 1977), *The Language of the Self: The Function of Language in Psycho-Analysis* (Johns Hopkins, 1968) and *Écrits: A Selection* (Norton, 1977). David Macey's *Lacan in Contexts* (Verso, 1988) is a sympathetic account of Lacan's ideas.

Interactionism 5

BEGINNING CHAPTER FIVE

In contrast to Parsonian functionalism, interactionism had much more modest aims, namely, the study of social interaction from 'the actor's point of view'. The chapter includes discussion of:

- the contribution of G.H. Mead;
- the early years of the Chicago School;
- the contribution of Herbert Blumer and the formulation of symbolic interactionism;
- studies of work and of deviance;
- the next generation: Becker, Strauss, and Goffman.

The approach to the analysis of society developed by those who became known as symbolic interactionists presents a stark contrast to the functionalist theories of Talcott Parsons and Robert Merton discussed in Chapter 2. Parsons and those who thought like him aimed to construct nothing less than an all-encompassing general theory of society which, they hoped, would ultimately resemble the theories of the natural sciences. Such an achievement would, they anticipated, lead to the recognition of sociology as a serious, scientifically based profession rather like medicine, psychology or economics, a discipline which could offer an objective understanding of the workings of society. In contrast, the symbolic interactionists were – for reasons that we shall discuss – sceptical about such grand pretensions. Indeed, the interactionists were suspicious of 'professionalisation' for what they regarded as good sociological reasons. As their own studies were to show, professionalisation was not simply to do with the development of specialised knowledge and services, but also involved attempts by particular occupational groups to monopolise the market for their services and so increase their own rewards and prestige. Professionalisation was rarely simply about applying knowledge for the public good.

There is also a marked contrast in the nature of the works produced by the interactionist school. In place of the bulky theoretical volumes produced by the leading functionalists, outlining complex theoretical schemes, the interactionists typically reported their work in the form of short essays containing a minimum of explicit theorising. It was during the 1940s and 1960s that these contrasting perspectives struggled to influence the character and future direction of American sociology. While Parsons and Merton sought to convert it into a scientific profession, Everett Hughes (1895–1982) and, later, Herbert Blumer (1900–87) were at the forefront of a resistance movement which argued that sociology should be an open association of scholars rather than an exclusive professional organisation. Moreover, both Hughes and Blumer saw valid sociological knowledge as much more likely to emerge gradually from the study of real people in real situations – that is, through the sort of fieldwork developed by social anthropologists – than from the abstract 'armchair theorising' of the functionalists.

The contrast between functionalist and symbolic interactionist perspectives in sociology has often been expressed in terms of the scale of the social phenomena which the respective approaches addressed. The word 'interaction' appears to suggest a primary focus on 'micro', small-scale, face-to-face encounters, as opposed to the large-scale patterns of social organisation with which the functionalists were concerned. It is this view of symbolic interactionism that has sometimes been the basis for criticism of the perspective, namely, that it cannot comprehend the more general 'macro' social processes, the structural and historical forces, which provide the settings and context in which face-to-face encounters take place. For their part, the interactionists countered, as did Max Weber, with the argument that all patterns of social organisation, indeed all human life, depend on the actions and interactions of real individuals: a theme to which we will return.

However, we wish to suggest that the fundamental contrast between the interactionists and those whom C.W. Mills referred to as the 'grand theorists' (Mills, 1959: 25ff.) has less to do with the scale or level of the social phenomena they dealt with and more with their basic, underlying assumptions as to how sociological research should be conducted, and about the nature of the knowledge it should aim to produce. For the interactionists, the categories and concepts of the 'grand theorists' were not only abstract but were created *a priori* through theoretical speculation and, moreover, postulated the existence of large-scale social forces and processes existing in a realm remote from the activities of real people going about their everyday lives. In this connection one has only to think of Durkheim's ideas which, among other things, went a long way toward reifying the notion of society as the external force constraining social behaviour. Moreover, while Parsons' argument, that in order to develop as a discipline it was necessary to develop a generally shared framework of general theory to organise and coordinate its programme of research was widely accepted, even by the interactionists, they nonetheless rejected the view that

Parsons' elaborate model of society could do the job. It was too abstract. It was a theoretical model constructed out of 'thin air', so to speak. For the interactionists, sociological theory could only be developed on the basis of a far more substantial knowledge of how social life is actually lived. Their preference, to put it briefly, was for the concrete over the abstract; a preference for doing actual studies rather than elaborating theories. In practice this led to studies of 'everyday' situations for it was in these that human society was actually manifested and patterns of social organisation enacted. For the interactionists, 'social structures' and large-scale social processes had to be understood as the outcome of such situations.

The interactionist perspective, we should emphasise at the outset, did not deny the importance of the processes so beloved of 'macro' theorists, such as power and constraint, or claim that individuals were free to act as they pleased. On the contrary, and as we shall see below, the tradition of symbolic interactionism emerged early in the twentieth century in the context of efforts by sociologists at the University of Chicago to understand the development of that city in a period of rapid growth, change and disruption. The massive effects of industrialisation, urbanisation, international migration and global economic change could all be seen on the streets of Chicago itself, in the turbulence of its social life, and in the successive appearances of new communities within the city. In the 1920s – the era of Prohibition, gangsters and Al Capone – the Department of Sociology at the University of Chicago initiated a programme of studies of the life of the city, especially its 'underside', under the leadership of major figures in early American sociology – Albion Small (1854–1926), W.I. Thomas (1863–1947), Robert Park (1864–1944), and Ernest Burgess (1886–1966). The studies were frequently based on fieldwork, and on a commitment to investigating the lives of those who were socially marginalised or morally outcast. These concerns were to remain important elements on the symbolic interactionist tradition, but its development as a coherent intellectual perspective also owed much to another major figure at the University of Chicago, the social philosopher George Herbert Mead (1863–1931).

G.H. Mead's 'social psychology'

As a young man, Mead's interests were in the fields of philosophy and psychology. He developed an early interest in physiological psychology, and travelled to Germany in 1888 to study in Leipzig with Wilhelm Wundt (1832–1920), then the leader in this field, before moving to the University of Berlin. Here he was exposed to the intellectual dispute between those who wished to develop psychology as an experimental, empirical discipline on the model of the natural sciences, and others, such as the philosopher Wilhelm Dilthey (1833–1911), who advocated an 'interpretative' approach for studies in the humanities (Joas, 1985: 18). By the time he returned to the USA in 1891, Mead had become deeply immersed in one of the main academic issues of the day, the question of whether, or how, it would be possible to develop scientific approaches to the study of human social life. Although he had been exposed to the ideas of leading thinkers in the German philosophical tradition, his arrival at the University of Chicago came about through the initiative of an American philosopher, John Dewey (1859–1952), who had been appointed to the Chair of Philosophy and Psychology in 1894.

Dewey, along with C.S. Pierce (1839–1914) and William James (1842–1910), was one of the founders of pragmatism, a philosophical movement which has been described as essentially American, and which took a down-to-earth, deliberately sceptical view of the great abstract, metaphysical schemes produced by European philosophers, and of German idealism in particular. For the pragmatists, the criterion by which actions or statements could be judged was whether or not they were effective in the real world, not whether they conformed to some ultimate, abstract standard of 'truth'. Pragmatists, for example, saw the age-old quest for definitions of 'good' or 'evil', 'truth' or 'freedom', as futile. Such notions were abstractions which bore no relation to the lived experience of real people. Instead, they argued, the way to judge actions was in terms of their practical consequences: did they produce good or bad effects, or achieve what they were intended to do, in real-life contexts? In their emphasis on the need to understand real-life situations, then, the pragmatic philosophers were providing an important foundation for the development of sociological thinking which rejected abstract theoretical systems and stressed the ways in which patterns of social organisation are created in and through the interactions of real people.

From the pragmatists' perspective, the 'meaning' of a concept, or the significance of a belief, lay essentially in the ways in which it could modify and direct people's actions; their view was that 'knowledge' was in the end a matter of establishing what worked in a practical sense – that is, how it allowed a person to do what he or she wanted to do rather than conforming to some ultimate standard of 'truth'. Human activity, moreover, was seen as having biological, psychological and ethical dimensions and as being directed towards particular purposes by a conscious agent, who had feelings and emotions. Once again, such a view of human action prepares the way for a sociological focus on the conscious actor as a self-steering creature, and for a rejection of theoretical perspectives which see human behaviour as essentially passive, in the sense that it is 'caused' by prior social forces, instinctual drives or other psychological mechanisms. Again the contrast with Durkheim's notion of 'social facts' is strong.

Mead's own perspective was much influenced by Dewey's essay 'The Reflex Arc Concept in Psychology', first published in 1896, which was a powerful early critique of the idea, then widely held by psychologists, that human action can be explained in terms of a stimulus–response sequence. Dewey argued, for example, that stimuli are not passively received by people: on the contrary, he emphasised the 'active character of perception' (Joas, 1985: 66) in the sense that we have to define for ourselves what is to count as a significant factor in choosing a course of action. We may see a red light, for example, but we still have to decide whether to stop at it. This is not an automatic response. Similarly, it follows that we do not just 'respond' to situations but have to formulate an appropriate course of action, taking into account what it is we wish to achieve, what the expectations of others are, and so on. Of course, in everyday life we perform countless actions 'without thinking' about them, and we may describe them as habitual or normal responses. But this does not alter the fact that we always have the capacity to do something different, and indeed to change our 'responses' when we perceive the need to do so. So, whereas the psychologists who advocated the 'reflex arc' concept saw behaviour in terms of three distinct phases (stimulus–internal processing–response), and as essentially passive in that responses were released by particular stimuli, Dewey argued for a view which placed emphasis on the *active* aspects of human agency, and took it to be a continuous process rather than sequences of distinct events.

These themes were important in the development of Mead's own perspective, in which he sought to preserve the idea of the active individual who experiences the world through what William James had called the 'stream of consciousness' (Joas, 1985: 77). For Mead this 'stream of consciousness' was constantly produced through the relationship between individuals and their significant environment, which includes the presence of other people. Thus society, for Mead, was 'an affair of consciousness', and necessarily so. But, and this is a point on which Mead insisted, this should not be taken to mean that the scientific psychology which he was concerned to develop must be concerned with the interior, 'subjective' realm of our experience. Of course we can, in this realm, imagine all sorts of things, and we can make choices and decisions according to our wishes and interests. At the same time, however, in order to realise any of our plans or wishes we have to bring them into alignment with an existing social framework, a framework in which we come up against the interests and commitments of others, existing conventions and relationships. In short, come up against all sorts of cultural and institutional constraints. In Mead's view, then, the experience of participating in human society involves developing a sense of ourselves as unique individuals, yet simultaneously becoming integrated into the wider sets of rules and shared understandings of the community and the social order. The issue was to provide a theoretical reconciliation of individual uniqueness with the inescapable requirements of social life. Mead's solution was to develop a view of the mind and the self as *emergent from* the constant flow of social life, and not as prior to or independent of it.

In pursuing these ideas, Mead was considerably influenced by Charles Darwin's (1809–82) work on evolution, and he retained his early interest in the physiological aspects of human psychology. Unlike those idealist philosophers who regarded abstract notions of mind or consciousness as the essential qualities of humanity, Mead regarded human beings first and foremost as animals who have evolved in such a way as to be able to engage in symbolic communication and so to co-operate in maintaining patterns of social organisation. However, human co-operation does not come about simply as a result of the biological characteristics of the human organism: if it did it would be impossible to explain the wide diversity of human cultures. In Mead's view, moreover, there is a fundamental difference between the conscious co-ordination of human social life and the instinctively co-operative patterns of organisation to be observed among insects, herds of deer, lions and other species. As we have seen, the pragmatist philosophers regarded humans as creatures who exercised choice and made decisions: not as creatures driven by instincts over which they had no control. Thus, for Mead, human action requires that individuals are capable of ascertaining and anticipating the actions of others, and of formulating appropriate actions on the basis of that knowledge. Human behaviour is not a matter of responding directly to others' actions but of reacting to the intentions that guide these actions, that is, to the likely future course of others' conduct.

The difference between human and other animal modes of interaction can be grasped if we contrast it with what Mead called the 'conversation of gestures' which may be observed among many animal groups. When a mother hen clucks, for example, her chicks will respond by running to her. This does not imply, however, that the chicks 'understand' the clucking, or that the mother intentionally clucks in order to guide the chicks to her: that is, she does not initially anticipate the viewpoint of the chicks towards her. In short, mother and chicks do not share the same experience. The chicks are responding to a signal rather than to a meaningful symbol. Among humans, however, gestures have symbolic content and therefore have to be interpreted, in the sense that we have to decide the meaning of actions in relation to others' intentions. If, for example, one person raises an arm, another can fill in the likely course of the act in his or her imagination by projecting the gesture into the future, perhaps as an intention to wave goodbye, or to strike a blow, or any other possible interpretation. The point is that the meaning of the gesture is not inherent in the gesture itself; we have, as we say, to 'make sense' of it within a particular social context.

However, in order for concerted action to take place among humans, each individual has to attach the same meaning to the same gesture. Unless there is sufficient consensus – that is, common or shared understanding of the meanings of gestures, acts and symbols – co-operative human action will be impossible. For Mead this is largely a matter of sharing the same images. 'Close the door!' presents the same image to the person giving the order and to the one receiving it. The imaginative completion of the act, which Mead understands as its 'meaning', takes place through 'role-taking'. To imaginatively complete the total act which a gesture represents, people must be able to place themselves in the position of the other person, to 'take the role of the other', completing in the imagination the part that the other plays. It is this, for Mead, which makes human behaviour social: that is, it has incorporated within it the actions of others, through our capacity to imaginatively participate in their conduct.

The self

Further, Mead points out that just as we are able to imaginatively interpret and so anticipate the likely actions of others, so we have the capacity to treat ourselves as if we were others; that is, to make ourselves the object of our own consciousness. This ability, which is of profound importance for Mead's understanding of human action, can be easily observed in phrases like 'I said to myself . . .', or 'I was really annoyed with myself', or 'I wonder if I should do *x* . . .' In such cases, Mead suggests, we are acting socially towards ourselves in the same way that we do to others: people can become the object of their own actions, as when we praise or blame ourselves, congratulate or condemn ourselves, and so on, and interpret our situation accordingly. It is, once again, this ability to 'take the role of the other' that enables us to 'get outside' ourselves, to see ourselves reflexively, as if we were an 'other', that enables us to imagine how we are viewed by others and so to take the same 'objective' view of ourselves as others do. It is in this way that humans can be said to have a 'self', in the sense that other animals do not. The self, however, has to be understood not as a static set of personal dispositions we are born with, but as a constant *process* of interpreting our own actions in relation to those of others, a process which is fundamental to our participation in social life, and which gives us an ongoing sense of our own identity.

The implication of Mead's analysis, then, is that the human 'self' cannot be adequately understood in individualistic or psychological terms. For him, the self is a process that arises in and through our inevitable involvement in social interaction. The capacity to engage in symbolic communication – which, as we have seen, is distinctively human – is realised through our use of language. It is in language that we can engage in the process of communication with others, and come to understand their points of view. By learning the shared symbols of language – the agreed meaning of the sounds we utter within particular linguistic communities – children come to adopt and accept as their own the meanings and definitions of the events and things that surround them, including their own actions.

So the human 'self' may be said to arise in and take its form through social interaction, and it is this view of the self as a social process that constitutes Mead's solution to the problem of reconciling the 'subjective' individual with 'objective' society. In fact, in Mead's analysis the opposition of 'individual' and 'society' is overcome by viewing of the emergence of selves as part of the social process. The minds of individuals, or in other words their psychological make-up, are constituted in the course of participation in society, through communication with others, and largely though the socially provided materials of language. It should be apparent not only why Mead's perspective was seen as a 'social' psychology, but why his ideas have exerted a major influence on sociological thought. Like Durkheim – although from a very different theoretical position – Mead had come to emphasise the process of 'internalisation', the idea that the conventions, values, expectations and beliefs of society were absorbed into the psychological make-up of the individual, constituting a very large part of the 'self'. For Mead, just as for Durkheim, society was prior to the individual.

The process of internalisation takes place through the 'socialisation' of children from the earliest days of infancy. At first, Mead suggests, infant behaviours are primarily biological reactions – such as crying because of hunger – but soon the developing child begins to imitate the behaviour of other people without knowing the meaning of what it does, or having any understanding of it. Nevertheless, this is the preparatory stage for being able to take on the roles of others and act appropriately in relation to their actions. This is followed by the 'play stage' (Mead, 1964: 284–5) in which actual role-playing occurs, as when children 'play at' being mothers and fathers, doctors and nurses, teachers, soldiers and so on; in so doing they are putting themselves in situations where they need to imagine other people and act out their roles appropriately. Through all this the child begins to form a conception of her- or himself as a distinct person, that is, they begin to direct activity towards themselves, even though at this stage the sense of self still lacks coherence. It is at the 'game stage' (ibid.) that the self develops in something like a complete form. In team games, as opposed to individual play, for example, the child must respond to the expectations of several people at the same time, and must imagine the intentions and expectations of several other players in order to work out what to do. Thus the child must develop the ability to take the roles of various others, rather than simply playing at being one of them, which is achieved by abstracting a composite understanding of the others involved. Mead called this the 'generalised other' (Mead, 1962: 154–63), which represents to the individual the perspectives and expectations common to the group, and is a means through which these 'external' points of view become part of the consciousness of the individual.

The sense of the generalised other leads the individual to act in an increasingly consistent and organised manner, and to go beyond particular situations by acting more in accordance with a generalised set of internalised expectations. What the individual thus acquires is the normative framework within which social action takes place, a framework formulated through the socially acquired self. For Mead, the process of acting involves the interaction of two basic aspects of the self, the 'I' and the 'Me'. Any human act (which, in Mead's view, it was the purpose of social science to explain) begins in the form of the 'I', that is, the initial, subjective impulse to do something before it comes under the control of the 'Me', the ongoing conception of one's self as an object, which incorporates the internalised expectations of others and so regulates the impulses of the 'I'. The 'I' is thus the creative aspect, giving acts their energy, while the 'Me' controls and directs this energy to ensure that actions, while oriented towards the achievement of the person's purposes, are formulated in ways which conform to the collective expectations of society, as represented by the 'generalised other'. So, importantly, a person's 'Me' is bound up with the person's conception of the 'generalised other'.

Within the self, then, there is the potential for both innovation (the 'I') and conformity (the 'Me'). It is as if, within the self, there exists a society in miniature. A person can engage in interaction with him/herself just as two separate persons can interact, and in so doing may bring about changes to the self. Moreover, despite Mead's account of the way in which processes of social control are internalised, human individuals are not seen as simply passive, responding to external pressures: we can autonomously initiate, or formulate, divergent courses of action as well as conform to others' expectations. Further, the possibility of conducting a dialogue with one's self means that there can be a realm of 'inner' experiences that need not result in overt expression or action. The social self thus creates the possibility of 'mind'.

In contrast to those individualistic psychological and philosophical approaches which assumed that the human mind or 'spirit' existed prior to social processes, Mead developed a perspective which aimed to show how both the self and the mind emerged as a *consequence* of humans' experience as fundamentally social animals. Of course, as we suggested above, Mead was concerned to emphasise how, unlike other animal species, humans as biological organisms had evolved in ways which gave them capacities of immense significance for the organisation of societies. Certain implications of this were important in the development of symbolic interactionist thought.

Firstly, both the self and the mind develop in the course of *symbolic* communication, and have to be understood not as fixed entities in people's heads – like memory banks or computer programs – but as ongoing, and thoroughly social, processes. The use of symbols is crucial here. Whereas other animals may respond to noises as signals to behave in particular ways, no other species has evolved the capacity for symbolisation which has enabled all human cultures to develop language by attaching of meanings to sounds in ways which are shared and sustained within linguistic communities. The implication of Mead's thought is that without this, it would be impossible for people to have the 'selves' and 'minds' that are generally considered basic aspects of the human condition.

Secondly, whereas humans and other animal species inhabit physical environments in which they are surrounded by things, it is only humans, Mead suggested, who can constitute elements of their environment as 'objects'. By objects he meant anything – physical or abstract, a chair or an idea – which we can designate or refer to. This seems fairly straightforward, but what Mead wished to stress was the key implication that the objects in our environment are not 'given' but, in the process of symbolic communication, are *constituted* in and through this process of designation. Other animals, because they cannot symbolise, may for example see only patches of colour or feel hard and soft things, but the environment of objects within the human 'stream of consciousness' is constituted though our shared cultural knowledge, our purposes at hand, our plans and intentions on a moment-to-moment basis, and so on. For human beings, Mead argues, objects, rather than appearing as elements in a fixed physical environment, are defined and brought into play, so to speak, on the basis of our purposes and plans of action as these emerge, develop, and fade away through time. The nature of objects, and their meanings, are not fixed or inherent in them, but depend on the concerns and commitments of individuals in the context of particular social interactions. A knife, for example, may be a kitchen tool or a murder weapon. Whatever the definition, nevertheless, objects may be said to represent shared, and commonly understandable, patterns of activity although they appear in our experience only in the process of being indicated – implicitly or explicitly – to ourselves and others. This should not, however, be taken as meaning that what we call objects, or other physical entities, do not exist independently of our indications. What is being suggested is simply that 'objects', as the term is being used here, become significant *in our experience* only on the basis of our plans and intentions as these develop over time.

Nor should any of this be taken to imply that individuals are able to define objects or situations in any way they choose, although in principle, or in imagination, they can. For most of the time established social conventions and constraints, represented by the generalised other and operating through the process of the self, ensure that most people in most situations accept the prevailing expectations of their social context.

It has been suggested, however, that in his initial formulation of these ideas Mead did in fact give undue emphasis to factors making for conformity and consensus in social life, to the neglect of innovation, change and deviance. Perhaps this was a reflection of his own background in the small-town America of the nineteenth century. However, as we have suggested even in this brief discussion of Mead's ideas, the basic model of the self and social order which he developed does not necessarily imply a bias towards conformity. Just as in the internal dialogue between the 'I' and the 'Me', the interactions among individuals can and do result in innovation and deviance, rather than conformity to the expectations of the 'generalised other'. We will return to these points as we consider some of the ways in which Mead's thought influenced sociological studies.

The early years of the Chicago School

Between 1850 and 1890 Chicago grew from a small town into the second largest city in the United States. It was the transport hub of access to the West and grew with the spread of railroads to become the business centre of the Midwest region.

From the 1850s onwards, migrants from rural areas of the USA and, increasingly, from Europe flooded into the city, which became home to Germans, Italians, Scandinavians, Poles, Jews, Czechs and, later, Blacks from the American South. Although a rapidly expanding metropolis, as the Chicago sociologists' own work was to show, the city was in effect a constellation of smaller ethnically homogeneous communities, each with its own distinctive way of life, and not a real 'melting pot' in which such cultural differences are dissolved into one homogeneous community, as many had hoped America would become. Chicago's rapid growth and economic change inevitably resulted in social disruption and significant groups of marginalised people, as well as in intensifying conflict between employers and workers, and in addition, from the first decade of the twentieth century, the growing potential for racial conflict (Bulmer, 1984).

Yet Chicago was also a city of learning and high culture. From an early date members of the city's business elite had prided themselves on their support for the arts and learning. This group was overwhelmingly made up of White, Anglo-Saxon, Protestant men (WASPs) who felt that their cultural dominance was coming under increasing threat from the city's new arrivals. More generally, at the beginning of the twentieth century there was considerable anxiety among American political and business leaders that the great influx of peasants, particularly from southern and eastern Europe, and the increasing numbers of industrial wage-workers in the cities might create the conditions for class conflict of the kind threatened by the European labour movements of the period, and for the weakening of American democratic institutions. In this context, the development of universities was seen not only as a way of producing expertise for the solution of social problems but also as a means of training people for positions of leadership in all walks of life.

The University of Chicago was one result of this initiative. Its Department of Sociology was founded in 1892 by Albion Small, and was soon a major force in the development of academic sociology, becoming renowned for its empirical studies of urban life. Both Robert Park and Ernest Burgess were concerned with the problems of social change and upheaval, and with the possibilities for social reform and the establishment of an ordered community. In addition, however, they became interested in the development of sociology as an empirical science. In effect, the Chicago sociologists were confronting in their own city exactly those issues – social change and social order in rapidly industrialising societies – which engaged the major European social theorists in the second half of the nineteenth century, but with a much stronger orientation to empirical research.

The social reform tradition

Although it never displayed the revolutionary fervour of Marxism, nor sought to develop a fundamental critique of American capitalism, the early work of the Chicago sociologists was characterised by strong reformist motivations. Their studies provided evidence for criticisms of racism, of industrial exploitation, of the depressed wages of immigrants and an educational system that mainly benefited the well-to-do. And their teaching was marked by an ethos of public service and a belief in the possibility of social improvement. This was also the era of the 'robber barons' who controlled the huge industrial corporations which dominated American industry, and of what came to be known as 'muck-raking' journalism which sought to expose the corruption and decadence which was hidden behind the respectable façade of economic and political institutions. From the outset, Chicago sociology reflected the idea that the effective scientific analysis of social problems was a necessary prelude to their solution. The two major figures were W. I. Thomas and Robert Park.

Thomas has been described as the major intellectual force in the early years of Chicago sociology, 'seeking to develop theories to explain different forms of social organisation and different kinds of social personality' (Bulmer, 1984: 37). Robert Park had begun his career as a journalist, moving into the academic world in 1913 – with Thomas' encouragement – to develop more solidly based research. For them, what Chicago faced was the classic problem of liberal political theory, namely, social justice; that is, simultaneously preserving social order in the face of potential conflicts while maximising the freedom of individuals. Both doubted that beneficial social change could be brought about solely by legislation. They also doubted that rational reflection would break down the barriers of racial prejudice and ethnic hostilities. Instead, they were committed to the idea that sociological research could make an important contribution to social reform by illuminating the issues as objectively as possible, so facilitating better communication among all social groups.

The early studies

Given their commitment to social reform, it is not surprising that one of the first – and subsequently most influential – studies undertaken by the Chicago sociologists was of the large Polish community in the city. Significantly, W.I. Thomas (1863–1947) and F. Znaniecki's (1882–1958) work on *The Polish Peasant in Europe and America* (1958; first published 1918–20), aimed to depict the community from its members' point of view, and was a landmark in at least the attempt at the integration of theory and empirical data, an immense and striking exemplar of the move away from abstract theorising towards the empirical study of social life. Utilising personal documents – notably letters to and from immigrants in the USA and the archives of a Polish newspaper – the study looked at migration from the point of view of those with experience of it. Polish immigrants largely brought to America the traditional values of rural villagers, only to experience the contrasts between these and the very different culture of the American city. The lack of correspondence between these sets of values led to symptoms of social disorganisation. For example, when family problems arose welfare and charity organisations were poor substitutes for the community and, as a result, many Polish immigrants became demoralised.

The aim of the sociologists was not to make external moral judgements about the activities of those they studied, but instead to seek an understanding of how things were perceived by the people themselves, what mattered to them and what affected their lives. Departures from social norms could be recognised as culturally patterned rather than as instances of individual deviance or law-breaking. To achieve an understanding of what it was like to be a migrant to Chicago from Poland, it was essential to understand how such migrants adapted to the changes in their social circumstances, and how this led them to develop the patterns of behaviour that they maintained, took up or invented. In other words, the migrants' activities, whatever others might think of them, could only be understood in terms of the way that they themselves made sense of their own situation and the challenges they faced in their new environment. It was in this context that Thomas later developed the formulation that was to become famous: 'if men define situations as real, then they are real in their consequences' (Thomas, 1923). In other words, people's actions in situations depend on *their own understanding* of the 'realities' that confront them, irrespective of how others might define the situation, or how the 'objective' facts might appear to the outsider. Thomas' insistence on the importance of understanding people's beliefs if we are to explain their actions, and his concept of the 'definition of the situation', were key elements in symbolic interactionism as a sociological perspective. It will be evident, too, that these ideas are consistent with Mead's more theoretical analysis of the ways in which human beings actively, and collectively, constitute the significant cultural 'objects' which make up their social environment.

In the early days of what came to be known as the 'Chicago School' of sociology, however, the concept of the definition of the situation, and its implications, emerged largely out of the empirical studies instigated by Thomas, Park and their colleagues, rather than from theoretical reflection. The empirical studies which are now regarded as fundamental to the development of the Chicago School were not a planned research programme, but were created through the researchers' practical efforts to work out how sociology could be done in ways which remained close to the experience of those being studied. From the beginning, research students were sent out into the city to discover at first hand the realities of people's lives, and the results of their work were treated as news that should be made available to the widest possible audience. Thus, out of a motivation to solve pressing social problems there arose a distinct research ethic which combined 'sociological curiosity' and a 'sympathetic understanding without moral horror' (Turner and Turner, 1990: 48).

The core of what came to be known as Chicago Sociology in the decade or so following 1918 comprised a series of studies based on fieldwork in the city. They were also written within the general perspective set out in Park's essay, 'The City' (1915) and Burgess' later essay, 'The Growth of the City: An Introduction to a Research Project' (1925). It was this latter paper that provided the framework for modern urban sociology, and which set out an influential 'ecological' theory of 'concentric zones' to describe Chicago as a conurbation. This model highlighted the ways in which the city could be seen as distinctly patterned into residential suburbs, industrial areas, immigrant districts, business and commercial zones, hotel and apartment areas, and so on. Each area was seen as a miniature society with its own traditions and culture, its own particular problems and aspirations. In other words, and contrary to the then received wisdom, large cities were not huge zones of disorganisation but conglomerations of zones of social organisation.

One of the first of the Chicago research reports was a policy-oriented study commissioned by the committee of inquiry into the race riots of July and August, 1919, first published in 1922 as *The Negro in Chicago: A Study of Race Relations and a Race Riot in 1919* (Chicago Commission on Race Relations, 1922; Bulmer, 1981). Other studies on aspects of life in the city followed, which gave the Chicago School its distinctive reputation. Like the earlier *Polish Peasant* study these investigations continued to reflect a basic commitment to achieving an understanding of, and describing, the point of view of the social actors being studied. It was an approach consistent with the philosophy of pragmatism, with its emphasis on the concrete and the particular as opposed to the abstract and universal, and its conceptualisation of human life as rooted in the actual practices of real people.

Actors' definition of the situation

As we have seen, Thomas and Znaniecki used the idea of the 'definition of the situation' as the key to understanding the social actor's point of view. It is an idea about which there are misunderstandings not dissimilar to those surrounding Weber's concept of 'Verstehen'. It has been taken to imply some sort of vague and mystical communion with the minds of the people being studied and, as such, of doubtful scientific value. However, for the Chicago sociologists this approach was specifically intended to overcome another major error in social science research, namely the substitution of the views and concepts of an external observer for the actual ideas and perspectives of those being studied, with the resulting distortion or neglect of the latter. (This aspect of their approach will be discussed more fully in the section on Herbert Blumer below.) From a sociological point of view, moreover, it became clear that – just as Max Weber had argued – any adequate explanation of human action requires an understanding of the 'subjective' factors which motivate it, however strange or irrational these may appear to the outside observer. That is, in contrast to the 'behaviourist' psychology criticised by Dewey and Mead, human conduct was seen as an active process: what people do depends on the ways in which they define and understand the circumstances in which they find themselves. What the Chicago sociologists discovered in the city is true in society more generally: different groups have different cultures, and it is only in terms of such cultures that the actions of real people can be explained.

At first, however, the need to understand the 'point of view of the actor' was treated very much as a piece of good practical advice for researchers, rather than a fundamental theoretical commitment. Nels Anderson, for example, in producing his exemplary study of *The Hobo* (1961; first published in 1923), was instructed simply to write down what he saw, heard and learned while living in the heart of Chicago's 'Hobohemia': that is, the area of the city where the homeless tried to survive. The aim of the study was to understand hobos in the social settings in which they lived, in the context of the larger urban community in which they were located, yet from which they were excluded. A little later, using a variety of methods, Frederick Thrasher began his study of the lives of members of boys' gangs (1927): he collected materials from organisations which had contact with the gangs, such as boys' clubs, the YMCA and juvenile courts, interviews with gang members, official records, and more. However, although there was little formal discussion of research methodology – and the Chicago sociologists were prepared to use almost any methods which enabled them to get close to the lives of those being studied – considerable efforts were made to ensure that data were scrupulously collected, information checked, and interpretations carefully weighed. For example, Shaw's research on *The Jack-Roller* (1966; first published 1930) was a study of 'Stanley', a young male delinquent whose story is told in the first person. Shaw interviewed Stanley extensively, compiling a list of the main events in his life – arrests, court appearances, custodial treatment, and so on – relating his experiences to the circumstances in which he lived: his home, his neighbourhood, the delinquent groups with which he came into contact, his experiences of penal institutions, and so on, which all played a part in shaping his behaviour. But Shaw also went to considerable lengths to verify what Stanley told him, checking his family history, official records, and others with whom Stanley had come into contact. Although this study was of only one person, it proved to be an immensely fruitful source of hypotheses that could be tested in further case histories. In addition, in its own terms it was seen as a demonstration of the importance of social, as well as individual, factors in accounting for delinquency.

The emphasis placed on researchers getting close first-hand experience of the social 'worlds' they were studying also raised the question of their own role: should the field-workers disclose that they were doing research, or should they remain concealed? Most of the Chicago sociologists, it seems, adopted the role of covert observer. Cressey, for example, in his study of *The Taxi Dance Hall* (1932), adopted the role of a regular patron of the 'taxi' dance halls, in which men paid young women to dance with them, mixing with the other patrons on a basis of equality but concealment. Although the ethics of such research methods continue to be debated, it was by such means that the Chicago sociologists aimed to secure first-hand knowledge, and the sort of experience that only regular participants could gain, aware that disclosing their status as researchers could significantly distort the data they obtained.

At this point it may be useful to point out two implications of the view of human action which gradually emerged from the early Chicago studies, since both were important in the more general development of interactionist thought in sociology. Firstly, as suggested above, the beliefs and ideas which motivate human conduct are not the properties of isolated individuals, so to speak, but are derived by them from the *shared* and *collective* understandings which constitute group cultures. It follows that an interactionist understanding of social order – contrary to many misunderstandings – is *not* primarily concerned with the unique or 'subjective' aspects of individuals' consciousness. As Mead's ideas suggest, it is concerned with the ways in which people fit their lines of conduct together to create orderly patterns of organisation, and a sense of social order.

Secondly, the empirical studies of real social situations, and the circumstances which people had to deal with, often suggested links between the nature of group cultures – their 'content', so to speak – and the particular problems or difficulties which the groups faced. Culture itself, then, could be seen not as a random assortment of beliefs and values, but as an emergent, collective response to the problems faced by specific groups of people.

Herbert Blumer: the formulation of symbolic interactionism

We have suggested that while the distinctive approach which has come to be regarded as characteristic of Chicago School sociology emerged gradually out of the series of studies carried out in the city, the perspective itself was in many respects consistent with G.H. Mead's philosophical view of the nature of human action. More than anyone else, however, it was Herbert Blumer who fashioned the two developing sets of ideas into a coherent sociological perspective. Blumer had studied with Mead at Chicago, and indeed took over Mead's lecture course after his death in 1931. Within six years, Blumer had used the term 'symbolic interactionism' in a published essay (Blumer, 1971: 1) and as time went by he became the leading advocate for the approach as it developed, particularly in the 1950s with the growing dominance of structural-functionalism in American sociology. By this time, the interactionist perspective was attracting some support from the minority of sociologists who dissented from the structural-functionalist orthodoxy, and it was largely through his criticisms – both theoretical and methodological – of this dominant school of thought that Blumer laid out with great clarity the alternative approach offered by symbolic interactionism.

Inevitably, Blumer drew heavily on Mead's intellectual legacy, and in a series of most influential papers he set out what he saw as the 'sociological implications' (Blumer, 1966; 1971: 61ff.) of Mead's thought. His point of departure was Mead's demonstration that 'human group life was the essential condition for the emergence of consciousness, the mind, a world of objects, human beings possessing selves, and human conduct in the form of constructed acts' (ibid.). Further, Mead had shown that humans' ability to 'take the role of the other', and their reflexive capacity to treat themselves as 'others', meant that humans' conduct could not be explained simply as a series of 'responses' to forces acting on them either from outside (as in the case of 'social forces') or inside (as in the case of psychological 'conditioning' or biological 'drives'). On the contrary, what is essential and distinctive about human beings is that:

> the process of self-interaction puts the human being over against his [*sic*] world instead of merely in it, requires him to meet and handle his world through a defining process instead of merely responding to it, and forces him to construct his action instead of merely releasing it. This is the kind of acting organism that Mead sees man to be as a result of having a self. (ibid.: 63–4)

Human beings, in other words, are not creatures whose patterns of conduct have been laid out in advance, whether by instinct or social training; instead these patterns are actively created through the process of working out what to do now and next, as we go along, adjusting what we do as circumstances unfold. We decide what to do by taking account of different things, indicating them to ourselves and to others, interpreting them and assessing their significance for our prospective action. It is ideas like these which develop earlier notions such as Thomas' concept of the 'definition of the situation', so that group or collective action may be understood as the fitting together of many individual lines of action. What is involved is the constant process through which individuals align what they do in relation to the actions of others, ascertaining as they go along what it is that others are doing or intend to do. All social groups, all societies, in the end consist of very complex patterns of interactions among individuals.

Such considerations led Blumer to present symbolic interactionism as resting fundamentally on three related premises. The first is that 'human beings act towards things on the basis of the meanings that the things have for them' (ibid.: 2). For all its apparent simplicity, says Blumer, the implications of this idea have been generally neglected by most schools of thought in both sociology (as when human action is 'explained' in terms of social pressures or forces bearing on the individual, status demands, cultural prescriptions or values, and so on), and in psychology (as when behaviour is 'explained' in terms of stimuli, attitudes, motives, etc). What such attempts at explanation neglect, Blumer argues, is precisely the essential characteristic of human social life, that is, the active process of interpretation and definition in and through which our meaningful world of experience is constituted. In fact, this crucial process is simply bypassed in all attempts at explaining action which treat prior conditions as 'causes' and actual behaviour as 'effects'.

The second of Blumer's premises is that things derive their meaning, and arise out of, social interaction. This idea is of fundamental sociological importance, and clearly differentiates symbolic interactionism from any individualistic approach to understanding social life. Conventional theories of meaning, says Blumer, tend to rest on one or other of two basic assumptions: either that meaning is inherent in things (so that through our senses we are made aware of their real nature or essence), or that as human beings we impose schemes of meaning on the things we confront in our environment (as a result of our basic mental capacities as thinking beings). The position of symbolic interactionism rejects both of these. Meaning is neither intrinsic to objects, nor is it a consequence of our psychological make-up as individuals – if either assumption were true, then all humans would experience things the same way, all the time. Rather, says Blumer, meaning arises 'in the process of interaction between people. . . . Thus, symbolic interactionism sees meanings, as social products, as creations that are formed in and through the defining activities of people as they interact' (ibid.: 4–5). In other words, the social world which we experience is *constituted* in and through the continuous process of definition and interpretation in which we engage with others. In emphasising the collective and collaborative aspects of this process, Blumer drew out the fundamentally sociological implications of Mead's thought.

This approach to understanding the nature of meaning has much in common with the perspective that later came to be called 'the social construction of reality' (Berger and Luckmann, 1966: 66) and we will consider this further below. At present, however, we simply wish to underline as we did earlier – because there have been many misunderstandings of this point – that in arguing for the notion of meanings as 'social products' arising out of 'the defining activities of people as they interact', Blumer is definitely *not* suggesting that as individuals we are free to define things however we want, or to interpret situations just as we please. On the contrary, it will be recalled that Mead was particularly concerned to show how members of human communities come to 'internalise' the basic ideas and beliefs of their cultures (as the 'generalised other'), and to experience them as part of their own 'selves', even though they are, as elements of a shared culture, ultimately social in origin. What is of interest to the sociologist, therefore, is not the unique subjectivity of individuals, but the *intersubjective* social world. The example of language may serve to make the point.

As humans, we have the capacity to make all sorts of sounds, but only a very few of these are organised into the significant symbols, or 'words' of a language. In order to participate normally in society, we must use words in socially approved ways (even though we could in principle create different sounds, or invent new words). In this way, interactionists have argued that our words (and thoughts) are shaped and constrained by the social practices of language use even though we may feel that 'speaking' in our language is both natural and spontaneous. To repeat, a focus on the processes of definition and interpretation which are held to be fundamental to human life, does *not* mean that the interactionist perspective neglects the 'massive facticity' of the social order which is 'a reality that confronts the individual as an external and coercive fact' (Berger and Luckmann, 1966: 76).

Blumer's third premise is that 'meanings are handled in, and modified through, an interpretive process used by the person in dealing with the things he encounters' (Blumer, 1971: 2). Following Mead, Blumer points to two phases of this process: firstly, actors must define, or indicate to themselves, the 'objects' with which they are dealing, and secondly they must interpret the meaning of these objects in the context of their social situation as it develops – that is, they must assess their significance in relation to possible courses of action. We have already considered this view of the nature of human action in the course of outlining Mead's ideas. Here we should simply note that this focus on the collaborative process of definition and interpretation is at the core of the symbolic interactionist perspective: from this point of view, human beings are essentially creatures who have to live in a cultural as well as a natural environment, and whose cultures are generated and sustained through the use of symbols in the collective process of meaning-creation.

On the basis of these three premises, Blumer developed a systematic outline of symbolic interactionism as a distinct perspective in sociology (see Blumer, 1971: 6ff., 78–89). As we have suggested, he did so in conscious opposition to the dominant trends in American sociology during the two decades following the Second World War, and it may be useful to outline the ways in which Blumer's approach contrasted with the structural-functionalism of that era, both in terms of its theoretical assumptions, and its methodological procedures.

Theoretical assumptions

As Blumer himself noted, most sociologists of his day neglected the study of 'acting units', instead treating society as made up of 'structure or organisation', and regarding social action as an outcome, or 'expression' of these (Blumer, 1971: 87). In other words, the observable parts of society – human beings and their actions – were explained in terms of properties of the whole – the social 'system' or 'structure'. From an interactionist point of view, the development of sociological theory required that the direction of this explanation be reversed: that is, that 'society' as a whole, and 'social structures' be understood as the *outcome* of the activities of people in interaction.

It should be said straight away that the intention is not to deny the existence of social structure or patterns of organisation in social life, in the sense of ordered and stable sets of social relationships which confront and constrain individuals as the realities of the social worlds in which they live. To deny these, as Blumer himself said, would be absurd. What the interactionist perspective rejects, however, is the treatment of such macro-sociological phenomena as formal organisations, institutions, social classes, corporations, and indeed whole societies, as if they were entities which existed apart from actual human beings, and operated in ways which are separate from their activities. Nor do they exist at a supra-individual level of social reality that controls people's actions. Rather, for the interactionist such collectivities must be understood as abstractions; that is, as concepts which allow us to think about important and extensive complexes of social relationships. Such complexes are in the end built up of many – perhaps thousands – of relationships between acting individuals, fitting their activities together in stable and regular ways which result in the stable and orderly patterns that are the foundation for social life.

To illustrate what is meant here, consider the nature of such collective entities as an army, or a church, or the family. None of these exists as a separate entity, that is, apart from the complex of activities and relationships which people engage in, yet each of these concepts is symbolically important, indeed essential, for us to make sense of significant areas of social activity. Armies are comprised of thousands of individuals, with different ranks and responsibilities, whose collective effectiveness depends precisely on their ability to fit their lines of action together. Similarly, churches may unite millions of 'believers' in a single faith, yet this does not mean that the existence of the whole does not depend on the collective action of all the individual members, or, for example, that there cannot be disputes between different factions over the interpretation of sacred texts. The family, too, is generally regarded as a fundamental institution in societies, yet it is apparent that its perpetuation depends on the activities and interactions of individuals, as they decide to marry, have children, and so on.

These examples should also serve to illustrate the point that this interactionist view of social order denies neither the extent of regularly patterned activity in society ('social structure'), nor the differences in power and resources among individuals and groups. An army general or a church bishop evidently has more power than a private soldier or a church member. What the interactionist would be concerned with are such questions as how such power differentials can arise, how they are sustained, how they may be challenged, and so on. As in most sociological perspectives, interactionist analysis seeks to illuminate the processes through which such routine, normally organised, aspects of social life are maintained in the endless succession of everyday encounters between people, and how established patterns of activity – including significant differences in power and resources – are symbolically legitimised (Prus, 1999).

Moreover, the interactionist focus on the collective activity of individuals as they pursue their everyday projects forces recognition of another vital aspect of human social life which is often taken for granted in conventional sociological analysis – the way in which all activities, no matter how routine or simple, must be *enacted* by real people. Social action, that is, cannot be explained as a result of the 'demands' of social roles or situations, which are held to 'produce' appropriate behavioural responses. It is true that many routine encounters, such as saying good morning or buying bread, may seem to involve no effort, and simply to be part of 'what we do' as normal members of society. But other activities, for example giving a speech or dealing with angry customers, may be experienced not only as highly stressful but as requiring specific planning and effort. The interactionists' point is that *all* activities, whether routine or extraordinary, require to be enacted, that is actually performed by real people in everyday situations.

From a theoretical point of view, then, the concept of social structure is understood by symbolic interactionists in a way which differs significantly from that of 'macro' sociological approaches, including the structural-functionalism which was often Blumer's target. For the interactionists social structures are not entities existing prior to individuals' actions, but are the outcome of them, and indeed are enacted through them. In Blumer's words (1971: 87–8):

> structural features, such as 'culture', 'social systems', 'social stratification', or 'social roles', set conditions for [individuals'] actions but do not determine their action. People – that is, acting units – do not act toward culture, social structure or the like; they act towards social situations. Social organisation enters into action only to the extent to which it shapes situations in which people act, and to the extent to which it supplies fixed sets of symbols which people use in interpreting their situations.

It is not surprising, therefore, that Blumer's basic objection to the sort of sociological theory which had come to dominate American sociology in the 1950s was that it had become divorced from the empirical world which it was supposed to explain. Theory, he complained, was being used to order the world, rather than the other way round, and was increasingly remote from what he took to be 'the empirical world of our discipline', that is, 'the natural social world of everyday experience' (Blumer, 1971: 148).

Methodological procedures

So the objections which Blumer and the interactionists had to the dominant 'macro' sociological thinking of the 1950s arose not so much from the scale of the social phenomena being considered, as from their claim that such 'macro' theorising fundamentally misconstrued and misrepresented the real nature of the empirical social world. A similar point may be made about the research methods which were being developed in the same period, often quite explicitly in an effort to make sociology an objective discipline on the model of the natural sciences. This effort involved the introduction, wherever possible, of quantification: the attempt to make social research 'scientific' by the precise measurement of social phenomena, and the analysis of data by ever more sophisticated statistical methods. As we indicated in Chapter 2, one of the leading figures in this movement was Paul Lazarsfeld (a colleague of Robert Merton at Columbia University, New York), and it was the vision of sociological research methodology held by Lazarsfeld and his school which Blumer chose to attack when, in September of 1956, he gave the Presidential Address at the annual meeting of the American Sociological Society (Blumer, 1956).

Blumer characterised the increasingly dominant approach to research taken by sociologists such as Lazarsfeld as 'variable analysis'. What this means is that theoretical concepts were translated into 'variables', that is, measurable properties of phenomena which can take different values, just as 'length' or 'weight' are measurable, as variables, properties of particular physical phenomena. Typical sociological 'variables' would be such things as social class position or years in formal education – properties which could be assigned to individuals, and given quite precise numerical values. Another variable, often used as an example, would be 'prejudice', with individuals ranked according to how 'prejudiced' they were on the basis of their responses to psychological tests or attitude surveys.

The logic of 'variable analysis' on the basis of these procedures now becomes apparent. First of all a theoretical idea, say for example one which suggests a link between race prejudice and education, is reformulated so as to produce a 'testable' hypothesis: in this case, perhaps that 'levels of prejudice are inversely related to levels of education'. (The more education you have, the less prejudiced you are, and vice versa.) This hypothesis implies an identifiable link between the variables – education somehow has an effect on prejudice – so the variables can be ordered accordingly: in this case, 'education' becomes the 'independent' variable (since it is held to produce the effect under investigation), and 'prejudice' the 'dependent' variable (since its value depends on individuals' amount of education). On this basis, the researcher is now able to 'test' the hypothesis by collecting data on individuals' levels of education and prejudice, and to discover whether there is a positive (or in this case negative) correlation between the variables. The outcome will be evidence which is either consistent with the original theory, or is not; in the latter case, the theory will have to be altered or rejected. (It should be noted that a correlation between two variables is not proof of a causal connection between them, only that there is a certain strength of association between them.)

It was this research procedure to which Blumer objected. Firstly, he argued that, unlike the situation in the natural sciences, sociologists seemed able to select virtually anything, no matter how vague, as a 'variable'. Ensuring that the 'variables' used in an analysis were actually relevant to the social processes being investigated would require 'intensive and extensive familiarity with the empirical area' in question (Blumer, 1971: 128). Typically, researchers using 'variable analysis' did not obtain this familiarity. Secondly, Blumer suggested that sociological analysis of this kind had failed to generate effective 'generic variables', that is, variables which could be used across a whole range of studies, and over time, to describe general, abstract properties of human group life. The sort of thing Blumer has in mind here, for example, is the concept of 'social cohesion' in a group or society – an idea which has played an important part in many studies (such as Durkheim's work on suicide, or Merton's explanation of deviance). Blumer's complaint is that various researchers have come up with different definitions of social cohesion, or integration, or something similar, have used different indicators of the concepts, and different ways of measuring them. As a result, these apparently 'generic' concepts, in practice, only relate to a variety of limited, local, and time-bound situations, rather than being universally applicable. This is quite different from the use of properly generic variables in the natural sciences, like the concept of 'weight', which can be applied to the whole range of relevant phenomena.

Moreover, the actual social significance of even such apparently generic variables as 'sex' or 'age' is not independent of specific social contexts; what it means to be 'female' or 'aged 18' is not constant across all societies or historical periods – on the contrary, the implications of such 'facts' about individuals depend on the cultural conventions of particular times and places. Once again, we can see Blumer's insistence that in order to produce valid sociological knowledge the researcher needs a detailed understanding of specific social contexts, of their cultures, and of the 'actor's point of view' within them. Blumer recognises the argument of those who support the methodology of 'variable analysis' that the approach is still in its infancy, and that through time more robust generic variables will be developed. But he rejects this view. It is not just a matter of time, or the accumulation of a sufficient number of studies. As is suggested by the previous point about the way in which social 'facts' are inevitably embedded in cultural contexts, Blumer's point is that the development of generic variables which will objectively describe the properties of human societies is impossible.

Finally, and arising from the points above, Blumer argues that since 'variable analysis' only results in findings which are applicable to particular, or 'here and now' situations, sociological understanding of their significance depends on detailed knowledge of their 'here and now' contexts. This, however, is what 'variable analysis' fails to provide: 'The variable relation is a single relation, necessarily stripped bare of the complex of things that sustain it in a 'here and now' context' (ibid.: 131). As we have seen, this sort of analysis neglects the ideas, beliefs and conventions of real people in real situations, but more than this – and of crucial importance for Blumer – what it also completely misses is the 'vast interpretative process by which people, singly and collectively, guide themselves by defining the objects, events and situations which they encounter' (ibid.: 132).

What 'variable analysis' provides is, in effect, exactly the sort of 'cause and effect' view of social life that the interactionist tradition has consistently rejected: 'independent variables' are seen as prior to actual behaviour, producing it in ways which can be described in terms of 'dependent variables'. What is actually central to human social life, the process of definition and interpretation which intervenes, is, says Blumer, 'ignored or . . . taken for granted as something that need not be considered' (ibid.: 133). What is more, the construction of relevant 'variables' is undertaken by the social analyst, not those whose lives are being studied, and the process of data collection is typically undertaken through questionnaires and interviews which, in themselves, are divorced from the real-life, situated activities of those being studied.

Overall, then, Blumer's challenge to 'variable analysis' amounts to much more than technical criticism of a particular methodology. Indeed, it would not be an exaggeration to say that what is at stake here is the nature of sociology as a scientific discipline. In Blumer's view, the introduction of quantitative methods, and hypothesis-testing by means of 'variable analysis' does not result in the establishment of objective, scientific procedures in social research. On the contrary, to those who have criticised the findings of interactionist ethnographic studies as small-scale and localised, Blumer responds that that is exactly what 'variable analysis' produces. To those who have argued that understanding 'the point of view of the actor' commits the sociologist to a 'subjective' perspective, Blumer's answer is that the application of 'variable analysis' simply results in the imposition on social life of a set of meanings and relevances which may have little or no relation to those of the actual people being studied. The 'point of view of the actor' is simply ignored or erased, to be replaced by the more or less arbitrary imposition of the analyst's 'point of view'. And this, for Blumer, is not objective science at all, but 'the worst form of subjectivism'.

Everett Hughes and the study of work

What emerged from Blumer's work was both an explicit theoretical commitment, to focus on social life as an interpretive process, and a methodological strategy, 'participant observation' in real social settings, in order to gain first-hand understanding of this process. Taken together, these contributed greatly to the formulation of symbolic interactionism as a distinct intellectual perspective within sociology, and its institutionalisation as a branch of the profession – albeit a minority one in the context of American sociology from the 1940s to the late 1960s. In retrospect, it is Blumer's writings on the theoretical and methodological implications of the interactionist approach which have established him as a major figure in the field. His own early empirical work – on such topics as the cinema, fashion, labour relations, and collective behaviour more generally – is now mostly forgotten, but it would be wrong to give the impression that the tradition of interactionist empirical studies, established in Chicago, was dormant during the period in question. On the contrary, the studies of Everett Hughes (1895–1982), with his associates and students, represents just the sort of work that Blumer was advocating, namely, emphasising the careful, naturalistic, and detailed examination of particular social settings, generally through fieldwork and participant observation. Much of Hughes' work displays a concern with aspects of occupational life, but this was not simply a personal preference on his part. Hughes recognised the centrality of work in contemporary societies, not just in the economic sense of giving people incomes, but from a more sociological point of view as providing individuals with their position in the social order. Moreover, Hughes developed a line of research which was to have considerable importance in later interactionist studies, examining the ways in which people's identities and sense of self were shaped by the kind of work they did, its status in the community, and their experiences of doing it.

Hughes recognised, too, that work organisations were both characteristic of, and pervasive in, modern societies. In studying them, we can learn much about how such institutions operate, and indeed about the patterns of organisation of society as a whole. Like Blumer, Hughes did not regard society or work organisations as large-scale entities with a life of their own; they were to be understood, rather, as complex outcomes of the collaborative activities of individuals, constantly being re-enacted, so to speak, and so also constantly changing. With a sociological vision not unlike that of Max Weber, Hughes saw patterns of social life as the dynamic results of a perpetual struggle for advantage among individuals and groups, with occupational groups of particular importance in modern societies. From this perspective, the most successful and powerful occupational groups were the professions, which had secured the right to control entry to their occupations, to license practitioners, to set standards and impose discipline, and in many ways to control their members' incomes. At the time of Hughes' work, the 'classic' professions – medicine, the law and the church – tended to be treated very respectfully by sociologists, in much the same way that their members expected to be treated by the general public.

Hughes and his students took a different, and much more sceptical, view. For them, those occupations which were fully professionalised were really the winners in a competitive struggle for power, prestige and material rewards among occupational groups. There was no essential difference between them and the work that they did, or their personal integrity, that could justify the privileged treatment they received or explain why other groups were not accorded such rewards and prestige. From this point of view, the job of the sociologist was to examine such professionals and their work in as disinterested a way as possible, thus revealing the essential similarities between 'professional' and other work activities, rather than accepting their distinctiveness at face value.

The basis of the professions' success was that they had managed – through effective use of regulations, exclusionary tactics, and symbolic legitimation of themselves – to acquire a 'licence' and a 'mandate' to carry out their 'professional' duties, and to represent themselves to the state and the public at large as 'higher' sorts of occupations. In reality however, members of professions may use their positions to further their own material or career interests rather than provide a 'service' to the public, yet because of their privileged positions, remain immune from the sort of scrutiny that members of other occupations have to accept. Hughes' approach may be regarded as a sociological development of George Bernard Shaw's famous remark that all professions are 'conspiracies against the laity'.

Later studies in this field pursued the theme of 'professionalisation' by examining the ways in which the established professions acquired and maintained their privileges and, more generally, the process through which a whole range of occupational groups, such as teachers, psychologists or accountants, attempted with varying degrees of success to achieve recognition as professions and the legal status that goes with this. Just as individuals can be upwardly or downwardly mobile within the occupational hierarchy, so too whole occupational groups can be seen to 'move' in this sense; the professionalisation of an occupation achieves this collective mobility by securing the right to the independent control of the occupation, the right to determine what the proper work of the profession is and to define what the public interest in their work might be (Hughes, 1981; first published in 1958).

Typically, members of the established professions, as a result of both their training and their occupational experiences, conceived of themselves as worthy, 'superior' sorts of people, a reflection of the hierarchy of occupational power and prestige recognised in the wider society. The occupational experience of individuals, that is, could be seen to shape their characters, giving them a distinct sense of identity, and in examining this theme Hughes initiated a tradition of interactionist research which expanded the concept of 'socialisation' so as to include, not only childhood learning, but the ways in which differential patterns of experience throughout individuals' lives could be seen to have significant effects on the kinds of people they became. Once again, the distinctively sociological emphasis of the interactionists' analysis is evident: the characters or personalities of individuals are not seen as fixed, or explainable in terms of psychological factors alone, but are understood as significantly influenced by the nature of their social experiences over time. As we shall see later, becoming a 'doctor', for example, not only involves learning a set of technical skills, but also involves becoming a certain sort of person, one who is able at the very least to carry out the public role of a doctor in the expected fashion. Of great significance for the interactionists, moreover, was the tendency for members of occupational groups, as a result of their training and experience, to acquire certain similar characteristics – that is, to 'identify' themselves with the occupation and to acquire distinct 'perspectives', or ways of understanding their work, their clients, and the world more generally. The studies undertaken by Hughes and his students thus stimulated an important research tradition which examined 'occupational ideologies', or the sets of ideas and beliefs which members of an occupational group typically came to share, and the effects of these on their work activities.

The studies of occupational groups thus illuminated the processes thorough which participation in work of various kinds contributed to the formation of individuals' identities and sense of self-esteem. For members of the established professions, these tended to be positive, giving individual members a sense of their own worth and dignity as people at the higher levels of the occupational hierarchy, and imbuing them with self-confidence. On the other hand, it was equally clear that the same sort of processes could produce very different sorts of outcome for people at the bottom end of the jobs market, who had to deal with economic insecurity, lack of autonomy, and the real possibility of humiliation in the course of their work.

One of the central themes of Chicago sociology in its earliest phase was the concern to achieve a sympathetic understanding of the point of view of those who were marginalised or excluded from mainstream society, and this concern to illuminate the social situation of the 'underdog' is similarly evident in Hughes' occupational research. His study of the work of the janitor in an apartment building is a useful example. Janitors are in a comparatively lowly occupational position, and are frank about the physically dirty nature of much of their work, which among other things involves dealing with the garbage produced by the buildings' tenants. However, this is not just a matter of the janitor and the garbage, but also involves the tenants who produce the garbage and who therefore impinge on the janitor's own 'dignified ordering of his life and work'. In the course of his job, and often through dealing with the garbage, the janitor gets to know details of the tenants' personal lives, their private habits, financial problems, love affairs and so on. This sort of knowledge gives the janitor the 'makings of a kind of magical power' over the tenant (Hughes, 1981: 51). This, however, is not integrated into any deeply satisfying redefinition of his role that might dissipate his antagonism to the people whose dirty work he does; on the contrary, on the basis of their knowledge of what goes on 'behind the scenes' in areas of people's lives that they would prefer to remain private, janitors (just like Hughes and his sociological colleagues) may come to have serious doubts about the claims of members of high-status occupations to moral and cultural superiority. Thus, one of the elements of the occupational ideology characteristic of janitors and many other members of low-status occupations whose work involves dealing with people in higher-status jobs is that the latter are not different or superior people at all. Indeed they may be perceived as hypocritical, giving impressions about themselves that do not withstand scrutiny, in contrast to straightforward, honest working people who do not make false claims about themselves.

As studies in hospitals showed, one of the sources of antagonism towards high-status professionals was the way in which others, usually in low-status, poorly paid jobs, were routinely called upon to do the 'dirty work' – cleaning, washing sheets, preparing food, etc. – in the cause of 'healing the sick' even though none of the prestige and monetary reward that derive from this service is given to them. The point may serve to illustrate another element of the occupational ideology characteristic of people in low-status positions, namely, a 'functional' view of the social order which emphasises the important, indeed essential, nature of 'dirty work', or of jobs which are tedious, demeaning, unpleasant or dangerous. Without these and the sacrifices made by people who perform such tasks, it is held, those in high-status occupations could not preserve their lifestyles, nor could the social order be sustained. Once again, the concern of the sociologists was to examine the ways in which people 'make sense' of their world, and come to terms with its harsh realities, in this case developing elements of an ideology which represent their own activities in a positive way, and legitimising their work by stressing its contribution to the overall functioning of society. As Hughes put it (1981: 48):

> Our aim is to penetrate more deeply into the personal and social drama of work, to understand the social and social-psychological arrangements and devices by which men make their work tolerable, and even glorious to themselves and others.

In the next section on deviance we shall consider further aspects of this process in which members of a marginalised social group may come to develop an ideology which serves to support their own position and activities. Before leaving Hughes' work, however, we should pause to consider his distinctive use of the concept of 'career', a notion central to his own thinking about the ways in which individuals' occupations are fundamental to their position in society, and which was to be extensively developed in later interactionist studies. Initially, it is clear that Hughes' interest in careers reflects the way the term is conventionally used, to indicate some kind of progression in an occupation, as when someone who starts out as a law student at the 'bottom' of the profession eventually becomes a judge at the 'top', or when we hear of people who began 'on the factory floor' and worked their way 'up' to a position in the boardroom. Such movement involves a passage over time through a conventionally designated series of stages and occupational statuses. Many sociologists have examined such patterns of 'social mobility' in industrial societies, but for Hughes the concept of career did not imply a static picture of the social world (such as 'social stratification' or the 'class structure'), but instead directed attention to the fluidity and dynamism of social life. In this, his thinking reflected the central interactionist emphasis on conceiving the social order as a *process*. Moreover, in Hughes' work the application of the concept of career was widened, to include not only recognised professions or occupations, but also informal patterns of social transition. Thus, for example, it may be said that there are typical criminal careers, as when someone begins as a petty thief, or 'enforcing' a small-time protection racket, and ends up organising armed robberies. Similarly, it was recognised that there can be identifiable career patterns in a whole range of social contexts, including those which represent the informal, often socially marginal aspects of urban industrial society – careers in begging or prostitution, for example, or in drug use or gambling. In the next section we will consider some of the ways in which this perspective was put to use in the study of deviance. For the moment, though, the essential point is that from a sociological point of view, all such careers, whether of captains of industry or drugs barons, involve the movement of individuals through a socially recognised hierarchy of status positions.

Given Hughes' concern with the ways in which occupational careers can shape individuals' identities, it is not surprising that he was also concerned to investigate the 'subjective' aspect of career movements, in the sense of individuals' experiences of them. Indeed, Hughes defined career as the 'moving perspective' through which people assess and evaluate their own social position and progress. This theme led to a further expansion of the use of the concept of career in sociological analysis, involving recognition of the ways in which people's own conception of themselves and others may be transformed by their experiences of passing through a recognisable sequence of 'status passages' (Glaser and Strauss, 1971). There have been interactionist studies of, for example, the processes of *becoming* a nurse, or a drug user, or of coming to define oneself as homosexual (Reiss, 1964), which have focused on the transformation of individuals' sense of their own identity. Similarly, researchers in this tradition have examined patterns of self-transformation in childhood, ageing, illness and dying which are not biologically determined, but shaped by the social contexts in which they occur. Goffman's study of the 'moral career of the mental patient' (Goffman, 1961a), which will be considered below, is perhaps the best-known, and certainly most influential, of these studies. Of considerable significance, too, are those studies which demonstrate ways in which a person's 'moral career' may develop even though their 'objective' occupational position does not. Faulkner, for example, has shown how orchestral musicians, full of enthusiasm and ambition when they first achieve a position in a major orchestra, can become disillusioned and frustrated as time passes and they realise that the position they worked so hard to achieve is not the beginning of a fulfilling career in music, but its end (Faulkner, 1971).

In developing studies of occupational life in ways consistent with the Chicago tradition of empirical research and with Blumer's more theoretical perspective, Hughes made a major contribution to the development of the interactionist perspective in sociology. The aim of these studies was to illuminate the wider patterns of social relationships which were fundamental to modern societies. Through his investigation of such topics as professionalisation, ideologies, identities and careers, in the context of the constant struggle for advantage which centres around occupational life, Hughes established generic research themes which were to play a significant part in the work of the next generation of interactionists. These themes formed the basis of many key studies in the fields of work organisations, health and illness and educational processes, among others, but were particularly influential in transforming sociological approaches to the study of crime and deviance.

Deviance

The contrast between Parsons' structural-functional perspective, and that of the interactionists, is very clear when their different approaches to the topic of deviance in society are considered. For Parsons, 'social control' was a functional mechanism that prevented disruptive individuals from doing too much damage to the 'social system'. For the interactionists, this was far too abstract a way to approach the matter, since it involved the reification of both the 'social system' and the 'mechanisms' of social control; that is, treating them as if they were acting entities in their own right. Social control, from an interactionist perspective, is not an abstract process operating independently of real people, but involves their collective activities, as they seek, for example, to pursue their interests by controlling the activities of others, or to gain control of their own situation (as is the case in attempts to 'professionalise' occupations). In this section, we will be concerned with the implications of this perspective for the sociological study of deviance.

In much of the early history of the social sciences, the study of what is now called deviance was restricted to instances of 'criminal' behaviour rather than non-conformity more generally, and as criminology it tended to focus on the perpetrators of crime and the 'causes' of their misdeeds, usually from a psychological point of view. A genuinely sociological approach, however, began to emerge with Durkheim's bold – and at the time shocking – claim that a certain level of crime was 'normal' in any society; in other words, that crime and other apparently anti-social activities were the result of the routine working of societal processes. Following Durkheim's lead, Robert Merton (1957) developed a highly influential structural-functionalist model of deviance, suggesting that in American society deviant or 'innovative' activities are likely to be undertaken by those whose access to the legitimate routes to material success is systematically restricted. The implication is that those, for example, whose educational achievements are low, or who are the victims of racial and ethnic discrimination, will be more likely to resort to illegitimate means in order to realise the 'American dream'. Rates of crime and deviance, then, are viewed as the consequence of structural properties of the society as a whole – institutionalised patterns such as social class differences in educational attainment, or racial discrimination.

Interactionists accepted – indeed developed – the sociological idea that crime and deviance were the normal products of the social process, but firmly rejected the notion that their causes were to be found in the structural properties of 'social systems'. In response to Merton, Edwin Lemert argued that American society was not integrated into a single value-system, but rather comprised a plurality of heterogeneous cultural groups, all competing for material and symbolic rewards, though some had greater resources than others. Thus the laws enacted by the state did not represent the abstract 'core' values of the society as a whole, but were in fact the result of political bargaining between interested groups. As Lemert put it, where incompatible values are involved, 'laws and rules represent no group's values nor values of any portion of a society. Instead they are artefacts of compromise between the values of mutually opposed, but very strongly organised, associations' (1967: 57). It followed that activities considered normal and acceptable by some groups would be condemned as wrong by others, and as a routine outcome of the political process would from time to time be 'criminalized' through being defined as illegal. The various economic, religious, cultural, ethnic, racial and regional interest groups which coexisted in America sought to establish their conception of what was right and proper, and sometimes they succeeded in having their views transformed into laws.

The most celebrated example of this sort of process of criminalisation was the enactment of Prohibition in the United States between 1920 and 1933. It was not the 'social system' or its 'structural' features that brought about the prohibition of the sale and consumption of alcohol, but the activities of specific middle class and religious pressure groups who for years had tried to have alcohol banned, and the inevitable negotiations inherent in state and national politics (Gusfield, 1986, 1996). From an interactionist perspective, making the consumption of alcohol illegal in the USA was not understood as a 'societal' response to a 'problem' of social control, nor, as Durkheim might have argued, due to legislation which expressed the 'core' values of the society. Rather, Prohibition was seen as the outcome of the activities of a specific coalition of pressure groups who for many years had been campaigning against alcohol consumption (Behr, 1997), and who were able to exploit the particular political situation at that time so as to have their demands made law.

The case of Prohibition illustrates the way in which the making of laws was seen by the interactionists as essentially a political process involving conflict and negotiation, and also the way in which specific laws could be said to represent the interests, not of the 'whole' society – or even a majority of its members – but of particular groups within it who were able to manipulate the levers of political power to their own ends. Prohibition, in other words, was the outcome of a 'moral crusade'.

Clearly, this interactionist analysis of deviant activities focuses on the 'real-life' activities of actual people, and has no need of an overarching conception of the 'whole' society as some sort of entity existing apart from them, or of large-scale social processes operating independently of them. Indeed, the idea of 'society' which emerges is not that of a more or less coherent entity (such as is implied by the analogy with a biological organism), but of a vast arena in which individuals and groups pursue their interests according to their 'definitions of the situation', and the resources which are available to them. The 'social structure' is reconceptualised as the pattern of institutionalised practices – including the constraints of the law – which emerges from this general process. In the present context, it is also important to emphasise the way in which the analysis has shifted away from a concern with the characteristics of criminals or the evil qualities of their acts, and moved firmly towards a focus on the more general social process through which laws and rules are established. Analytical attention, that is, has moved from the domain of the psychological to that of the sociological, as the following, now famous, remarks by Howard S. Becker (1963: 9) make clear:

> I mean, rather, that social groups create deviance by making the rules whose infraction constitutes deviance, and by applying those rules to particular people and labelling them as outsiders. From this point of view, deviance is not a quality of the act a person commits, but rather a consequence of the application by others of rules and sanctions to an 'offender'. The deviant is one to whom the label has been successfully applied: deviant behaviour is behaviour that people so label.

As countless commentators have indicated, the implications of this thoroughgoing sociological analysis are clear. Neither individuals nor actions are *inherently* deviant: what makes them so is the social response – the 'societal reaction' – to them. Drinking beer was not a crime, but was redefined as such with the advent of Prohibition; those who drank alcohol in 1932 were criminals, and law-abiding citizens the following year when Prohibition was repealed. Even in the extreme case of killing, it is evident that there are some situations in which this is allowed (as in war), some in which it is the most serious crime (for example 'first-degree' murder), and others in which there may be some legal debate about it (as in the case of euthanasia, or 'mercy killings'). Deviance in societies, therefore, is seen as above all the outcome of processes in which situations are *defined* in particular ways, and individuals and groups are publicly 'labelled' as deviant (Becker, 1963: 9). It is on these social processes that interactionist analyses of deviance focus, on the assumption that it is through these that patterns of conformity and deviance are established in societies, and that the characteristics of individuals – while important – are a secondary consideration.

To illustrate this point, we may turn to Becker's analysis of 'becoming a marijuana user' (Becker, 1953: 235–42). Like Merton, Becker accepts the influence of 'structural' features of societies in producing patterns of deviance, but analyses this influence in a radically different way. Whereas Merton's position is that structural conditions give rise to differential patterns of deviance, Becker suggests that such conditions do not, in themselves, bring about deviant responses: a person's lack of financial success, for example, does not automatically mean that he or she will become a thief or a drug addict. A person's movement into a deviant career must be understood as a series of steps in which he or she responds to the contingencies of various circumstances and situations. In accounting for the 'career' of the marijuana user, for example, Becker argues that we must first establish how it is that individuals get into situations in which marijuana is available, and then why it is that only some individuals are willing to experiment with it, and why, of these, only some will progress to become habitual users. At each step of the way the person is confronted with a choice concerning what to do next, and the outcome of such choices is not predetermined – especially as initial experience of the drug (like most others) is not pleasurable. One has to *learn*, that is, through experience in specific social contexts, how to derive pleasure from use of the drug. What is more, becoming a regular user also involves redefining both the drug itself and aspects of one's own self. Where 'structural' sociologists speak of the effects of social 'forces', then, Becker sees a career of contingencies in which individuals make choices, some of which may have significant consequences.

A further set of contingencies, of course, are those which arise not so much from the process through which rules and laws are established, but from the various ways in which they may – or may not – be enforced. Once again, the interactionists' focus is less on the particular qualities of deviants or their actions, and more on the contingencies of the application of sanctions or the enforcement of laws. Some examples may serve to illustrate the idea. Most drivers of cars will admit, if asked, to the violation of traffic rules – notably speeding – from time to time. Yet whether a particular individual is 'caught' or not may depend very greatly on luck, or the policy of the police in different areas. What is more, police response may vary in accordance with officers' definitions of the offender, rather than the offence – with, for example 'respectable' white ladies less likely to be charged than young black men. From time to time, too, the police devote their resources to organising a 'crackdown' on certain sorts of offences, and at all times police services have to decide how to allocate their resources in order to deal with their perceptions of significant crime. In this, they have to take account of the changing concerns of members of the public, politicians and the media. It follows that the 'rates' of various crimes recorded in different areas at different times will fluctuate considerably: but this does not mean that the actual phenomenon – the crime itself, so to speak – has fluctuated, or that people have become more or less deviant in their activities. What it does mean is that the recorded 'rates' tell us as much, if not more, about the organisation of social control as they do about 'actual' deviance, and it is these processes of social control which have been the focus of the interactionists' attention. Once again, that is, deviance is seen as being constituted in the 'societal reaction' to it, rather than in the characteristics of individual offenders.

Considerations such as these have reinforced the scepticism of most interactionists concerning the validity of official statistics as measures of the 'rates' of crime and deviance. Such rates, it is argued, are not only the outcome of complex processes of definition in which both people and their actions are classified by those in authority, but are in addition produced by agencies of social control in ways which reflect their own policies and priorities. This theme was developed in some detail in a later study, Cicourel's *The Social Organisation of Juvenile Justice* (1968) which documented the ways in which police definitions of young people's behaviour were variable – being influenced particularly by perceptions of social class – and how the rates of juvenile crime in different cities reflected police policies and procedures rather than the 'real' phenomena of crime. Findings such as these were consistent with the interactionists' idea that 'deviance' and 'social control' were inextricably linked, and led sociologists like Cicourel to a fundamental critique of quantitative methods as tools of sociological research (Cicourel, 1964). For the reasons considered above, it was argued that the attempt to 'measure' social phenomena, particularly through the use of official statistics, in order to achieve scientific objectivity was misguided, and resulted only in a spurious 'objectivity' which ignored the social process through which the statistics were produced. In short, the strong suggestion was that statistics did not 'measure' such phenomena as crime but actually *constituted* them.

A further important link between deviance and social control was illustrated by studies which showed how efforts to control patterns of behaviour defined as deviant could actually lead to more, rather than less, deviance. Edwin Lemert, for example, distinguished between behaviour which comprises a 'primary' deviation, such as taking illegal drugs or brewing illegal alcohol, and that which is 'secondary', which arises from the attempt to pursue the primary deviation in the face of attempts to control and suppress it (Lemert, 1951, 1967). For example, illegal drug use, the primary deviation, gives rise to smuggling and money laundering not to mention the odd assassination or two: these are examples of secondary deviations. There has also been talk of 'deviance amplification', that is, the way in which the reaction against an identified deviance 'feeds back' to the deviant and exacerbates the deviant inclination still further. Lemert's classic paper, 'Paranoia and the Dynamics of Exclusion' (in Lemert, 1967) argues that people who have difficulty relating to colleagues in the workplace are caught in a cycle of mutual suspicion in which the colleagues' only partially concealed hostility and distrust 'feeds back' into the individual's own suspicions, and intensifies that individual's alienation from the group and, eventually, *can* drive him or her into a paranoid outbreak.

Similarly, the hostile social pressure experienced by individuals engaged in deviant activities, such as drug use or prostitution, could lead to their greater involvement in the culture and lifestyle of the deviant groups as a means of self-defence. In such cases, individuals are likely to identify with the values of the marginalised group (as opposed to those of the authorities), to enjoy solidarity with fellow-deviants, and to adopt an ideology which offers a justification for their activities. More generally, it was argued that attempts to control deviant activities could produce more crime as an unintended consequence: a process spectacularly illustrated by the link between Prohibition and the spread of organised crime in the USA. Similar points have been made more recently in relation to attempts to control drugs legally classified as dangerous. The persistent demand for these drugs creates a 'black market' around which other criminal activities can flourish.

Overall, the interactionists' studies of crime and deviance constituted a formidable body of sociological work which demonstrated convincingly that these phenomena had to be understood as social processes rather than, as had previously been the case, as resulting from the psychological problems of individuals. It should be clear, too, that while the interactionist studies – in the Chicago tradition – emphasised the importance of understanding the actor's point of view, and the ways in which some people were 'labelled' as deviants by others, the major implication of their work was that socially recognised deviance was above all a consequence of rule-making and efforts at social control. So despite the undoubted sympathy of many of the researchers for the 'underdogs' whose worlds they studied, it would be wrong to conclude (as some have done) that the interactionist approach to deviance simply describes the plight of victims, rather than engaging with the 'macro' issues of social power (Gouldner, 1968). On the contrary, as Becker makes explicit, a sociological understanding of deviance requires an analytical focus on those who make laws and rules, and those who enforce them (Becker, 1963). It is through their activities that deviance is socially constituted, and 'rates' of it produced. Indeed, far from avoiding issues of power in society, it may be argued that what the interactionist studies of deviance concentrated on was precisely how power relationships are established, enacted and challenged in real-life situations.

A view of society

The interactionists' analysis of deviance is an expression of their more general views, particularly about *personal* identity and about the nature of society. The emphasis upon the way that the course of an individual's life can be decisively shaped – brought to a 'turning point' – by the individual's being publicly stigmatised as an outsider is paralleled by individuals who are publicly identified as socially superior, privileged and worthy, as in the case of the collective organisational achievement of the professions. Deviance is bestowed by interactional, collective and organised processes of labelling because 'deviant' is one kind of identity, and identities in general are all bestowed by 'labelling' processes.

Far from it being the case that the interactionists conceived social life as composed only of interactions *among individuals*, it ought to be clear to anyone who reads them that they *do* have a particular conception of *society* – not systematically spelled out, but very much derived from the United States. Such a conception is implied in numerous studies and discussions, and was shaped both by the history of Chicago sociology and by the interactionists' theoretical principles. The central emphasis is upon social life as process, that is, as constant, renewed and transformed flows of 'collective action' (Becker, 1974). The notion of 'structure' is to be understood as a derivative one: some processes of activity result in the establishment of stable, durable patterns of social organisation, but only *some* processes generate such structures. Many processes are much more fluid and transient. Further, social reality exists in 'the definition of the situation', and society is constituted through a plurality of such definitions: studies of deviance are investigations of the contrasting definitions of the situation that prevail in the deviant, straight, and law-enforcement settings for example. The society is (to some extent) a unification, though not an integration, of the plurality of different definitions, with unification being achieved through the dominance of some definitions over others, through the attainment of control – for longer or shorter periods – with more or less extensive penetration of positions of power in economic life, the legislature, judiciary and other key institutions. Thus, for example, the imposition of Prohibition was a political triumph for sections of the religious middle classes, but only a temporary one. More generally, Lemert viewed the process of law-making as one in which groups with various interests and cultures were in competition to have their 'definitions of the situation' established in law. Often the result was a politically acceptable compromise (Lemert, 1967).

There is a clear contrast here with Parsons' picture of America as an integrated, consensual society. For the interactionists, America was a society of immigrants from very different cultures. It was a stratified society, often on the basis of ethnicity, religion and cultural diversity as much as on the economic basis of class. Society was portrayed as a loose federation of culturally heterogeneous groups, with some more strategically placed by securing and controlling positions of power to pursue their interests in the legal and administrative apparatus of the society as a whole, and thus to dictate official definitions of the situation – though those official definitions were never to be taken as expressions of a thoroughgoing consensus. Those in power were far from being in complete control of society. Indeed, an important element in this view is that the official or prevailing definitions – of what is legal, for example – are often the achievements of (to use Howard Becker's term) 'moral entrepreneurs' (Becker, 1963). Once again a concept from the world of business – 'entrepreneur' – is, like other concepts, such as that of 'career', given far wider application. The moral entrepreneur is, like the business one, an individual who initiates and develops activity and organisation, creating – in the 'moral' case – pressure groups, lobbies, political parties and so on, to promote some concern: stamping out drinking or drug use, for example. The aim of such 'moral entrepreneurs' is to have their cause recognised in legislation and established in administrative structures. Of course, whether anything that the 'moral entrepreneur' pursues is recognised and established depends upon the whole range of contingencies that can affect the rise, recruitment and influence of social movements, and whether what does get installed is anything like what the entrepreneur originally wanted will depend upon all the contingencies affecting the politics of legislation and government.

Further, if the 'moral entrepreneur', or the social movement, is successful and does get legislation passed and agencies set up, the entrepreneur then often loses interest in and involvement with the cause. Rule-making is the entrepreneur's enthusiasm. Enforcement passes into the hands of those who characteristically lack the entrepreneur's enthusiasm for the moral cause, and for whom enforcement is only their daily work, with the practice of enforcement then depending upon priorities other than the moral purpose of the work, such as bureaucratic infighting, workloads, etc.

The next generation

The atmosphere created at Chicago by Blumer and Hughes was an inspiration to a large number of younger sociologists, three of whom were particularly important in taking their ideas forward, each developing their own distinctive 'take' on the tradition as well as having a significant influence on sociology more widely. The career of one of these, Howard S. Becker, has stretched from the 1950s to the present day. Two others, Anselm Strauss (1916–96) and Erving Goffman (1922–82), were active researchers throughout their careers, and their studies continue to be recognised as major achievements.

Howard Becker and Anselm Strauss – in their different ways – both reflect the attempt to formulate ideas that captured the view of society outlined above. Both had long careers, and their interests changed or developed over time, and both were less than enthusiastic about being tied down to some programmatic sociological position by being titled 'symbolic interactionists.' As far as they were concerned, symbolic interaction, if one is to talk of such a thing, was only a loose association of independent investigators.

Howard S. Becker

Much of Becker's earliest sociological work was concerned to develop Hughes' work on occupations, professions and personal identities. Becker studied teachers in the Chicago school system, examining their careers and the way in which they came to adopt an occupational ideology which reflected the problems they faced in dealing with their 'clients' – the school pupils. Teachers' perceptions of pupils often reflected the extent to which they were seen as accepting the teachers' expectations of them (the 'ideal pupil'), or rejecting them. Becker pointed out (in work which anticipates the later studies of the French sociologist, Pierre Bourdieu) that pupils' conformity (or not) to the teachers' expectations is often a matter of culture rather than academic ability as such – with differences of class and ethnicity particularly important, since these contribute to a situation in which many pupils, perhaps the majority, fail to meet the schools' expectations of them (Becker, 1952a, 1952b). The ultimate outcome is the familiar pattern of social class differentials in educational attainment. This work helped to stimulate a considerable body of influential research on classroom interaction, in which the social organisation of the school, and the routine interactions within it, may be seen to produce regular patterns of 'success' and 'failure' (Rist, 1973; Cicourel and Kitsuse, 1963). In the present context, such studies provide a good example of the way in which interactionists have focused on the 'everyday' social practices which, taken cumulatively, result in well-documented patterns of social class, ethnic, and gendered, variations in educational attainment. For 'structural' sociologists, these patterns and the statistical rates which describe them may appear to be independent 'social facts', or properties of the society as a collectivity; from an interactionist perspective such 'structural' features are in the end simply the outcome of innumerable everyday encounters.

Similarly, the contrasts between these approaches are apparent in Becker's later studies of university students. Becker and his colleagues (who included Hughes and Strauss) examined the careers of medical students, producing a book – *Boys in White* (1961) – which is far less respectful of 'professional' training than *The Student Physician* (1957), written by Robert Merton, G. Reader and P. Kendall. Reflecting the Chicago tradition, *Boys in White* shows how the original idealism of medical students is transformed into a primarily practical concern to survive the exceptionally demanding requirements of medical school and to obtain the qualification. Moreover, the study also demonstrates the ways in which the students, like members of other occupations, developed a culture which was in large part a response to the problems they faced within a particular institutional context. This theme was central to the analysis of student culture in *Making the Grade* (Becker at al., 1968), which links the students' concern to achieve good grade point averages with the emergence of the particular 'perspectives' which are a major element of the student culture. The basic idea, as Becker has put it, is that 'people with common problems who can communicate with each other about them will create shared understandings and practices, a culture . . .' (Burgess, 1995).

As we have seen, this theme is also apparent in Becker's analysis of deviant groups, including the musicians who saw themselves as 'outsiders' in relation to mainstream society. Becker's early experience of the world of music (as a professional pianist), together with his later interest in photography, also contributed to his later development – in *Art Worlds* (1982) – of a general perspective on the whole process of cultural production. In the tradition of interactionism, Becker views the production of art – or indeed any process in which cultural products are created – as 'collective action'. For Becker, the myth of the individual as the sole creator of an art work (as when we speak of, say, a 'Michael Cimino' film) bears no relation to the sociological reality of the complex pattern of coordinated activities without which no cultural object could be created, distributed or appreciated – as is evident from the list of credits for a Hollywood film, which reminds us just how many people are involved in its production. In fact, every 'art world' – that is, the social networks concerned with the production of such things as books, paintings, films, photographs, plays, styles of music, poetry, and so on – is a complex division of labour involving many people, each of whom makes a contribution to the realisation of the 'work'. This division of labour inevitably generates a set of 'conventions' – accepted ways of doing things – which all the participants have to take account of (even if they aim to challenge them, as radical artists do, though often at the cost of unpopularity). Thus the set of conventions established in any given art world influences what can and cannot be done in that world, so influencing the nature of artistic production, and also becomes part of the taken-for-granted assumptions which are 'internalised' by participants and provide the basis for their aesthetic experiences.

Through the concept of art worlds, then, Becker aims to capture the sociological reality of those social circles or networks which develop around the production and consumption of cultural products. But such forms of social organisation are not well captured in the standard schemes of structural sociology – indeed, they are often taken for granted or simply ignored. Becker's approach offers a sociological account of how, according to the ever-changing criteria of art worlds, some things come to be defined as art and others not; how judgements concerning artistic value are made according to these criteria, and how every cultural product depends on the 'collective action' of large numbers of people. Indeed, the character of art works themselves is influenced by the conventions around which the art world itself is built, those conventions shared with consumers of the products, as to how things are to be done, and upon which the producers can draw in putting together their works. They can rely upon their audience to understand what they are doing when they can depend upon their knowledge of a convention, just as they can provoke reactions when they violate those conventions. In general, this is a perspective which – in a way characteristic of Becker's work, and interactionism more generally – leads us to see artistic production as *work*, and 'artist' as an *occupation*.

Anselm Strauss

In his early work, Anselm Strauss was also concerned with 'identity' and his small book *Mirrors and Masks* (1959), is a classic and lucid statement about the way in which identity is not something intrinsic to the individual, but subsists in the relation to a social context and in the interactions between individuals – the 'mirrors' in the title perhaps alluding to Cooley's 'looking glass self' (Cooley, 1978). A main interest of Strauss, in the middle period of his work from the 1950s until the 1970s, was in the organisation of the professions, with Strauss contesting the idea of the professional occupation as a unified, consensual body. The heading 'Professions in Process' was one that Strauss (together with Rue Bucher) used to encapsulate an interest in the way that the medical profession was in a constant process of definition and redefinition, emphasising the extent to which medicine was segmented into different specialisms (Strauss and Bucher, 1961). This was a kind of fragmentation of the profession in that each specialism had its own interests and its own perspectives, with new specialisms having to struggle to assert themselves and gain a recognised place in the profession.

Together with a team of colleagues, Strauss was then involved in the study of relations amongst different 'segments' of the psychiatric profession as they were involved in the activities of a large hospital (Strauss et al., 1964). The study was directed toward identifying the different ideologies associated with different specialist groups, and to seeing how those ideologies worked out in practical conduct. The study was, however, most notable for the formulation of a concept – 'negotiated order' – that has been very influential and found much more general application than to psychiatric hospitals alone. The concept of 'negotiated order' was designed to recognise that the affairs in the hospital were orderly, but that they did not simply correspond to the broad lines of authority and unofficial function set down for the hospital. It sought to bring out the extent to which that order was the product of being constantly 'worked on' by the employees at the level of daily operation, the extent to which the official division of labour was modified in practice, and to show the actual distribution of work at any point in time – who will do exactly what just now? The order was being worked out relative to a whole variety of considerations and contingencies. There was a continuing process of 'negotiation' over the distribution of work. The hospital organisation was conceived as an arena within which the interests of different individuals and groups played out their interests. Thus, the 'structure' of the hospital – its official designation of lines of authority and communication and its division of labour – is real enough, but this does not capture the reality of the hospital's social organisation. This is a composite of groups, each of which has its own interests and points of view, and it is only through the understanding of the way they relate to each other and to the official structures that one grasps the hospital as a social organisation.

Strauss continued his interest in medical work, producing classic studies of the social relations surrounding the experience of pain and the occurrence of death in the medical setting, but his dominant interests latterly turned toward methodological issues. Strauss accepted Blumer's idea that field studies were of indispensable value to sociology, regarding as a major folly the attempt to propound general theories about human affairs of which one had only the faintest empirical knowledge. However, for Strauss, field studies were not an end in themselves, and should be – but were not – a means of producing better theories. The attempt to correct this situation resulted in probably his most influential work, a collaboration with Barney Glaser, *The Discovery of Grounded Theory* (Glaser and Strauss, 1967), in which it is argued that sociology should seek to create formal theory of the kind that positivist sociologists had envisaged but had failed to deliver. The way to achieve this objective was to change the relationship between theory and research: to cease thinking of research data as of use only in *testing* theories, and instead to think of research as a means of *creating* theories, ones which are first of all specific to the area of social life one is studying in the field, but which will have the potential to become generalised as one explores a wide range of social domains. The book was a guide to the way in which theory could be generated from and firmly anchored in field materials, providing advice that Strauss himself took as he attempted to develop formal theories – one for 'negotiation' for example.

The notion of 'formal theories', and the need to develop more generic concepts out of the localised fieldwork typical of symbolic interactionism, brings us to the work of Erving Goffman, who is often associated with the perspective, but whose work, in significant ways, represents a rather different approach to the questions of sociology.

Erving Goffman

Erving Goffman – always wary of being labelled a symbolic interactionist – became widely known in the 1960s and 1970s, as his *The Presentation of Self in Everyday Life* (1959) became an international bestseller. He was certainly influenced by the Chicago tradition, but also strongly affected by thinkers like Durkheim and Simmel, especially by the former's emphasis on the importance of ritual in social life, and the latter's ambition to develop a *formal* sociology, that is, one which seeks to analyse social relations in terms of their formal patterns rather than their content. For example, whereas symbolic interactionists aim to take 'the point of view of the actor', to capture the particular experience of being a student doctor, a musician, a prostitute, or whatever, in order to see the world through their eyes, formal sociology is much more interested in the generic properties of interaction.

Although the distinction between 'form' and 'content' can be overdone, it is a difference that can be illustrated using one of Goffman's own striking examples, namely, the concept of 'total institution' (Goffman, 1961a). This concept sought to show that the *same* patterns of social relationships developed in such diverse settings as mental hospitals, naval vessels, military schools and monasteries – despite the great differences in the practical purposes, cultures, and even the moral status of these settings – as a result of the formal necessities of administering people who are kept together for 24 hours a day.

Nevertheless, Goffman was much influenced by the general conceptions of the interactionists, and also by the kinds of studies that had been made in Chicago, which provided much of the illustrative material for his general ideas. Goffman *was* centrally concerned with interpersonal interaction, and for the first half of his career developed a specialised field within sociology, one that analysed the general form of relations within the face-to-face encounter, which, he complained, was, as far as sociology was concerned, a 'neglected situation' (Goffman, 1983). Goffman wanted to highlight the fundamental importance of face-to-face interaction in human social life, and to study it in naturally occurring settings: there are many studies of 'languages', he once argued, but relatively few of actual speech, and the same point could be made about real-life social interaction.

Goffman's aim was to develop a field of study which he envisaged would fit into sociology more generally, and which might be related to some more general theory of social structure or social order, such as Parsons' account of the social system. His initial concern, however, was to try to identify those properties of social relationships that are specifically created by the nature of the face-to-face encounter, though he was well aware that this meant taking account of the context within which such encounters occurred. Many of Goffman's works were attempts to tackle, in different ways, the same problem, namely that of developing a general frame of analysis for the examination of face-to-face situations.

His most famous work, *The Presentation of Self in Everyday Life*, and a number of related studies – *Stigma* (1964), *Asylums* (1961a), *Encounters* (1961b) – focused on one of the interactionists' central topics: personal identity. *The Presentation of Self* dealt with the ways in which people attempt, through 'impression management', to project to others the identity in which they wish to be seen. This study drew on a theatrical metaphor not least in its exploitation of the contrast between 'front stage' and 'back stage' to draw attention to the ways in which social actors 'manage' the impression they give. What goes on backstage is kept from the theatrical audience the better to ensure that the illusion being created by the on-stage performance is effective. So, too, in social life we attempt to control the information we 'give off', attempt to give a convincing 'impression' of who we are, and to hide information incongruous with or discrediting to that impression. 'Back regions' are places – such as bathrooms, bedrooms, studies and other areas where we can be private – where we can do the things which help us assemble the impressions we want to convey in the more public 'front regions'. One persistent interactionist theme was centrally present: the projection of what is supposedly an individual's own identity is often a collective, collaborative matter, something done through team work. Moreover, the successful presentation of self involves the acceptance of one person's identity-claims by others.

The everyday situation of most of us contrasts with that of the inmate of the asylum for whom, in that environment, the difference between front and back regions has been broken down. It contrasts, too, with the position of those who have 'spoiled identity', who are in one way or another 'stigmatised' by, for example, physical deformity, or skin colour in a racist society, where those persons have to try to live with or escape from the fact that their socially discrediting characteristic is readily apparent to those with whom they come into contact. Yet again, there are those who occupy a particular identity and who are required to engage in activities associated with that identity but who – like a growing child who tries to dissociate itself from the 'childish' things imposed upon it – do not want to be absorbed into that identity and seek to display 'role distance'.

These situations involve, of course, the ordering of the interactions, and Goffman's concern with identity was paralleled by attention to the ways in which people sustain the identity of the social occasion, keep it going as the kind of occasion that it is. Thus, a further theme of *The Presentation of Self* was a concern with the way in which the failure to sustain separation of front and back regions results in embarrassment, a disruption of the interaction. Another book, *Behavior in Public Places* (1963) was based on the study of etiquette books and described the conventions to be found there for the effective management of social occasions, what Goffman called 'focused encounters' in which a small group of people share a common, focal involvement. *Frame Analysis* (1974), his biggest and perhaps most ambitious work, was an attempt to provide a systematic analysis to describe the ways in which people manage to sustain a common frame of reference – a shared sense of reality – in an interaction; how they manage to keep going, for example, the sense that this particular encounter is between pupil and teacher or that the activity involved is a matter only of play, and not something serious.

A 'frame' is a principle of organisation that defines a situation, tells us 'what is happening here' and enables us to distinguish, for example, a casual chat from a more formal interview. The things that are said in both may be similar but their import and sense are different. Any given frame is maintained by the nature of the physical world, the ecology of the situation and the institutional setting. 'Natural frameworks' define situations in terms of the physicality of the world, such as the weather, and the 'ecological dimension' focuses on the persons who happen to be present. People must always pay attention to others in their presence for even 'when nothing eventful is occurring, persons in one another's presence are still nonetheless tracking one another and acting so as to make themselves trackable' (Goffman, 1981: 103).

The most fundamental of frames are 'primary frameworks'. These can be 'keyed' whenever their meanings are transformed into something patterned on, but independent of, them. Thus, 'children playing at house' is patterned on the primary framework that defines the episode as 'family life' but is transformed into a playful, make-believe episode. Indeed, social interaction is very often a superimposition, or 'lamination', of frames, each manipulating the understanding of the others.

Frames can also be fabricated, that is, made to convey a false idea about what is happening. Fabrications can be benign or exploitative. Both fabrications and keyings can undermine our confidence in frames, though our trust in frames is maintained by procedures such as 'brackets' which define when a frame begins and ends, close identification with the roles involved, the residue that activities leave behind, and the assumption that we all have a constant identity – these 'anchor' frame activity to ensure that the frame's purported meaning and its actual meaning are the same. In subsequent studies Goffman explored ideas set out in *Frame Analysis*, as for example, in *Gender Advertisements* (Goffman, 1979), where he looked at 'gendered interactions'; that is, how men and women interpret their interactions with each other.

Recent work in symbolic interactionism

Despite the achievements of interactionist researchers in the 1950s and 1960s, by the 1970s the perspective was to a great extent eclipsed by Marxian and other macro-conflict theories of society which developed out of the critique of structural-functional perspectives. However, reports of the demise of symbolic interactionism (Mullins and Mullins, 1973) proved to be premature. Although the approach has returned to its somewhat marginalised position, its themes and concerns have been resurgent, rediscovered and adopted by very different traditions in social thought. The widely influential work of Michel Foucault, for example, highlights the socially constituted nature of the self, and ways in which social constraint and power relations are 'inscribed' in the routines and practices of everyday life. In the 1980s and 1990s, the widespread interest in the ideas of postmodernism also revived interest in these themes, in cultural studies generally, and in such specific topics as the contemporary role of the mass media. What is evident is that the perspective of the symbolic interactionists has much to offer here, and in turn it has been argued that the ideas of the post-structuralists and postmodernists have much to contribute to the revitalisation of the perspective (Denzin, 1992).

Further, there are many studies being produced today that may be considered developments of the tradition. Just two examples from what could be a very long list are those on youth by Gary Allen Fine (1987) and on economic activity by Robert Prus (1989a, 1989b). In particular, interactionists have been leaders in sociological fields which have now developed into busy areas of activity: Arlie Russell Hochschild's (1983) work exploring the sociology of emotions is a prime example as an initial contribution to a now thriving interest in emotions. Given symbolic interactionism's commitment to Mead's social psychology, with its emphasis on the socialisation of impulses, it is perhaps surprising that the study of emotions was relatively late in becoming an interest. Be this as it may, from its perspective emotions can be seen as orderly, as interactionally regulated, in a word, as actions. In other words, there are rules – 'feeling rules' – or conventions such as that we should feel sad at funerals, happy at weddings, ecstatic at passing an examination and miserable at having failed one, which govern how people feel or try not to feel in ways appropriate to the situation in which they find themselves (Hochschild, 1979). Hochschild's work was very much in the symbolic interactionist tradition, pointing out that what might look like natural physiological reactions are normatively regulated.

It is true that by the 1970s the main concepts of symbolic interactionism had been developed, and most recent substantive work using this approach has tended to involve the application of its concepts. Moreover, the brief popularity it had enjoyed in the 1960s by virtue of its critical attitude to positivism in sociology, and its scepticism toward those in authority, was over. By then, many sociologists – including the prominent theorist Alvin Gouldner (1968) – were condemning symbolic interactionism as a merely liberal venture, when something much more politically radical was called for. Much of the criticism repeated two points: first, that symbolic interaction 'reduced' society to a mere collection of individuals and could not comprehend the larger picture that more so-called 'macro' sociological theories could provide; secondly, that symbolic interaction could not comprehend the role of power and consequent constraint in social relations. Allegedly, it unrealistically emphasised the spontaneity and freedom of individuals to innovate in their conduct, and thus deluded people about the true extent of their freedom. In focusing, for example, on the front-line regulators of deviance, such as the cop on the beat or the attorney in the courtroom, it failed to appreciate the way in which deviance is related to the economic interests, real powers and governing forces that run the whole society. It was argued that symbolic interactionism wrongly imagined that mere local and specific reforms could achieve what in fact only a transformation of the whole society could achieve. As a result, interactionists have often been on the defensive, reacting against what they regard as unjustified criticism, but their responses have not prevented the continuing repetition of very similar complaints.

Criticism in sociology often confuses two very different questions: whether an approach *does* do a certain kind of study, and whether an approach is *capable* of doing that kind of study. For example, it has been pointed out that symbolic interactionism – despite its name, Mead's original ideas, and the nature of its project – did not actually pay very much attention to language use, the 'symbolic' medium of interaction (Watson, 1994). At most, there was patchy and superficial attention. The late interest that Goffman took in language (Goffman, 1981) was almost certainly provoked in a competitive spirit but was also certainly inferior to the work being done by Conversation Analysis which emerged from ethnomethodology through the work of Harvey Sacks (1930–75) and his colleagues (who had formerly been Goffman's own students).

However, the fact that symbolic interactionism did not pay much attention to language does not mean that it could not have done: such an interest could have been taken and substantially developed within the symbolic interactionist framework. The same may be said about the frequently repeated complaints concerning the alleged neglect of power and 'large scale social structures'. While it is true that attention was given to organisation on a societal scale only occasionally, as in Gusfield's study (1986) of the Prohibition movement, this does not mean that symbolic interactionists could not take account of such things. As we have seen, at the heart of symbolic interactionism is the focus on collaborative interaction as the basis for *all* social organisation, and on the idea of social life as *process*. These analytic commitments do not entail a denial of the enormous and enduring differences between groups and individuals in the power, wealth and other resources which they can command. Rather, from the symbolic interactionists' perspective such structured patterns of inequality are the outcome of the social process as it has developed over time. Indeed the pursuit of wealth, power, status, security, and so on is precisely what motivates individuals to participate in the 'worlds' which are the basis of their social experience.

Thus, there have been relatively recent reminders that Herbert Blumer's own empirical interests included 'macro' topics such as industrialisation and industrial relations, and the mass media. Randall Collins – not, himself, an interactionist – argued that symbolic interactionism could comfortably be integrated into mainstream sociology, and that Weberian themes, conflict theory and the notion of 'interaction ritual' (Goffman's conception, derived from Durkheim) complement each other effectively (Collins, 1981). From within symbolic interactionism itself, Hall (1987) has reminded these critics of the numerous studies of power, class, status, gender, race and collective action in the bibliography of the approach. Similarly, Maines (1982) argued that the macro–micro distinction was inapplicable in this case, and coined the term 'mesostructural' to subvert the dichotomy, proposing an intermediary or connecting level at which most interactionist studies locate themselves, focusing on how institutional and societal forces mesh with localised interactions (frequently in organisational and administrative settings). Sam Gilmore (1990) proposed that the notion of 'worlds' could be generalised from Becker's treatment of art worlds to deal with all kinds of networks of social relations organised through a division of labour; an idea independently proposed by Anselm Strauss. He noted, too, that the concept of 'world', far from excluding considerations of power, recognised the extent to which the pursuit of fame, wealth and power are central to these worlds.

Further, it may be argued that the general emphasis of symbolic interactionist studies was on the *enactment* of power relations, with the way in which differences in power were (to use a term of Michel Foucault's) *inscribed* in social relations – in the areas of work, crime and deviance, medicine, mental illness, education, and race, to name but a few. It should also be noted that Hughes coined the term 'dirty work' on the basis of his early awareness of the racial persecution practised by the Nazis (in Hughes, 1981). Indeed, there are strong parallels between the symbolic interactionist approach and that of Foucault, which has been so influential across a range of contemporary disciplines, with his focus on the organisation of discipline (and the possibilities of resistance to it) in prisons, schools, business, the military and so on. Moreover, certain areas where Foucault's work has been criticised – for example, his neglect of resistance to power or his over-determined conception of the self (McNay, 1994) – are areas with which symbolic interactionism is well equipped to deal.

Symbolic interactionism has been marginalised at the time when many of its themes are, through the influence of cultural studies and postmodernism, resurgent. We have mentioned the parallels with Foucault, and there are also strong points of contact with the British tradition in cultural studies (in which Stuart Hall is a key figure), with its emphasis on resistance to and subversions of power. Further, the idea of 'the social construction of reality', also widely influential in recent years, is one to which symbolic interactionism made early contributions and which retains strong resonances. For example, it argued that many of the things often regarded as biological conditions – such as mental illness or criminality – might often more fruitfully be seen as 'social constructions'. It should not be forgotten, either, that one of the key sources for the idea of 'social construction' – Berger and Luckmann's striking book (1966) – was an attempt to fuse a Meadian approach with the kind of approach Marx and Durkheim had taken. Equally, the postmodern emphasis on the importance of identity and the 'fluidity' of the self is substantially prefigured in the interactionists' treatment of identity as created situationally, and transmuted through social experience and by organised social processes, as well as with collective behaviour that asserts and promotes revised and new conceptions of the self (Fine, 1990; Reese, 1993).

Symbolic interactionism's association with qualitative research has continued to thrive, and the users of qualitative research have continued to proliferate. Some leading figures in contemporary symbolic interactionism have attempted the fusion of its analytic interests with some of those prominent in postmodern writings. Thus, Manning has proselytised from connections with semiotics, whilst Denzin (1997) has seized on the importance of the idea of 'interpretation' in both traditions as a basis for grafting a connection between them through the concept of ethnography – as fieldwork is often more grandiosely called.

Perhaps the best that symbolic interactionism can plead is that of priority, for though there are these striking parallels in recent sociological developments they have often come from many other, and very different sources, especially European social theory, generally without an awareness of symbolic interactionism's earlier achievements. More positively, one could follow Gary Alan Fine in noting the extent to which the central concepts and themes of symbolic interactionism have now become accepted elements of mainstream sociology: 'if the ultimate goal is to develop the pragmatic approach to social life – a view of the power of symbol creation and interaction – then symbolic interaction has triumphed gloriously' (Fine, 1993: 81).

CHAPTER FIVE SUMMARY

- Symbolic interactionism, in contrast to the 'grand theory' efforts of such as Parsons, argued that sociological theory could only be developed on the basis of a substantial knowledge of how social life was actually lived. Its preference was for the concrete over the abstract.
- Symbolic interactionism as formulated by Blumer, following Mead, stressed three principles: human beings act toward each other on the basis of meanings; meanings arise out of interaction; meanings are mediated through an interpretative process. Using these principles interactionism sought to illuminate the processes through which social organisation was maintained as an endless succession of everyday encounters between people.
- Symbolic interactionism pioneered studies of work and deviance as well as anticipating a number of current preoccupations with identity and emotion and, of course, from the beginning, made contributions to the idea of the social construction of reality.

Select bibliography and further reading

Good introductions to the Chicago School and its influences include Martin Bulmer, *The Chicago School of Sociology: Institutionalisation, Diversity, and the Rise of Sociological Research* (University of Chicago Press, 1984); R.E.L. Faris, *Chicago Sociology: 1920–1932* (Chandler, 1967); and D. Smith, *The Chicago School: A Liberal Critique of Capitalism* (Macmillan, 1988). S.P. Turner and J.H. Turner's, *The Impossible Science: An Institutional Analysis of American Sociology* (Sage, 1990) is a very good, and short, account of the debates and issues surrounding the professionalisation of sociology in the United States.

Among the studies for which the School is well known, though they are not always easily available, are Nels Anderson, *The Hobo* (University of Chicago Press, 1961), F. Thrasher, *The Gang: A Study of 1,313 Gangs in Chicago* (University of Chicago Press, 1927) and C. R. Shaw's, *The Jack-Roller: A Delinquent Boy's Own Story* (Chicago, University of Chicago Press, 1930).

General texts on symbolic interactionism must include the two volumes edited by Ken Plummer, *Symbolic Interactionism, Vols 1: and 2* (Edward Elgar, 1991). The first volume deals with foundations and the second with more recent developments, including its engagement with postmodernist and structuralist social thought. Earlier edited collections which also include studies are J.G. Manis and B.N. Meltzer (eds), *Symbolic Interactionism: A Reader* (Allyn and Bacon, 1978) which reprints a number of the classic statements. Hans Joas' 'Symbolic Interactionism', in A. Giddens and J. Turner (eds), *Social Theory Today* (Polity Press, 1987) is worth reading. Paul Rock's *The Making of Symbolic Interactionism* (Macmillan, 1979) is also still worth reading. B. Fisher and A. Strauss provide an informed account of the history of symbolic interactionism in their 'Interactionism', in T. Bottomore, and R. Nisbet (eds), *A History of Sociological Analysis* (Heinemann, 1979). Robert Prus' *Symbolic Interaction and Ethnographic Research: Intersubjectivity and the Study of Human Experience* (State University of New York Press, 1996) is a good textbook account of the tradition and where it is now.

George Herbert Mead's contributions can be found in his *Mind, Self and Society* (University of Chicago Press, 1962; first published 1934), *Selected Writings* (Bobbs-Merrill, 1964; first published 1924-25), and *Movements of Social Thought in the Nineteenth Century* (University of Chicago Press, 1936). His paper 'Cooley's Contribution to American Social Thought' is reprinted in Plummer, op.cit. Vol. 1 and was originally published in the *American Journal of Sociology* (35, 1930: 693–706). John Dewey's paper, 'The Reflex Arc Concept in Psychology', appeared in the *Psychological Review* (3, 1896: 357–70). Useful commentaries on Mead include H. Joas, *G.H. Mead: A Contemporary Re-examination of his Thought* (MIT Press, 1985). 'The Social Psychology of George Herbert Mead' by B.N. Meltzer is reprinted in Manis and Meltzer (eds), op.cit.

Many of Blumer's seminal papers are to be found in his *Symbolic Interactionism* (Prentice-Hall, 1971). Others of note are his 'Psychological Import of the Human Group', in Muzafer Sherif and M.O. Wilson (eds), *Group Relations at the*

Crossroads (Harper and Row, 1953); 'What Is Wrong with Social Theory' (*American Sociological Review*, 19, 1954: 3–10); 'Sociological Analysis and the "Variable"' (*American Sociological Review*, 21, 1956: 683–90), reprinted in Manis and Meltzer (eds) op.cit.; 'Society as Symbolic Interaction' in A. Rose (ed.), *Human Behavior and Social Processes* (Houghton Mifflin, 1962, pp. 179–92); 'Sociological Implications of the Thought of George Herbert Mead', *American Journal of Sociology*, 71, 1966: 535–48.

Everett Hughes' research is contained in his *Men and Their Work* (Greenwood Press, 1981) originally published by The Free Press, 1958; *The Sociological Eye* (Aldine Atherton, 1971); and 'The Professions in Society', *Canadian Journal of Economics and Political Science* (26, 1960: 54–61). Other studies of work include B. Glaser and A. Strauss, *Status Passage* (Aldine-Atherton, 1971); R.R. Faulkner, *The Hollywood Studio Musician* (Aldine-Atherton, 1971) and also his *Music on Demand* (Transaction, 1983). *Boys in White* (Chicago University Press, 1961) by Howard S. Becker, Everett Hughes, Blanche Greer and Anselm Strauss is usefully compared with Robert Merton, G. Reader and P. Kendall, *The Student Physician* (Harvard University Press, 1957). Becker's edited collection *Institutions and the Person* (Aldine, 1968) contains some useful and interesting material.

Works on deviance are voluminous. More than useful is Becker's *The Outsiders: Studies in the Sociology of Deviance* (Free Press, 1963); Joseph Gusfield, *Symbolic Crusade: Status Politics and the American Temperance Movement*, 2nd edn (University of Illinois Press, 1986) and *Contested Meanings: The Construction of Alcohol Problems* (University of Wisconsin Press, 1996). 'Secondary deviance' and 'deviance amplification' are elaborated in Edwin Lemert, *Social Pathology* (McGraw-Hill, 1951) and *Human Deviance, Social Problems and Social Control* (Prentice-Hall, 1967). A.V. Cicourel's, *The Social Organisation of Juvenile Justice* (Wiley, 1968) is a study of the 'social construction' of criminality and criminal statistics.

Erving Goffman's corpus includes not only the famous *The Presentation of Self in Everyday Life* (Anchor, 1959) but a series of books, often collections of essays, exploring themes to do with face-to-face interaction. These include *Asylums* (Anchor, 1961), *Behavior in Public Places: Notes on the Social Organisation of Gatherings* (Free Press, 1963), *Relations in Public: Microstudies of the Public Order* (Harper and Row, 1971), *Frame Analysis: An Essay on the Organisation of Experience* (Harper and Row, 1974) and his *Gender Advertisements* (Macmillan, 1979). Commentaries on Goffman include P. Drew and A. Wootton's edited collection, *Erving Goffman: Exploring the Interaction Order* (Polity Press 1988), and Peter Manning's, *Erving Goffman and Modern Sociology* (Polity Press, 1992).

Among the second generation of interactionists discussed, the following are worth reading: Becker's *Art Worlds* (University of California Press, 1982) as well as his earlier work with Hughes, Greer and Strauss on medical students, *Boys in White* (Chicago University Press, 1961) and Becker et al., *Making the Grade: The Academic Side of Student Life* (Wiley, 1968). Anselm Strauss' work includes *Mirrors and Masks* (Free Press, 1959), *Negotiations: Varieties, Contexts, Processes and*

Social Order (Jossey-Bass, 1978), and with Barney Glaser, *The Discovery of Grounded Theory: Strategies for Qualitative Research* (Aldine, 1967). Gary Fine's, *With the Boys: Little League Baseball and Preadolescent Culture* (University of Chicago Press, 1987), Robert Prus', *Making Sales: Influence as an Interpersonal Accomplishment* (Sage, 1989) and *Pursuing Customers: An Ethnography of Marketing Activities* (Sage, 1989) are all worth a look at. The pioneering work on emotion by Arlie Russell Hochschild is to be found in 'Emotion Work, Feeling Rules, and Social Structure', *American Journal of Sociology* (1979, 85,3: 551–75) and *The Managed Heart: The Commercialisation of Human Feeling* (University of California Press, 1983).

Concluding Remarks 6

Having reviewed the developments of the 'middle period' of sociology up to the eve of another transformation growing out of Structuralism and Critical Theory particularly, we find the discipline to be highly pluralised – some would say fragmented. For those who strove so hard to provide a unifying framework for the discipline, this state of affairs has been a major disappointment. For others it is one to be celebrated as the final collapse of the constraints bequeathed by the Enlightenment that have proved so difficult to eradicate from our thinking. For yet others, though perhaps a very small number even including the authors of this book, it is a state of affairs that is only to be expected given the overweening ambitions that sociology has often inflicted upon itself. It is less the passing of an epoch that is involved in the collapse of confidence in the 'scientific' or 'grand narrative' conception of sociology and more of a predictable deflation of ambition. For it is worth remembering that, outside of the USA, sociology as a numerously staffed enterprise is still less than half a century old. The loss of faith, especially in Marxism, may signal only the final disintegration of the unrealistic expectations with which many entered the newly established community of sociology in the fateful days at the end of the 1960s and the beginning of the 1970s. However, the important question at this point is: what relevance does understanding these supposedly outdated schools of sociology have for us today?

One answer is, we think, straightforward but certainly not, these days, an uncontentious one. It is that these ideas, like the ones reviewed in *Understanding Classical Theory*, represent considerable and ingenious achievements even though they were, in crucial respects, found wanting and have been superseded by what are regarded as progressive intellectual developments. Further, a number of them, particularly Critical Theory and structuralism, represent a reworking of classic ideas, especially ones derived from Marx but also from Weber and Durkheim, and in this respect are an unfolding of sociology's intellectual tradition.

It is in this evocation of the idea of sociology's intellectual tradition that we have been accused of holding to the currently unfashionable view that sociology has, or should have, a 'canon'; that is, a set of classic texts that are acknowledged to be the founding and prevailing authorities for the discipline as a whole. In this supposedly 'postmodern' era such a view would certainly be regarded as an outmoded one. The very idea of a supposed 'canon' of texts that are purportedly exemplary and universally acceptable in defining the nature of a field is in bad repute and perhaps in terminal disintegration in other humanistic and literary studies. Why should sociology be any different?

There may be reasons why sociology could be different from literary and humanistic studies. Decisions as to whether a canon is obsolete should not be made on the basis of what holds elsewhere. In any case, it is no part of our motivation in writing these two books to elevate any sociological studies or traditions to canonical status. It seems to us that a challenge to the idea of a canon for sociology need not necessarily spring from postmodernism – or any 'post-' movement for that matter – but from a much simpler and more basic question: has there ever been, or are there promises that there will soon be, any genuine unity and coherence in the sociological pursuit?

The sociologists we have portrayed in these books were engaged with very different kinds of ambitions and, accordingly, envisage what sociology might be in very different ways. Their diversity has not been resolved by the rash of synthesising efforts that have been so popular in recent years in sociological theory; efforts which include, most prominently, those of Jürgen Habermas, Jeffrey Alexander, Anthony Giddens, Pierre Bourdieu and Randall Collins. In our view 'victories' in sociology are seldom thorough or final. Sociologies that are rejected as supposedly outmoded and surpassed do not simply go away entirely and for good. Indeed, they often have difficulty in recognising themselves in the pictures that are painted of them by those who proclaim themselves the makers of radical new advances in sociological thought, and, they therefore persist and await either a resurgence or a rediscovery that has, in the way of things, a good chance of occurring. Scholars continue to engage in or attempt to reinstate traditions of work that have, often with no little derision and no little misreading, been previously dismissed. What better example of this than Marxism?

Notwithstanding one or two exceptions, Marxism in the 1940s and 1950s was arguably moribund, largely because the working class – upon whose usurpation of power the revolutionary emancipation of humankind depended – had effectively been 'incorporated' into Western societies which were becoming increasingly dominated by an expanding middle class. However, Marxism experienced a resurgence after the mid-1960s – with students now in the vanguard of emancipatory prospects – only to meet its nemesis no more than twenty years later with revelations about the *gulag archipelago* – the vast network of slave labour camps scattered like a chain of islands throughout the Soviet empire – which exposed the Soviet Union as a repressive society and disillusioned many French theorists (who were to play a key part in the next series of theoretical developments). The final disintegration of the Soviet Union after the fall of the Berlin Wall in 1989 precipitated further decline in Marxist politics. But that did not mean that Marx's ideas were off the agenda altogether, for many of the more recent ways of thinking have been effectively updatings of Marx's ideas in the light of some of the grosser changes in the nature of society since the end of the Second World War. Thus, Marx's thought might be 'outdated' in the sense that it proposed the analysis of society through class, treating people's social identities and political interests as functions of their economic location, with the latter being designated on the basis of people's position in production. Marx is 'outdated' because the role of production in defining people's social locations is of diminishing significance as we have moved into a 'consumer society', one in which our identities are now defined by what we buy, wear, eat, play with; that is, our part in the 'sphere of consumption'. But, of course, the idea proposed by Marx, and also by Weber, that the structure of economic relations generates changes in the culture of society, lives on in the attempts by many sociologists to understand the rise and meaning of the 'consumer society'.

Marx's theories are a leading, and in some ways really the only, example of the 'grand narratives' that, we are told, because of the conditions of contemporary (that is, postmodern) society it is impossible for us to believe in any longer (Lyotard, 1984). Of course, this does not mean that Marx's influence has been entirely dissipated, not least because – as noted – many of his postmodern critics were themselves Marxists who rejected certain emphases in his thought but were driven to their criticism of Marx, and in the further development of their own ideas, by seeking to extend other aspects of Marx's logic. Nor does the derision for 'grand narratives' mean that there are no longer any 'card carrying' Marxists who remain explicitly and enthusiastically sure that the real answers are to be found in Marx, and are therefore undiscouraged by the setbacks, and resolute in their belief that the correct interpretation of Marx can be found.

Just as there are active Marxists, so too there are active functionalists, or at least those who are functionalist in practice, if not necessarily in name. Repeated attempts are made to recover Parsons' reputation, to establish that he was a better sociological theorist than critics have given him credit for, as well as attempts to justify functionalism as a general mode of analysis and dissociate it from the 'inherently conservative' approach it was often made out to be. It has been argued more than once that much of Marx's method of analysis was functionalist in nature, which point has been regarded as identifying the major, and deeply damaging deficiency of classic Marxism, but has also been made in an attempt to validate the strength and relevance of Marx's historical theories (Elster, 1985). There have even been attempts, as we have seen, under the label of neo-functionalism, to revive the Parsonian legacy, albeit in moderated ways. Further, within sociology, systems analysis plays a part in the work of Habermas, whose own intellectual objective was to give new life to the Frankfurt School by showing that the emancipatory project was still possible through a critical appraisal of society.

Symbolic interactionism, although it has lost the impetus it had in the 1950s and 1960s, continues to be productive, refusing to think of itself as outmoded in favour of much more fashionable 'postmodern' developments. The tradition can claim considerable credit for encouraging the growth in, and supplying the rationale for, contemporary enthusiasm for qualitative sociological research. As part of this it can also claim credit for eroding sociology's premature ambitions for scientific methods in the form of variable analysis. It was also one of the stimulating sources for the now popular, though often misunderstood, notion of 'social construction'.

Structuralism was influential across a range of disciplines in the humanities as well as in social studies, and the structural analysis of myth continues. However, it is not structuralism as such that matters these days. Rather, it is the transmuted form the approach has taken since the 1960s as 'post-structuralism' that tends to dominate at the present time. In the transformation structuralism has been changed out of all recognition. Lévi-Strauss' dissections of myths are no longer the model for what now goes on. Nevertheless, many recent developments started from the place the structuralists had reached, eventually calling into question the very assumptions upon which the structuralists had originally made their 'gains', and pressing the logic of structuralism to the point at which it could be turned on structuralism itself.

The ideas of the Frankfurt School about the 'administered society' live on in the work of many who have been more or less directly influenced by the School, whose ideas are certainly prominent, if not dominant, in cultural studies and in many other academic disciplines such as literature, history, aesthetics and musicology that cultural studies have penetrated. They also hold very wide application as a result of their independent reinvention by the French philosopher and social theorist who is surely the most influential of individual thinkers in social thought today, Michel Foucault. There is a close kinship, if not always direct inheritance, between so much of the thinking that now goes on in the social and human studies and the thought of the Frankfurt School.

Earlier we suggested that being 'rejected' in sociology does not necessarily result in the total demise of a particular approach. Rather it generally signifies its, perhaps temporary, decline from fashion with it living on even though marginalised from the mainstream. Even more importantly, however, we think that understanding these 'earlier' approaches serves not merely to help us understand how sociology got to where it is today, but also enriches the understanding of what sociologists are nowadays talking about. What goes on at the moment not merely originates in, but is often deeply shaped by, attempts at the continuation of, or even opposition to, earlier tendencies.

Some years ago we spoke of sociology as being an argument rather than a knowledge subject (Anderson et al., 1985). By this we meant that rather than produce findings, sociology mainly consists in the production of arguments and in this respect is probably closer to disciplines like philosophy and literary studies than to disciplines such as chemistry, physics or biology which, it can be said, produce facts about the world. Though this is a distinction which can be overdone, it is one which attempts to draw attention to the non-canonical nature of the discipline. Further, it has implications for the evaluation of sociological approaches. Too often – and we have discussed many examples of this in the preceding chapters – criticism of different sociological approaches typically begins by misrepresenting them. Hopefully, what we have done here will serve to correct that in some small way. But, of course, the disputes between sociological approaches are rarely just about their theories. More often than not they are also disputes about what we might term their 'metatheoretical' elements: that is, ideas about, among others, the nature and role of theory itself, the tasks theory should fulfil, what problems it should solve, what standards of veracity it should set itself, and more. From this point of view, there cannot be any canon in sociology. There is not much by way of common ground among the various sociological approaches. Rarely are the disagreements set against a background of agreement. Invariably disagreements between approaches involve a host of matters both great and small. Criticising an approach from the point of view of another generally comes down to reaffirming the differences between them, showing that the parties have very different ideas about sociology itself. Very different ideas, to put it another way, of how the sociological project is to work itself out.

Select bibliography and further reading

Much of the reading relevant to this short concluding chapter has already been cited in the previous chapters.

Of the efforts to synthesise various sociological approaches Jürgen Habermas', *Knowledge and Human Interests* (Beacon Press, 1971) is challenging. Jeffery Alexander's four-volume *Theoretical Logic in Sociology* (Routledge, 1983–84) is daunting and very thorough. Bourdieu's *Sociology in Question* (Sage, 1992) is a good example of his extensive corpus reflecting on sociology. Anthony Giddens, likewise, has written extensively. See his *Central Problems in Sociological Theory: Action, Structure and Contradiction in Social Analysis* (Macmillan, 1979) for an earlier statement and his *In Defence of Sociology: Essays, Interpretations and Rejoinders* (Polity Press, 1996) for a more recent one.

Bibliography

Abel, T. (1959), 'The Contribution of Georg Simmel: A Reappraisal', *American Sociological Review*, 24: 473–9.

Adorno, T.W. (1973), *Negative Dialectics*, London, Routledge. Trans. E.B. Ashton. First published 1966.

Adorno, T.W. (1984), *Aesthetic Theory*, London, Routledge. Trans. C. Lenhardt, Ed. G. Adorno and R. Tiedemann. First published 1970.

Adorno, T.W. (1987), *Philosophy of Modern Music*, London, Sheed and Ward. Trans. Anne Mitchell and Wesley Bloomer.

Adorno, T.W. (1991), *The Culture Industry: Selected Essays on Mass Culture*, London, Routledge. Translated and edited, J.M. Bernstein.

Adorno, T.W. and Horkheimer, M. (1997), *The Dialectic of Enlightenment*, London, Verso. Trans. John Cumming. First published 1942.

Adorno, T.W., Frankel-Brunswick, E., Levinson, D.J., and Sanford, R.N. (1950), *The Authoritarian Personality*, New York, Harper.

Alexander, J. (1983–84), *Theoretical Logic in Sociology, Vols 1–4*, London, Routledge.

Althusser, L. (1969), *For Marx*, Harmondsworth, Penguin. Trans. Ben Brewster. First published 1965.

Althusser, L. and Balibar, E. (1970), *Reading Capital*, London, New Left Books. Trans. Ben Brewster.

Anderson, N. (1961), *The Hobo*, Chicago, University of Chicago Press. First published 1923.

Anderson, R.J., Hughes, J.A., and Sharrock, W.W. (1985), *The Sociology Game: An Introduction to Sociological Reasoning*, London, Longmans.

Ashenden, S. and Owen, D. (eds) (1999), *Foucault contra Habermas*, London, Sage.

Badcock, C. (1975), *Lévi-Strauss: Structuralism and Sociological Theory*, London, Hutchinson.

Bales, R.F. (1950), *Interaction Process Analysis*, Cambridge, Mass., Addison Wesley.

Bannet, E.T. (1989), *Structuralism and the Logic of Dissent: Barthes, Derrida, Foucault, and Lacan*, London, Macmillan.

Barnes, H.E. and. Becker, H. (1938), *Social Thought from Lore to Science*, Boston, D.C. Heath.

Barthes, R. (1967), *Elements of Semiology*, New York, Noonday Press. Trans. Annette Lavers and Colin Smith.

Barthes, R. (1972), *Mythologies*, London, Cape. Trans. Annette Lavers.

Barthes, R. (1975), *S/Z*, London, Cape. Trans. Richard Miller.

Barthes, R. (1983), *The Empire of Signs*, London, Cape. Trans. Richard Howard.

Barthes, R. (1985), *The Fashion System*, London, Cape. Trans. Matthew Ward and Richard Howard.

Becker, H.S. (1952a), 'Social Class Variations in the Teacher–Pupil Relationship', *Journal of Educational Society*, 25: 451–65.

Becker, H.S. (1952b), 'The Career of the Chicago Public School Teacher', *American Journal of Sociology*, 57: 470–7.

Becker, H.S. (1953), 'Becoming a Marijuana User', *American Journal of Sociology*, 59(53): 235–42.

Becker, H.S. (1963), *The Outsiders: Studies in the Sociology of Deviance*, New York, The Free Press.

Becker, H.S. (1982), *Art Worlds*, Berkeley, CA, University of California Press.

Becker, H.S. (ed.) (1968), *Institutions and the Person*, Chicago, Aldine.

Becker, H.S. (1974), 'Art as Collective Action', *American Sociological Review*, 6: 767–76.

Becker, H.S. and Greer, B. (1957), 'Participant Observation and Interviewing: A Comparison', *Human Organization*, 16: 28–32. Reprinted in Manis, J.G. and Meltzer, B.N. (1978), Boston, MA, Allyn and Bacon, pp. 109–19.

Becker, H.S., Hughes, E., Greer, B. and Strauss, A. (1961), *Boys in White*, Chicago, Chicago University Press.

Becker, H.S., Hughes, E. and Greer, B. (1968), *Making the Grade: The Academic Side of Student Life*, New York, Wiley.

Behr, E. (1997), *Prohibition: The Thirteen Years that Changed America*, Harmondsworth, Penguin.

Bell, D. (2000), *The End of Ideology: On the Exhaustion of Political Ideas in the Fifties*, Cambridge, Mass., Harvard University Press. Rev. edn. First published 1960.

Benton, T. (1984), *The Rise and Fall of Structuralist Marxism: Althusser and His Influence*, London, Macmillan.

Berelson, B. and Steiner, G.A. (1964), *Human Behavior: An Inventory of Scientific Findings*, New York, Harcourt, Brace and World

Berger, P. and Luckmann, T. (1966), *The Social Construction of Reality*, New York, Anchor.

Bernard L.L. and Bernard, J. (1965), *Origins of American Sociology: The Social Science Movement in the United States*, New York, Russell and Russell.

Bernstein, J. (1994), *The Frankfurt School: Critical Assessments*, 6 vols, London, Routledge.

Black, M. (ed.) (1961), *The Social Theories of Talcott Parsons: A Critical Examination*, Englewood Cliffs, NJ, Prentice-Hall.

Blumer, H. (1953), 'Psychological Import of the Human Group', in Sherif, Muzafer and Wilson, M.O. (eds), *Group Relations at the Crossroads*, New York, Harper and Row.

Blumer, H. (1954), 'What Is Wrong with Social Theory', *American Sociological Review*, 19: 3–10.

Blumer, H. (1956), 'Sociological Analysis and the "Variable"', *American Sociological Review*, 21: 683–90. Reprinted in Manis and Meltzer (eds) (1978), *Symbolic Interactionism: A Reader*, Boston, MA, Allyn and Bacon.

Blumer, H. (1962), 'Society as Symbolic Interaction', in Rose, A. (ed.), *Human Behavior and Social Processes*, New York, Houghton Mifflin, pp. 179–92.

Blumer, H. (1966), 'Sociological Implications of the Thought of George Herbert Mead', *American Journal of Sociology*, 71: 535–48.

Blumer, H. (1971), *Symbolic Interactionism*, Englewood Cliffs, NJ, Prentice-Hall.

Bottomore, T.B. (1984), *The Frankfurt School*, London, Ellis Harewood.

Bourdieu, P. (1992), *Sociology in Question*, London, Sage.

Buckley, W. (1967), *Sociology and Modern Systems Theory*, Englewood Cliffs, NJ, Prentice-Hall.

Bulmer, M. (1981), 'Charles S. Johnson, Robert E. Park and the Research Methods of the Chicago Commission on Race Relations, 1919–22: An Early Experiment in Applied Social Research', *Ethnic and Racial Studies*, 4: 289–306.

Bulmer, M. (1984), *The Chicago School of Sociology: Institutionalisation, Diversity, and the Rise of Sociological Research*, Chicago, University of Chicago Press.

Burgess, E.W. (1925), 'The Growth of the City: An Introduction to a Research Project', in Park, R.E. and Burgess, E.W. (eds), *The City*, Chicago, University of Chicago Press, pp. 47–62.

Burgess, R.G. (ed.) (1995), *Howard Becker on Education*, Milton Keynes, Open University Press.

Burnham, J. (1945), *The Managerial Revolution*, Harmondsworth, Penguin.

Caws, P. (1988), *Structuralism: The Art of the Intelligible*, Atlantic Highlands, NJ, Humanities Press.

Checkland, P. (1981), *Systems Thinking, Systems Practice*, London, Wiley.

Chicago Commission on Race Relations (1922), *The Negro in Chicago: A Study of Race Relations and a Race Riot in 1919*, Chicago, University of Chicago Press.

Cicourel, A.V. (1964), *Method and Measurement in Sociology*, New York, The Free Press.

Cicourel, A.V. (1968), *The Social Organisation of Juvenile Justice*, New York, Wiley.

Cicourel, A.V. and Kitsuse, J.I. (1963), *The Educational Decision-Makers*, Indianapolis, Bobbs-Merrill.

Clarke, S. (1981), *The Foundations of Structuralism*, Brighton, Harvester Press.

Cohen, P. (1968), *Modern Social Theory*, London, Heinemann.

Collins, R. (1975), *Conflict Sociology*, New York, Academic Press.

Collins, R. (1981), 'On the Microfoundations of Macrosociology', *American Journal of Sociology*, 86: 984–1014.

Collins, R. (1988), 'The Micro-contribution to Macro-sociology', *Sociological Theory*, 6: 242–53.

Colomy, P. (ed.) (1990a), *Functionalist Sociology*, Aldershot, Edward Elgar.

Colomy, P. (ed.) (1990b), *Neofunctionalist Sociology*, Aldershot, Edward Elgar.

Connerton, P. (1980), *The Tragedy of Enlightenment: An Essay on the Frankfurt School*, Cambridge, Cambridge University Press.

Cooley, C.H. (1964), *Human Nature and the Social Order*, New York, Schocken. First published 1902.

Cooley, C.H. (1978), 'The Looking-Glass Self', in Manis, J.G. and Melzer, B.N. (eds), *Symbolic Interaction: A Reader in Social Psychology*, Boston, Allyn and Bacon. First published 1902.

Coser, L. (1965), *Georg Simmel*, Englewood Cliffs, NJ, Prentice-Hall.

Cressey, P. (1971), *The Taxi-Dance Hall: A Sociological Study in Commercialized Recreation and City Life*. New York, AMS Press. First published 1932.

Crick, M. (1976), *Explorations in Language and Meaning: Toward a Semantic Anthropology*, London, Malaby Press.

Culler, J. (1975), *Structuralist Poetics*, London, Routledge.

Dahrendorf. R. (1958), 'Out of Utopia: Toward a Reorientation of Sociological Analysis', *American Journal of Sociology*, 74: 115–27.

Dahrendorf, R. (1959), *Class and Class Conflict in Industrial Society*, London, Routledge.

Davis, F. (1968), 'Professional Socialisation as Subjective Experience', in Becker, H.S. (ed.), *Institutions and the Person*, Chicago, Aldine.

Davis, Kingsley (1966), *Human Society*, New York, Macmillan.

Davis, K. and Moore, W.E. (1945), 'Some Principles of Stratification', *American Sociological Review*, 10: 242–9.

Demerath, N.J. and Peterson, R.A. (eds) (1967), *System, Change and Conflict: A Reader on Contemporary Sociological Theory and the Debate over Functionalism*, New York, The Free Press.

Denzin, N.K. (1992), *Symbolic Interactionism and Cultural Studies: The Politics of Interpretation*, Cambridge, Mass., Blackwells.

Denzin, N.K. (ed.) (1997), *Cultural Studies: A Research Volume*, Greenwich, CT: JAI Press.

Dewey, J. (1896), 'The Reflex Arc Concept in Psychology', *Psychological Review*, 3: 357–70. First published in 1896.

Dosse, F. (1997), *History of Structuralism Vols 1 and 2*, Minneapolis, University of Minnesota Press.

Drew, P. and Wootton, A. (eds) (1988), *Erving Goffman: Exploring the Interaction Order*, Cambridge, Polity Press.

Durkheim, E. (1976), *The Elementary Forms of the Religious Life*, London, Allen and Unwin.

Easton, D. (1965), *A Systems Analysis of Political Life*, New York, Wiley.

Elster, J. (1985), *Making Sense of Marx*, Cambridge, Cambridge University Press.

Faris, R.E.L. (1967), *Chicago Sociology: 1920–1932*, Chicago, Chandler.

Faulkner, R.R. (1971), *The Hollywood Studio Musician*, Chicago, Aldine-Atherton.

Faulkner, R.R. (1983), *Music on Demand*, New Brunswick, Transaction.

Feenberg, A. (1981), *Lukács, Marx and the Sources of Critical Theory*, Oxford, Robertson.

Fine, G.A. (1987), *With the Boys: Little League Baseball and Preadolescent Culture*, Chicago, University of Chicago Press.

Fine, G.A. (1990), 'Symbolic Interactionism in a post-Blumerian Age', in Ritzer, G. (ed.), *Frontiers of Social Theory*, New York, Columbia University Press.

Fine, G.A. (1993), 'The Sad Demise, Mysterious Disappearance, and Glorious Triumph of Symbolic Interactionism', *Annual Review of Sociology*, 19: 61–87.

Fisher, B. and Strauss, A. (1991), 'The Chicago Tradition and Social Change: Thomas, Park and Their Successors', *Symbolic Interaction*, 1: 5–23. Reprinted in Plummer, K. (ed.), *Symbolic Interaction, Vol. 1*, Aldershot, Edward Elgar, 1991, pp. 73–94.

Fisher, B. and Strauss, A. (1979), 'Interactionism', in Bottomore, T. and Nisbet, R. (eds), *A History of Sociological Analysis*, London, Heinemann.

Foucault, M. (1972), *The Archaeology of Knowledge*, London, Tavistock. Trans. A.M. Sheridan.

Foucault, M. (1977), *Discipline and Punish: The Birth of the Prison*, London, Allen Lane. Trans. A.M. Sheridan.

Freud, S. (1930), *Civilisation and its Discontents*, London, Hogarth Press.
Frisby, D. (1981), *Sociological Impressionism: A Reassessment of Georg Simmel's Social Theory*, London, Heinemann.
Frisby, D. and Featherstone, M. (eds) (1997), *Simmel on Culture: Selected Writings*, London, Sage.
Galbraith, J.K. (1960), *The Affluent Society*, Cambridge, Mass., Riverside Press.
Geuss, R. (1981), *The Idea of a Critical Theory: Habermas and the Frankfurt School*, Cambridge, Cambridge University Press.
Giddens, A. (1979), *Central Problems in Sociological Theory: Action, Structure and Contradiction in Social Analysis*, London, Macmillan.
Giddens, A. (1996), *In Defence of Sociology: Essays, Interpretations and Rejoinders*, Cambridge, Polity Press.
Gillmore, S. (1990), 'Art Worlds: Developing the Interactionist Approach to Social Organization', in Becker, H. and McCall, M. (eds), *Symbolic Interaction and Cultural Studies*, Chicago, The University of Chicago Press, pp. 148–78.
Glaser, B. and Strauss, A. (1967), *The Discovery of Grounded Theory: Strategies for Qualitative Research*, Chicago, Aldine.
Glaser, B. and Strauss, A. (1971), *Status Passage*, Chicago, Aldine-Atherton.
Glucksmann, M. (1974), *Structuralist Analysis in Contemporary Social Thought*, London, Routledge.
Goffman, E. (1951), 'Symbols of Class Status', *British Journal of Sociology*, 11: 294–304.
Goffman, E. (1959), *The Presentation of Self in Everyday Life*, New York, Anchor Books.
Goffman, E. (1961a), *Asylums*, New York, Anchor.
Goffman, E. (1961b), *Encounters: Two Studies in the Sociology of Interaction*, Indianapolis, Bobbs-Merrill.
Goffman, E. (1963), *Behavior in Public Places: Notes on the Social Organisation of Gatherings*, New York, The Free Press.
Goffman, E. (1964), *Stigma: Notes on the Management of Spoiled Identity*, Englewood Cliffs, NJ, Prentice-Hall.
Goffman, E. (1971), *Relations in Public: Microstudies of the Public Order*, New York, Harper and Row.
Goffman, E. (1974), *Frame Analysis: An Essay on the Organisation of Experience*, New York, Harper and Row.
Goffman, E. (1979), *Gender Advertisements*, London, Macmillan.
Goffman, E. (1981), *Forms of Talk*, Oxford, Basil Blackwell.
Goffman, E. (1983), 'The Interaction Order', *American Sociological Review*, 48: 1–17.
Gouldner, A.W. (1959), 'Reciprocity and Autonomy in Functionalist Theory', in Gross, L. (ed.), *Symposium on Sociological Theory*, New York, Harper and Row.
Gouldner, A.W. (1968), 'The Sociologist as Partisan: Sociology and the Welfare State', *The American Sociologist*, 3: 103–16.
Gouldner, A.W. (1970), *The Coming Crisis of Western Sociology*, New York, Basic Books.
Gurvitch, G. (ed.) (1947), *La Sociologie aux Xxe siècle*, Paris, Presses Universitaires de France.
Gusfield, J. (1986), *Symbolic Crusade: Status Politics and the American Temperance Movement*, 2nd edn., Urbana, University of Illinois Press.

Gusfield, J. (1996), *Contested Meanings: The Construction of Alcohol Problems*, Madison, WI, University of Wisconsin Press.

Habermas, J. (1971), *Knowledge and Human Interests*, Boston, Beacon Press.

Hall, P. (1987), 'Interactionism and the Study of Social Organisation', *Sociological Quarterly*, 28: 1–22.

Harland, R. (1991), *Superstructuralism: The Philosophy of Structuralism and Post-structuralism*, London, Routledge.

Harris, R., (2001), *Saussure and his Interpreters*, Edinburgh, Edinburgh University Press.

Hawkes, T. (1977), *Structuralism and Semiotics*, London, Methuen.

Held, D. (1980), *Introduction to Critical Theory: Horkheimer to Habermas*, London, Hutchinson.

Hobbes, T. (1991), *The Leviathan*, Cambridge, Cambridge University Press. Edited by Richard Tuck. First published in 1651.

Hochschild, A.R. (1979), 'Emotion Work, Feeling Rules, and Social Structure', *American Journal of Sociology*, 85(3): 551–75.

Hochschild, A.R. (1983), *The Managed Heart: The Commercialisation of Human Feeling*, Berkeley, CA, California University Press.

Holmwood, J. and Stewart, A. (1991), *Explanation and Social Theory*, London, Macmillan.

Honneth, A. (ed.) (1991), *Cultural-political Interventions in the Unfinished Project of Enlightenment*, Cambridge, Mass., MIT Press.

Honneth, A. (ed.) (1992), *Philosophical Interventions in the Unfinished Project of Enlightenment*, Cambridge, Mass., MIT Press.

Horkheimer, M. (1974), *Eclipse of Reason*, New York, Oxford University Press. Reprinted Seabury Press. First published 1947.

Horkheimer, M. (1973), *Aspects of Sociology*, London, Heinemann.

Horkheimer, M. (1993), *Between Philosophy and Social Science: Selected Early Writings*, Cambridge, Mass., MIT Press. Trans. G. Frederick Hunter, M.S. Kramer and John Torpey.

Horkheimer, M. (1995), *Critical Theory: Selected Essays*, New York, Continuum.

Horowitz, I. (1974), *The Rise and Fall of Project Camelot: Studies in the Relationship between Social Science and Practical Politics*, New York, Cambridge University Press.

Hughes, E. (1971), *The Sociological Eye*, Chicago, Aldine-Atherton.

Hughes, E. (1981), *Men and Their Work*, Westport, Conn., Greenwood Press. Originally published by The Free Press, 1958.

Hughes, E.C. (1960), 'The professions in society', *Canadian Journal of Economics and Political Science*, 26: 54–61.

Hughes, H. Stuart (1959), *Consciousness and Society: The Reorientation of European Social Thought, 1890–1930*, London, MacGibbon and Kee.

Hughes, H. Stuart (1974), *Consciousness and Society: The Reorientation of European Social Thought, 1890–1930*, London, Paladin. First published 1959.

Hughes, J.A., Martin, P. and Sharrock, W.W. (1995), *Understanding Classical Theory: Marx, Weber and Durkheim*, London, Sage.

Jarvis, S. (1998), *Adorno: A Critical Introduction*, Cambridge, Polity.

Jay, M. (1973), *The Dialectical Imagination: A History of the Frankfurt School and the Institute of Social Research, 1923–50*, London, Heinemann.

Joas, H. (1985), *G.H. Mead: A Contemporary Re-examination of his Thought*, Cambridge, Mass., MIT Press.

Joas, H. (1987), 'Symbolic Interactionism', in Giddens, A. and Turner, J. (eds), *Social Theory Today*, Cambridge, Polity Press.

Johnson, Chalmers A. (1964), *Revolution and the Social System*, Stanford, Stanford University Press.

Katovitch, M.A. and Reese, W.A. (1993), 'Postmodern Thought in Symbolic Interaction', *Sociological Quarterly*, 34: 391–411.

Kendon, A. (1988). 'Goffman's Approach to Face-to-Face Interaction', in Drew, P. and Wootton, A. (eds), *Erving Goffman: Exploring the Interaction Order*, Cambridge, Polity Press.

Kornhauser, W. (1964), *The Politics of Mass Society*, Glencoe, The Free Press.

Kurzweil, E. (1980), *The Age of Structuralism: Lévi-Strauss to Foucault*, New York, Columbia University Press.

Lacan, J. (1968), *The Language of the Self: The Function of Language in Psycho-Analysis*, Baltimore, Johns Hopkins University Press. Trans. Anthony Wilden.

Lacan, J. (1977a), *Écrits: A Selection*, Baltimore, Norton. Trans. A.M. Sheridan.

Lacan, J. (1977b), *The Four Fundamental Concepts of Psycho-Analysis*, London, Hogarth Press. Trans. Alan Sheridan.

Lane, M. (1970), *Structuralism: A Reader*, London, Cape.

Lavers, A. (1982), *Roland Barthes: Structuralism and After*, London, Methuen.

Leech, E.R. (1974), *Lévi-Strauss*, London, Fontana Modern Masters, rev. edn.

Lemert, E. (1951), *Social Pathology*, New York, McGraw-Hill.

Lemert, E. (1967), *Human Deviance, Social Problems and Social Control*, Englewood Cliffs, NJ, Prentice-Hall.

Lévi-Strauss, C. (1962), *The Savage Mind*, London, Weidenfeld.

Lévi-Strauss, C. (1964), *Structural Anthropology*, New York, Basic Books. Trans. Claire Jacobsen and Brook Grundfest Schoeph.

Lévi-Strauss, C. (1967), *The Scope of Anthropology*, London, Jonathan Cape. Trans. S.D. Paul and R.A. Paul.

Lévi-Strauss, C. (1969), *The Elementary Structures of Kinship*, London, Eyre & Spottiswoode. Trans. and ed. R. Needham. First published 1949.

Lévi-Strauss, C. (1970), *The Raw and the Cooked: Introduction to a Science of Mythology*, New York, Harper and Row. Trans. John and Doreen Weightman.

Lévi-Strauss, C. (1973a), *From Honey to Ashes*, London, Jonathan Cape. Trans. John and Doreen Weightman.

Lévi-Strauss, C. (1973b), *Totemism*, Harmondsworth, Penguin. Trans. Rodney Needham.

Lévi-Strauss, C. (1978), *The Origin of Table Manners*, London, Jonathan Cape. Trans. John and Doreen Weightman.

Lévi-Strauss, C. (1981), *The Naked Man*, London, Jonathan Cape. Trans. John and Doreen Weightman. First published in 1971.

Lipset, S.M. (1964), *The First New Nation*, London, Heinemann.

Lockwood, D. (1956), 'Some Remarks on "The Social System"', *British Journal of Sociology*, 7: 134–46.

Luhmann, N. (1995), *Social Systems*, Stanford, Stanford University Press. Trans. John Bednarz and Dirk Baecker.

Lukács, G. (1971), *History and Class Consciousness: Studies in Marxist Dialectics*, London, Merlin Press. First published in 1923. Trans. Rodney Livingstone.

Lyotard, J.-F. (1984), *The Postmodern Condition: A Report on Knowledge*, Manchester, Manchester University Press.

Lyotard, J.-F. (1993), *Towards the Postmodern*, New York, Humanities Press.

Macey, D. (1988), *Lacan in Contexts*, London, Verso.

Maines, D. (1982), 'In Search of Mesostructure: Studies in the Negotiated Order', *Urban Life*, 11(3): 267–79.

Malinowski, B. (1921), 'Ethnology and the Study of Society', *Economica*, 2: 208–19.

Malinowski, B. (1944), *A Scientific Theory of Culture*, Oxford, Oxford University Press

Malinowski, B. (1948), *Magic, Science and Religion and Other Essays*, Glencoe, The Free Press.

Manis, J.G. and Meltzer, B.N. (eds) (1978), *Symbolic Interactionism: A Reader*, Boston, MA, Allyn and Bacon.

Manning, P. (1992), *Erving Goffman and Modern Sociology*, Cambridge, Polity Press.

Marcuse, H. (1941), *Reason and Revolution: Hegel and the Rise of Social Theory*, New York, Oxford University Press. Republished in 1960 by Beacon Press.

Marcuse, H. (1966), *Eros and Civilisation: A Philosophical Inquiry into Freud*, Boston, Beacon Press.

Marcuse, H. (1991), *One Dimensional Man: Studies in the Ideology of Advanced Industrial Society*, London, Routledge. First published Beacon Press, 1964.

McCarthy, T. (1978), *The Critical Theory of Jürgen Habermas*, London, Hutchinson.

McNay, L. (1994), *Foucault: A Critical Introduction*, Cambridge, Polity Press.

Mead, G.H. (1930), 'Cooley's Contribution to American Social Thought', *American Journal of Sociology*, 35: 693–706. Reprinted in Plummer, K. (1991), *Symbolic Interactionism, Vol. 1*, London, Edward Elgar.

Mead, G.H. (1936), *Movements of Social Thought in the Nineteenth Century*, Chicago, University of Chicago Press.

Mead, G.H. (1962), *Mind, Self and Society*, Chicago, University of Chicago Press. First published 1934.

Mead, G.H. (1964), *Selected Writings*, Indianapolis, IN, Bobbs-Merrill. First published 1924–25.

Meltzer, B.N. (1978), 'The Social Psychology of George Herbert Mead', in Manis, J.G. and Meltzer, B.N. (eds), *Symbolic Interactionism: A Reader*, New York, Allyn and Bacon.

Merquior, J.G. (1986), *From Prague to Paris: A Critique of Structuralism and Post-structuralism*, London, Verso.

Merton, R.K. (1957), *Social Theory and Social Structure*, New York, The Free Press.

Merton, R.K., Reader, G. and Kendall, P. (1957), *The Student Physician*, Cambridge, Mass., Harvard University Press.

Mills, C.W. (1956), *The Power Elite*, New York, Oxford University Press.

Mills, C.W. (1958), *The Causes of World War Three*, New York, Simon and Schuster.

Mills, C.W. (1959), *The Sociological Imagination*, New York, Oxford University Press.

Mills, C.W. (1960), *Listen, Yankee: The Revolution in Cuba*, New York, McGraw-Hill.

Mullan, B. (1987), *Sociologists on Sociology*, London, Croom Helm.
Mullins, N. and Mullins, C. (1973), *Theories and Theory Groups in Contemporary American Sociology*, London, Harper and Row.
Musolf, G.R. (1992), 'Structure, Institutions, Power and Ideology', *Sociological Quarterly*, 33: 171–89.
O'Connor, B. (ed.) (2000), *The Adorno Reader*, Oxford, Blackwell.
Olsen, P. (ed.) (1963), *America as a Mass Society: Changing Community and Identity*, New York, The Free Press.
Palmer, D. (1997), *Structuralism and Post-structuralism for Beginners*, New York, Writers and Readers.
Park, R.E. (1915), 'The City: Suggestions for the Investigation of Human Behavior in the Urban Environment', *American Journal of Sociology*, 20: 577–612. Reprinted in Park, R.E. and Burgess, E.W. (eds), *The City*, Chicago, University of Chicago Press, 1925, pp. 1–46.
Park, R.E. and Burgess, E.W. (1921), *Introduction to the Science of Sociology*, Chicago, University of Chicago Press.
Parsons, T. (1952), *The Social System*, London, Routledge.
Parsons, T. (1954a), *Essays in Sociological Theory*, rev. edn, New York, The Free Press.
Parsons, T. (1954b), *Social Structure and Personality*, New York, The Free Press.
Parsons, T., (1964), *Societies: Evolutionary and Comparative Perspectives*, Englewood Cliffs, NJ, Prentice-Hall.
Parsons, T. (1968), *The Structure of Social Action*, 2nd edn, New York, The Free Press. First published 1937.
Parsons, T. (1971), *The System of Modern Societies*, Englewood Cliffs, NJ, Prentice-Hall.
Parsons, T. and Shils, E. (eds) (1951), *Toward a General Theory of Action*, Cambridge, Mass., Harvard University Press.
Parsons, T. and Smelser, N. (1956), *Economy and Society: An Integration of Economic and Social Theory*, London, Routledge.
Parsons, T., Bales, R.F. and Shils, E. (1953), *Working Papers in the Theory of Action*, New York, The Free Press.
Parsons, T., Bales, R.F., Olds, J., Zelditch, M., and Slater, P.E. (1955), *Family, Socialization and Interaction Process*, New York, The Free Press.
Payne, M. (ed.) (1986), *Dictionary of Cultural and Critical Theory*, Oxford, Blackwell.
Peter, M.R. (1992), *Max Horkheimer: A New Interpretation*, Hemel Hempstead, Harvester Wheatsheaf.
Plummer, K. (ed.) (1991), *Symbolic Interactionism, Vols. 1 and 2*, London, Edward Elgar.
Poggi, G. (1993), *Money and the Modern Mind: George Simmel's Philosophy of Money*, Berkeley, University of California Press.
Prus, R. (1989a), *Making Sales: Influence as an Interpersonal Accomplishment*, London, Sage.
Prus, R. (1989b), *Pursuing Customers: An Ethnography of Marketing Activities*, London, Sage.
Prus, R. (1996), *Symbolic Interaction and Ethnographic Research: Intersubjectivity and the Study of Human Experience*, New York, State University of New York Press.
Prus, R. (1999), *Beyond the Power Mystique: Power as Intersubjective Accomplishment*, New York, State University of New York Press.
Radcliffe-Brown, A.R. (1922), *The Andaman Islanders*, New York, The Free Press.

Radcliffe-Brown, A.R. (1952), *Structure and Function in Primitive Society*, London, Cohen and West.

Rasmussen, D. (1990), *Reading Habermas*, Oxford, Basil Blackwell.

Rasmussen, D. (1996), *Handbook of Critical Theory*, Oxford, Basil Blackwell.

Reese, A. (1993), 'Postmodern Thought in Symbolic Interaction', *Sociological Quarterly*, 34: 391–411.

Reiss, Ira J. (1964), 'The Social Integration of Queers and Peers', in Becker, H. (ed.), *The Other Side: Perspectives on Deviance*, New York, The Free Press, pp. 181–210.

Rex, J. (1961), *Key Problems of Sociological Theory*, London, Routledge.

Reisman, D. (1950), *The Lonely Crowd: A Study of the Changing American Character*, New Haven, CT, Yale University Press.

Rist, R.C. (1973), *The Urban School – A Factory for Failure; A Study of Education in America*, Cambridge, Mass., MIT Press.

Rocher, G. (1972), *Talcott Parsons and American Sociology*, London, Nelson. Trans. S. and B. Mennell.

Rock, P. (1979), *The Making of Symbolic Interactionism*, London, Macmillan.

Rossi, I. (1981), *The Logic of Culture: Advances in Structural Theory and Methods*, London, Tavistock.

Ryan, A. (1970), *The Philosophy of the Social Sciences*, London, Macmillan.

Shaw, C.R. (1966), *The Jack-Roller: A Delinquent Boy's Own Story*, Chicago, University of Chicago Press. First published 1930.

Shibutani, T. (1988), 'Herbert Blumer's Contributions to Twentieth Century Sociology', *Symbolic Interaction*, 11: 23–31. Reprinted in Plummer, K. (ed.), *Symbolic Interaction, Vol. 1*, Aldershot, Edward Elgar, 1991, pp. 215–23.

Simmel, G. (1950), 'The Field of Sociology', in *The Sociology of Georg Simmel*, New York, The Free Press. Trans. and edited K.H. Wolff.

Smelser, N. (1959), *Social Change in the Industrial Revolution: An Application of the Theory to the Lancashire Cotton Industry, 1770–1840*, London, Routledge.

Smelser, N. (1962), *Theory of Collective Behaviour*, London, Routledge.

Smith, D. (1988), *The Chicago School: A Liberal Critique of Capitalism*, London, Macmillan.

Spykman, N.J. (1966), *The Social Theory of Georg Simmel*, New York, Atherton Press.

Stirk, Peter M.R. (1992), *Max Horkheimer: A New Interpretation*, Hemel Hempstead, Harvester Wheatsheaf.

Strauss, A. (1959), *Mirrors and Masks*, Glencoe, The Free Press.

Strauss, A. (1978), *Negotiations: Varieties, Contexts, Processes and Social Order*, New York, Jossey-Bass.

Strauss, A. and Bucher, R. (1961), 'Professions in Process', *American Journal of Sociology*, 66(4): 325–34.

Strauss, A., Schatzman, L., Bucher, R., Ehrlich, D. and Sabshin, M. (1964), *Psychiatric Ideologies and Institutions*, Glencoe, The Free Press.

Sturrock, J. (1993), *Structuralism*, 2nd edn., London, Fontana.

Thomas, W.I. (1923), *The Unadjusted Girl*, Boston, Little Brown.

Thomas, W.I. and Znaniecki, F. (1958), *The Polish Peasant in Europe and America*, New York, Dover. The five-volume edition was published by the University of Chicago Press and Richard Badger in Boston in 1918–20.

Thrasher, F. (1927), *The Gang: A Study of 1,313 Gangs in Chicago*, Chicago, University of Chicago Press.

Turner, S.P. and Turner, J.H. (1990), *The Impossible Science: An Institutional Analysis of American Sociology*, Newbury Park, Sage.

Watson, R. (1994), 'Symbolic Interactionism', in J.-O. Östman, J. Verschueren and J. Blommaerts (eds), *The Handbook of Pragmatics*, Amsterdam, John Benjamin, pp. 520–7.

Waxman, C. (ed.) (1968), *The End of Ideology Debate*, New York, Funk and Wagnalls.

Whyte, W.H. (1957), *The Organization Man*, London, Cape.

Wiggergaus, R (1994), *The Frankfurt School: Its History, Theories and Political Significance*, Cambridge, Polity Press.

Williams, R. (1960), *American Society: A Sociological Interpretation*, New York, Knopf.

Winch, P. (1958), *The Idea of a Social Science*, London, Routledge.

Wolin, R. (1992), *The Terms of Cultural Criticism: The Frankfurt School, Existentialism, Poststructuralism*, New York, Columbia University Press.

Index